Fields of Play

Fields of Play

Sport, Literature and Culture

Edited by

Poonam Trivedi

and

Supriya Chaudhuri

Orient BlackSwan

FIELDS OF PLAY: SPORT, LITERATURE AND CULTURE

ORIENT BLACKSWAN PRIVATE LIMITED

Registered Office
3-6-752 Himayatnagar, Hyderabad 500 029 (Telangana), India
e-mail: centraloffice@orientblackswan.com

Other Offices
Bangalore, Bhopal, Chennai, Ernakulam,
Guwahati, Hyderabad, Jaipur, Kolkata,
Lucknow, Mumbai, New Delhi, Noida, Patna

First published 2015

ISBN 978 81 250 5755 0

Typeset in
Adobe Jenson Pro 11/13.2
by Le Studio Graphique, Gurgaon 122 001

Printed in India at
Rakmo Press, Greater Noida

Published by
Orient Blackswan Private Limited
1/24 Asaf Ali Road
New Delhi 110 002
e-mail: delhi@orientblackswan.com

Contents

Illustrations

Acknowledgements

This collection of essays emerged out of a national seminar, '"The game's afoot" ... Sport, Literature and Culture' which was organised by the Department of English, Indraprastha College for Women, University of Delhi, Delhi, from 10 to 12 March 2011. Thanks and deep appreciation are due to many for the event: to the Principal, Dr Babli Moitra Saraf, who welcomed the idea of the seminar and facilitated it in every respect, to all members of the English Department who worked tirelessly to make the event a success, to the students of English Honours and especially the office-bearers of the English Literary Society for their enthusiastic contribution, to the speakers and paper–readers, many of whom travelled long distances for the occasion, and to many friends and colleagues who rallied round to contribute to the event in different ways. Our thanks to Professor Dev Swarup of the UGC for his unwavering support, without which the seminar would not have been possible. Special mention must be made of the seminar committee: Sonali Agarwal who oversaw the printing of the posters, folders, abstract booklet and the programme; Nitoo Das who designed the much appreciated poster and arranged for the exhibition of the Delhi Commons Postcards and Debjani Sengupta who provided invaluable liaison between all. Warm thanks are also due to all the contributors to the book for their co-operation, patience and dedication in seeing it through. The volume is dedicated to the workers and sportspersons of the Commonwealth Games who provided the primary stimulus for the seminar and the book.

Our grateful thanks to Iram Ghufran, curator of the Delhi Commons, for permission to reproduce seven postcards designed for the exhibition, to Mohammed Shafiq for the hockey and football photos and to Mukta Arts, Producers, for the reproduction of stills from the film *Iqbal*.

Poonam Trivedi
Supriya Chaudhuri
Editors

Introduction

Poonam Trivedi

> The constitution of a field of sports practices is linked to the development of a philosophy of sport which is necessarily a political philosophy of sport. ... sport like any other practice is an object of struggles among the factions of the dominant class and also among the social classes.
>
> Pierre Bourdieu, 'How Can One be a Sportsman?'

Sports, games and play are activities which have long been considered essential to society: they are held to be integral to education and indispensable for leisure and recreation. Yet these words/terms have come to acquire a range of meanings which challenge a singular attitude towards them: the Collins Cobuild Dictionary lists thirty-eight entries for 'play', six with subsections for 'game' and four for 'sport'. These refer, among other things, to a rule bound physical practice, a spectacle, a ritual, a way of life, an ideal of a body-culture, a performance, a metaphor or a symbol. The range of reference of these words has expanded further with the professionalisation and internationalisation of sport, but has also sharpened the ambiguities inherent in the concept of 'sport' which is basically a playing which involves a letting go, a 'mis-ruling' but usually within the rules of the game, a pleasure with pain.

The Greeks differentiated this complexity in terms of *paidia* (free play) and *ludus* (rule-bound play). Johan Huizinga in his *Homo Ludens* argued for 'play' as constitutive of the human.[1] Roger Caillois structures this in terms of *agôn*, games of competition; *alea*, games of chance; *mimicry*, games of simulation and *ilinx*, games of vertigo (as in roller-coaster rides).[2] Freud sees the 'play' impulse as an instinct for mastery. Victor Turner referred to 'play' as the joker in the deck, both creative and untrustworthy.[3] Jeremy Bentham used the term 'deep play' to describe the placing of astronomical stakes in return for intangibles like esteem, honour and status.[4] Psychologists refer to 'dark play' as that which entails high risk, deception or sheer thrill.[5] The recognition of probability as a founding principle in science and the Derridean positing of an absent centre has further led to 'play' being identified with both uncertainty and infinite substitution.[6] In Indian philosophy, too, play, sport, drama as connoted by *lila* signify both the process and mode of cosmic generation, a divine play, with rules but also uncertainty.[7] In a further shift of configuration of meaning, Pierre Bourdieu has linked sport to field in his theoretical analysis of cultural production. For Bourdieu, sport is part of a cultural 'field', a structured social space, with its own rules of domination and struggle. It is a force which is used by agents to produce a demand and supply, by instituting 'fields' of competition and distinction, imposing definitions of legitimate body use and sporting practice to create areas of social and cultural capital. Thus, according to him, sport is ultimately, a political philosophy: amateurism, for instance, is the promotion of an aristocratic ideal of sport as disinterested practice.[8] Hence among the numerous 'fields of play' which structure and control our lives today there are many which are constituted by the specific game/play/sport fields being worked out on the playing fields of the world.

The essays in this collection emerge largely from a seminar[9] which brought this gamut of significations of sport to critical attention. The impetus for the venture came from the ferment around the Commonwealth Games in Delhi in October 2010, but the project has developed beyond them. Since the 1970s, there has been increasing interest in analysing the place of sport in modern society and Sports Studies have become a recognised sub-field in history and sociology. While institutionalised sport has received considerable academic attention in the areas of sport history and anthropology, media and cultural studies, the engagement of literature and the creative arts with the field of sports is still a fledgling area of study especially here in India. The book therefore attempts to redirect attention from the 'representation' of sport in various media to its 'mediation' in literature; focusing not just on how various sports have evolved, are commented upon and presented to consumers in print and on television, but also on what discourses and ideologies structure and critique the engagement with sport especially in art, literature, culture and film. It looks to go beyond sports reportage, to the embedding location of the games, the 'fields' of play and the 'habitus' or the dispositions and convictions through which the cultural capital of sports is generated.

The objective of the seminar was to investigate and interrogate what goes into the making of the institutions, practices and cults of modern sport, their nationalising, and now globalising, agendas which simultaneously unite and divide. It opened up for discussion the commercialisation and corporatisation of sport which has brought into being a seamy side of doping, cheating, gambling, match-fixing, the ill-effects of athletic training regimes etc., all consequences of competitive sport with its emphasis on victory and records. It also led to the questioning of the almost irresistible creation and excessive adulation of an alternate surrogate world of sporting 'heroism' which is projected as the acme of human achievement, but which may not necessarily be free of classism, racism and sexism. It therefore brought to the forefront the costs and the payoffs of the development of sporting cultures and bodily practices, especially the need to confront the continuing neglect of women's sport and the access to sports for the marginalised, minority and differently abled groups. Further, it provoked investigation into how internet technologies are radically changing the way 'gaming' is configured today; how multiple engagements across time and space are possible, cartographical categories are questioned and individuals can become different *avatars*. Thus it became evident that there was almost no aspect of sport that did not touch some part of life and society and vice versa and that it was imperative to bridge the polarisation between academics and athleticism, not just in education but in critical discourse and creative arts too.

The state of writing and discourse on sport in India, though lively and informative, is mainly confined to the journalistic which dominates print and electronic media. However, while there is now a perceptible ground-swell of popular interest in the sports story as opposed to the sports news, and is manifest in a spate of publication of a range of histories, biographies and autobiographies (mostly ghost written though with superstars cashing in on their limelight), the line between life-writing by sports celebrities and the serious sports book is still to be breached, despite the record crowds for Rahul Dravid at the 2013 Jaipur Literary Festival. Critical or investigative accounts are still too few and far between. *Batting for the Empire* on Ranjisinghji by Mario Rodrigues, is a notable exception, which confronts the irony that the figure called the greatest Indian cricketer and honoured with the premier league championship being named after him was an active opponent of the freedom struggle.[10] And though a beginning has been made in the more considered and scholarly analyses by historians and cultural anthropologists like Ashis Nandy and Ramachandra Guha, followed by Boria Majumdar, Kausik Bandyopadhyay, Joseph Alter and others, the study of sport in India remains a barely tilled vast field awaiting discovery on many fronts.

Sport, in the Indian context, is particularly apt for investigation as a social, cultural and economic field since the ideals of individual masculinity and moral athleticism are not so universally subscribed to. Rather, sporting activity is more closely aligned to the creation and assertion of identity and class mobility, to nationalism, decolonisation, border crossing and modernity, i.e. the alternative sociologies of sport. Further, sport in India, is not just a preserve of the playing field but embeds many of the critical flash-points of today's society like corruption and gender discrimination. Effects like match-fixing, doping, sex testing are part of the larger issues being played out in a developing society with competing interests: the Indian Premier League betting scandals cannot be divorced from the growing corruption in high places and the harassment of the athlete, Pinki Pramanik, by the police and the attempt to medically 'fix' her gender, an unfortunate instance of the anxieties stoked by unconventional female sexualities. As a matter of fact, the place of all women in sport—players, coaches, commentators and spectators—is marked by a deplorable absence of coverage and discourse. They attract notice only as eroticized bodies: recall the fuss over the skimpily dressed gyrating 'cheerleaders' introduced in the IPL cricket matches. On the other hand, examples of social empowerment through sport are increasingly to be found: the establishing of the football club, YUWA, for young tribal girls in, Ranchi, Jharkhand, is like a fairy tale come true. Some have been selected for the under sixteen team and many have set a goal of earning a living through football.[11] The selection of the first cricketer from Kashmir, Parvez Rasool, for the national team was hailed as a step towards national integration. Test cricketer and scorer of 6 sixes in 6 balls, Yuvraj Singh's book, *The Test of my Life: Cricket to Cancer* had the indirect though welcome effect of sensitising the public towards an openness about cancer. Play, games and sport constitute the veritable fields of life being played out today.

While the representation of sport in Indian literature is yet to have a Philip Roth like *Great American Novel* with baseball both as centre of plot and as a metaphor of life, the Game of Dice in the *Mahabharata* is not far behind. It is the pivot of the whole epic, the one identifiable cause of the great war forming a point of no return; simultaneously ritualistic, symbolic and realist, stoking both duty and passion, *dharma* and greed, obsession and lust and provoking immutable questions of legality and rights. It forms the primal instance of match-fixing as also an archetypal representation of '*bhaga*' versus '*bhagya*',[12] the playoff between achievement and fortune, skill and luck—the crucial cornerstone of all games. Literary treatments, which can go behind the scenes and into the heart and mind of the players and the spectators, can expose and exploit these ambivalences and their tensions, even as they comment and critique them. They can turn sport into political and moral metaphors e.g. in the well known stories by Premchand, *Shatranj ke Khiladi* and *Gulli Danda*. Further, a direct interactivity and intertextuality of a most unusual and striking kind between literature, even high brow literature, and sports practice is to be found in the book, *Shakespeare the Coach*, by the famous hockey player and now key coach Ric Charlesworth which tells us how he has consistently found in Shakespeare's plays and sonnets apt words and lines for stimulating motivation and management in sportspersons.

The fields of the study of sport are therefore as extensive as varied. This book is one of the first of its kind to emerge from India. In attempting to mine these fields, it not only takes all sport as its arena of study and foregrounds India as a location for most of its discussions, but also it adopts an interdisciplinary perspective to engage with the representation of sport in art, literature and film. The essays are divided into four parts which represent the main areas of investigation. Part 1 'Sporting Cultures,' locates sport and sporting events in culture, society and history. It begins with a discussion of the 'Delhi Commons,' a public and participatory exhibition of artwork and photographs conceived and curated by Iram Gufran, film maker and artist, as a riposte to the experience of the Commonwealth Games of 2010 in Delhi. The Games, CWG, as (mis)termed locally, served as a springboard for the book. As a matter of fact, the seminar and the resultant book were provoked by the frustration of the common citizen being at the receiving end of the hoopla of the games, at being turned into a hapless spectator of the chaos in a city being torn apart by the refurbishing of stadia, roads and even sewers, of the gross mismanagement and scams which followed, and of experiencing a huge disconnect with the world of administrators and athletes in which the rest of the people did not count—could not even get tickets for events which were finally performed to half-full stadia. The art work and photographs of 'Delhi Commons'—the title playing and punning on the fractured collectivity of the 'Commonwealth' and the 'commons'—which are included in the book are a sample of the sharp and witty articulation of such responses bringing out into the open the other, undocumented dimensions of mega nationalised events where the actual sports become fleeting memories amidst permanent legacies of dug up environments and displacements. They are graphic narratives which memorialise moments in the sporting history of the city.

Cricket is, of course, the premier game in India, judging by its massive following throughout the country. It is also representative of the new postcolonial India in its complete appropriation of a colonial game where the centre of power has shifted to India. This is a consequence of its newest format the Indian Premier League (IPL) which, like Kerry Packer's one-day matches of a generation ago, has transformed the sport by its T20 matches. It has moved the cricket economy, in India an estimated three billion dollars,[13] towards the big finance of football leagues. However, its shine has been somewhat tarnished by the controversies around spot fixing and corruption which emerged in its seasons V and VI (2012/13). Boria Majumdar's essay here 'The Indian Premier League and the Future of Indian Cricket' is an apt corrective to the current doomsters about the sport. It traces the growth of IPL, its revolutionizing effect on the economics, marketing and the attraction of the new avatar of the game for players and spectators. He argues that the seeming commodification of the 'gentleman's game' is infusing new life into a game which was increasingly playing to emptying stands; that the infusion of glamour through Bollywood franchises, female commentators and cheerleaders has lead to a jump in and diversification of viewership and that finally it is the fans who will save the game—as was witnessed in their nationwide protests forcing the chairman of the BCCI to step aside after the most recent expose of his involvement in the conflict of financial interests.[14]

'Sporting Legacies in India: Mohun Bagan's 1911 Football Victory *versus* Olympic Hockey Medals' by Novy Kapadia takes us through a historical recap of the sporting successes in Indian hockey and football followed by a searching review of the varying fortunes of the two sports. He focuses on their paradoxical trajectories that despite the spectacular early victories of hockey—gold medals in successive Olympics—as opposed to the one very early historic win of Mohun Bagan over the East Yorkshire Regiment, hockey has never been able to garner and sustain that passionate support and fan base as football, and now, cricket. Kapadia's analysis offers cogent cultural, political and institutional reasons for this: the emigration of the Anglo-Indians who were a mainstay of the early hockey teams, the nationalistic celebration of hockey as opposed to the regional rooting fervor surrounding football, the rise of cricket after the 1983 World Cup victory, the coming of colour television, but most crucial of all, the governmental control and administrative failures to promote the games in a now globalised media driven world.

Part 2 'Sport and Literature,' shifts emphasis to examining how literary writings can encapsulate a larger picture of sport embedded in the trials and dilemmas of human history and society. Since literature both represents and constructs and is able to mirror and critique simultaneously, creative writing/film become more suitable for the articulation of the darker shades behind the glamorisation of sports, for exposing the inevitable politics of sporting cultures and the presentation of alternate world views where winning is not necessarily success and losing can be winning. Supriya Chaudhuri's 'Other Histories: Modernity, Literature and Football in India' argues that a full account of the place of football in Bengal is best found in the short stories and novellas of Moti Nandy. She elaborates and theorises the development of organised sport in India as a marker of modernity. Unlike cricket, football, especially in Bengal, has always been a subaltern sport, patronised largely by the working class. Its following grew with partition refugees who developed a deep identification and loyalty to the game, its clubs, players, and their struggles to establish themselves. The 'gritty realism' of Moti Nandy's writings, characteristic of literary modernism in India which was not divorced from the popular, she argues, is not of a triumphalism but of suffering and pain, and depicts a connect with the everyday reality of the local sport, doubly significant in the light of the fact that now most sport is experienced through a globalised media.

Literature is also a powerful means of critique and Sanam Khanna's 'Sport, Surveillance and Speed in the *Hunger Games* Trilogy' explicates how Suzanne Collins' futuristic and dystopic novels (2008–10), now adapted into two films (2012/14), expose the contemporary celebrity culture in sports and its mediatisation and manipulation by technology. Bringing the concept of chronoscopic time, the result of the telescoping of time and space in live transmission, which creates an instantaneous mode of production and consumption, argues Khanna, technology has created an era of eye-lust demanding faster and newer action and images at high speed which ultimately devolve into the violent. Such media control is the focus of the trilogy. It projects a future in which games are used by a totalitarian society to assert control over its people: young representatives hunt and kill each other in a competition—the prize is food for their districts—which is telecast live, but selectively, to provide entertainment dope for the rest. Its scathing satirical perspective on the extent of the commercialisation and degradation of sporting values is seen in the end when the distinction between war and games is collapsed.

Quidditch, the fantasy game of the biggest success of children's fiction of current times, the Harry Potter series by J. K. Rowling, is the subject of Paromita Patranobish's essay 'Quidditch Incorporated: Sports, Fantasy and the Consumer Child'. It explores a singular instance of the development of a sport which has been born out of fiction, and which not only forms a convergence of fantasy and fact, of performance and material culture, of play and the consumerised child, but also of deep narrative structures of the quest and a moral compass registering the resistance as well as the collusion of child's play with the commodification of sport.

The popular genre of the British schoolgirl story which evolved out of the schoolboy stories and hence placed organised sports as central is surveyed and contextualised by Aishwarya Subramanian in 'The New Girl and the British School Story'. She argues that the growth of women's education in the late nineteenth and early twentieth centuries incorporated the prevailing emphasis on the sports ethic in schools, despite Victorian society's reservations against women's strenuous physical activity. This new sporting culture for young girls is reflected in the school stories too and leads to a redefinition of femininity, giving girls access to 'masculine values' like leadership, discipline and team spirit. Though not quite 'feminist' in their perspective, these stories were radical in the Victorian context in their depiction of shifts in gendering based on a revaluation of sports for women.

The final essay in this section chooses the primal sport of running as its concern. Sohini Banerjee in 'The Long Run: The Modernist Experience as Long Distance Running' discourses on the two iconic texts on long-distance running, Alan Sillitoe's 'The Loneliness of the Long Distance Runner' and Haruki Murakami's *What I Talk About When I Talk About Running* juxtaposed with the film *Forrest Gump*, all of which she finds enframed in postmodern narrative structures but hankering towards a modernist awareness and affirmation of the self. Long-distance running, she argues, becomes in these texts a metaphor for life itself, a process and an equivalence of the search for meaning.

Part 3 'Sporting Bodies', analyses the impact of sport on the psychology and the corporeality of the performing bodies of the sportsperson, on identity and behaviour of sports bodies/clubs and on the transpositions between virtual and other realities in computer gaming. Maitri Baruah in her essay, 'The Expressive Body: Notes on Individualism and Solitude in Sport' looks at the oft disregarded underside of the habitus of the sporting body, particularly the practices, contexts and histories of spin bowlers and goalkeepers. She points out that the beauty, glamour and celebration of the sporting body conceals the fragility of its skills and a haunting melancholia about their loss. She investigates the life histories of Sonny Ramadhin, Jack Iverson and Robert Enke, all solitary individuals who scaled heights with their special and unclassifiable skills, but could not take the loss of form: Iverson put a gun to his chest and Enke walked into a train.

The sporting bodies of clubs, especially of football, and of cities that house them are perhaps more significant in modern sport than the players themselves. The passion and rivalries they evoke is the driving force of the sport. The tensions between the football clubs and fandoms of Bengal are well known: matches between Mohan Bagan, East Bengal and Mohammedan Sporting have always set the city of Kolkata on edge and often resulted in violence. Debjani Sengupta's 'Refugee City: Football and Other Divides of the Self in Post Partition Kolkata' however provides an alternative view on these sporting bodies of fans and their passions stroked by football. She argues, basing her perspective on literary evidence, that the sub-regional rivalries between the *ghotis* and *bangals* (West and East Bengalis) which were exacerbated after partition were in fact dissipated on the football field. The football arena in the nineteen-fifties and sixties Calcutta worked as a therapeutic space allowing the defusing of tensions which may otherwise have spilled on to the streets.

E-Sports or computer and digitally inspired games, whose popularity and innovative dimensions are well established today, have radically challenged the notion of the 'sporting body' through their problematisation of the material with virtual reality. Aratrika Das in 'The *Matter* that Matters—Re-thinking Corporeality in a Computer Game' initiates us into the burgeoning theoretical discourses of cyberspace and games studies in an attempt to define and refine the nature of the 'embodied experience' of playing computer games. Probing concepts like 'inter human', 'posthuman', 'techno social', 'body-in-code', 'interobjective', 'flickering signifiers' and 'haptic visuality', she argues that thinking *through* the body in analysing digital gaming critically reconfigures the nature of corporeality.

Cricket and Bollywood. Inevitably, these two have become the markers of modern India in the age of globalisation. Their twinning has rubbed off on each other, most obviously seen in sportspersons being endowed with a transferred 'star' rating and film celebrities competing with sportspersons for media endorsements. Part 4 'Sport and Cinema,' has three essays which delve into the cinematic investigations into the interstices of sporting cultures. They present the inner scenarios of individuals involved in sport. '*Shoonya* (The Zero Zone)' by producer/director Arindam Mitra is a personal account of the making of this film (2007), the first on match-fixing and gambling in cricket which won praise and awards at film festivals but could not be released in India and which, however, is uncannily congruent with the current moment with spot fixing scandals breaking out every year and in almost every country. *Shoonya*, which is not a documentary but a journey into match-fixing, focuses on the ironies of the aftermath: the anxiety of the player to confess and come clean versus the trauma of his family and friends to live with the taint. Unfolded in a series of flashbacks, it locates and enters into the crux of the problem, the heart and mind of the player, his slow but steady seduction by the bookies, his growing but false sense of an invincibility and finally the tragic inability to stop. Poonam Trivedi's 'Playing Fair, Playing for Money: A note on the film *Shoonya*', which complements Mitra's piece, is an enquiry into the dilemma of not only the individuals caught in the betting networks but also into the double-edged role of capital, the consequent changing notion of 'fairplay' in sport, and the problematic nature of ethics in cricket in particular.

'The Underdog Bowling to the Cultural Field in Kukunoor's *Iqbal*', an analysis based on the Lacanian theory of language and entry into the Symbolic, by Anas Tabraiz, gives depth to the understanding of the narrative of a film which is apt to be relegated to the fantastic and the utopian by the viewer. It argues that sport can provide empowerment to the minority and the differently abled communities by transforming them into 'desiring subjects' and thus incorporating them into the Symbolic nation/al. Iqbal, hearing and speech impaired, overcomes his physical and social obstacles to become a successful bowler by inserting himself into the imaginary: he closes his eyes to imagine that he is playing for the country and 'hears' the cheers of the crowd which spur him on. This keeps him going and he struggles to hone his skills by practicing bowling among the buffaloes he has to tend. The cricket field as a field of cultural and national desire becomes in the film a liberating and inclusive metaphor.

Women's interface with sports has always been limited in India, and even though their participation is now increasing, patriarchal society continues to pose stumbling blocks. 'The Gender Games: A Study of *Chak De! India* and *Meerabai Not Out*' by Mithuraaj Dhusiya looks at an alternative genus of the sports film which focuses on the sportswoman and the female sports fan. It finds that though ostensibly these two films valorise female participation and seemingly fashion new female subjectivities—the women's hockey team wins the tournament against all odds, and Meerabai helps her father-in-law win a cricket quiz with her encyclopedic knowledge of the game—they end by stabilising and straight jacketing the subversive female. The women players win because of the coach, Shah Rukh Khan, and Meerabai agrees to close her cricketing innings and get married. Hopefully, the projected film on boxer and Olympic medalist, Mary Kom, will do better.

The myriad meanings and moments of sport, play and game cannot hope to be encompassed in a single volume but enough interest and issues would have been generated by the essays to establish a case for the study of sport in its multiple significations. As in 'wordplay' the layering and doubleness of 'play' needs to be caught and elucidated. For instance, amidst the verbiage produced by the Commonwealth Games there was one epiphanic moment, Joseph Alter's article in the *Indian Express*, historicising the success of the Indian wrestlers in the Games. He reminded us that exactly a century ago, a young boy, named Gama, from a very small town in MP, had wrestled his way to the heart of the empire—becoming world champion in London in 1910, and how, later, in 1928 he again brought down his 300 lb opponent in a mere fortyfive seconds to become the indisputable world champion once more.[15] 'Gama pehlvan' a mythic storybook hero of our childhood days suddenly sprang into a real and radical persona, and the wrestling victories of 2010, and, later, of the 2012 Olympics which had exhilarated the whole country, could connect to those of 1910 and 1928.

Sports are there everywhere dovetailing into politics, society, culture, commerce and the arts. It is this instrumentality, of collusion and containment along with a simultaneous combativeness and creativity which accounts for their power and pull. Research and reflection, whether from the historical, sociological, anthropological, philosophical, psychological, literary, cinematic or creative perspective, serves to enhance the value of sport and realise its fullness not just as physical and aesthetic, but also as social and cultural capital. Sports today is a lens through which to understand and unpack people and society, something which books like James Astill's *The Great Indian Tamasha: Cricket, Corruption and the Turbulent Rise of Modern India* ambitiously try to accomplish. Hence it is imperative to play on.

Notes

1. Johan Huizinga, *Homo Ludens* (Boston: Beacon Press, 1970).
2. Roger Caillois, *Man, Play and Games* (New York: Schocken Books, 1979).
3. Victor Turner, 'Body, Brain and Culture', *Zygon* 18, no. 3 (1983), 221–45.
4. Jeremy Bentham, *Theory of Legislation*, 1789. This concept was further developed by Clifford Geertz in *The Interpretation of Cultures* (New York: Basic Books, 1973).
5. Brian Sutton-Smith, *The Ambiguity of Play* (Cambridge: Harvard University Press, 1997).
6. Jacques Derrida, *The Derrida Reader: Writing Performances* (Lincoln: University of Nebraska press, 1998).
7. Margaret and James Stutley, *A Dictionary of Hinduism* (London: Routledge and Kegan Paul, 1977).
8. Pierre Bourdieu, 'How can one be a Sportsman?' in *Sociology in Question* (London: Sage, 1993), pp. 117–31.
9. 'The game's afoot'... Sport, Literature and Culture' held at Indraprastha College for Women, University of Delhi, Delhi, 10–12 March 2011 and sponsored by the UGC.
10. Mario Rodrigues, *Batting for the Empire: A Political Biography of Ranjitsinghji* (New Delhi: Penguin, 2003).
11. Yuwa Football Club and Trust established by American coach Franz Gastler for poor tribal girls in Ranchi, Jharkhand, uses education and sport to tackle the issues of child marriage and trafficking. It has been widely successful: 'Over the last three years, Yuwa has managed to ensure that the kitchen has been firmly replaced by the glorious football field in the lives nearly 300 young women' writes Saadia Azim, 'Tribal girls see football as a game changer,' *One World South Asia*, 13 July 2013, http://southasia.oneworld.net/features/with-new-spikes-and-footballs-tribal-girls-as-game-changers#.UhjenX95dIY (accessed 20 Aug. 2013).

12. As observed by Romila Thapar in *From Lineage to State: Social Formations in the Mid-First Millennium B.C. in the Ganga Valley* (New Delhi: Oxford University Press, 1990), p. 57.
13. Ayaz Memon, 'Rip the Veil of Silence', *The Times of India*, 30 May 2013.
14. Boria Majumdar, 'Don't take Cricket Fans for a Ride', *The Times of India*, 9 June 2013.
15. Joseph S. Alter, 'The Akhara Earth', *The Indian Express*, 12 October 2010.

Part I

Sporting Cultures

1

Delhi Commons: A Public Art Project on the Commonwealth Games

Iram Ghufran

Postcards for All

Niha Masih

It has been four years since the mega event and the subsequent corruption scandal around the Commonwealth Games 2010 in New Delhi. What do we remember of that time? And how important is it to remember?

Come Out and Play

With this seemingly innocuous phrase, the *aam janta* was invited to participate in the sporting event of the decade. Not since the Asian Games of 1982, had the city witnessed an overdrive to revamp itself structurally. The ensuing saga of potholed roads, crashing overbridges, and flooded stadia is part of the larger story. The city had to live up to the standards of Beijing, the venue of the 2008 Olympics. That particular event had been a monstrous $33 billion dollar spectacle. Of course what didn't merit a mention in the applauding chorus was a simple corollary event—the mass displacement of more than a million people as its fallout. The irony here of course is that Delhi tried to outshine Beijing in this regard as well. Accurate figures for displacement in Delhi of course do not exist. But as we know, that just like how many 'inconvenient' things are brushed aside—'unwanted' people were pushed to the edges, and the ones on the periphery got pushed out of the city altogether.[1] Making the issue more complex were the narratives of struggle, aspiration and success from the sporting world.

The reaction to the Games was surely wide-ranging. Television and the print media produced a certain narrative more often than not reflecting the interests of the government. There was extensive reportage on the initial euphoria at bagging the mega event, to more serious concerns about how the infrastructural work would finish on time for the Opening Ceremony. Issues of corruption cropped up much later. And questioning the State's megalomaniacal desire to stage the spectacle of the century barely made it to the editorials. However there were some more reflective expressions from within the visual media and the arts. One such eclectic response was Delhi Commons.

A public art project, Delhi Commons was initiated by filmmaker and artist Iram Ghufran, and supported by Arts Network Asia [ANA]. The project brought together a range of practitioners—graphic artists, photographers, painters, and urban researchers into dialogue with each other in order to comment on the complex narrative of the South Asian city and the shaping of its specific modernity.

The etymological significance behind the title Delhi Commons has to be understood for a more interesting reading of the project. While obviously deriving from the Commonwealth Games, the title also borrows from the idea of the 'Commons' and hence the project sought to produce a shared resource in the shape of an 'image commons'.

While the title addressed the many contours of the discourse, the project tried to create an understanding of the relationship of contemporary cities to mega events and 'memory making'. 'Delhi Commons' addressed issues concerning that itinerant flux of our times and ultimately how a city is inhabited, experienced and understood. This experience extended to having a world class Metro which connected the city in ways earlier unimaginable. The peripheries became a part of the centre though many of those who made up the centre ultimately could not hold. Shanty owners alongside the same Metro flyover were banished behind huge Commonwealth hoardings. Those who couldn't be evicted were conveniently covered up. The incongruity of the hoardings proclaiming 'Come out and play' was of course lost upon the Commonwealth Games Organising Committee. They had the most challenging task of procuring treadmills, chairs and toilet paper (among others) at 100 times the usual cost. (The cost of hiring a treadmill for a month and a half (being paid by the OC)—Rs 9,75,000, a chair at Rs 8,378 apiece and a 100 litre refrigerator at Rs 42,202.)

While the figures did not quite add up, neither did pretty much anything else.

The project had two key elements—an online photography show, and a postcard series. To be able to reach out to the maximum people, the project had its own website, a Flickr account, and a popular Facebook page. The website hosted the photographs for which entries were invited. People were encouraged to send in cell phone images keeping in view the penetration of the mobile network in the country. While stand alones were admitted as well, people were asked to submit a series of 8–12 images for the weekly photo show.

Calls for submitting postcard designs too received a huge feedback. People were encouraged to take photos, surf the internet, work with found images and words, work with crayons and paint, cut, copy, paste, remix. It was felt that only with the involvement of spontaneous responses like these could the project really hope to traverse across various spectrums of society, and keep up with the pace at which the city was changing, minute by minute into a behemoth, swallowing anything and anyone in its way. And as and when designs were submitted by artists and others through email and Facebook, the postcards were printed.

Distribution of this material was also done in different ways. They were kept in shops such as the People Tree and Yodakin, to be picked up, given out in other places, displayed in other locations. The idea was to try and intervene in as many kinds of spaces as possible. The postcards were also posted to art centres, universities, individuals, activists, artists, filmmakers and workers of all kinds. The image of the Games was to be a message that travels to a range of contexts and practices. On request they were also mailed to people who wrote in. The Facebook page was an important tool as it helped to connect with a range of people as well as get responses to the work. All photographs and postcards received comments, feedback and brickbats.

As with most artworks, the project tried to go beyond documentation in an attempt to make an intervention. The idea was to produce an artwork that outlasted the Games, and travelled to other cities, and contexts carrying with it some stories, images, and expressions on the Commonwealth Games of 2010. The disconnect that the city experienced because of the structural and social transformation at the time preceding and during the Games was played around through various mediums. Delhi Commons succeeded in creating a more evocative understanding of the same through this body of work.

The photographs produce an image of the Delhi of 2009–10, which in the first instance of the plethora of imagery around us may seem superfluous. A closer inspection reveals nuanced camera work by professional and amateur photographers.

The project succeeded in drawing artists like Amitabh Kumar and Bhagwati Prasad from the Sarai Media Lab-CSDS and independent artists like Vishwajyoti Ghosh, Pradip Saha and Priya Sen were some of the other contributors. Besides, there were scores of entries from students, amateur photographers, designers, artists, poets et al. Photojournalism students from the Mass Communication Research Centre of Jamia Millia Islamia (batch of 2010) too were involved in this process.

The Postcards travelled. They carried messages, stories, secrets and rumours of the Commonwealth Games across cities and continents. Far from being emblematic of the picturesque, the sanitised and the iconic, the Delhi Commons postcard series is provocative and sensitive to the current flux. The imagery produced by the project ultimately hopes to have created an abiding memory of the Delhi that will never be the same.

Note

1. See the report of the Housing and Land Rights Network, Habitat International Coalition, February 2011, 'Planned Dispossession: Forced Evictions and the 2010 Commonwealth Games' which estimated that more than 200,000 people were evicted from 19 sites in Delhi leading not just to displacement but also rampant violation of human rights. Ironically, these are the very people whose labour runs the city.

Illustration 1.1 *Artist*: Pradip Saha *Courtesy*: Delhi Commons

Illustration 1.2 *Artist*: Bhagwat Prasad *Courtesy*: Delhi Commons

Illustration 1.3 *Artist*: Mitoo Das *Courtesy*: Delhi Commons

Illustration 1.4 *Artist*: Deepankar Gohain *Courtesy*: Delhi Commons

Illustration 1.5 *Artist*: Iram Ghufran *Courtesy*: Delhi Commons

Illustration 1.6 *Artist*: Ranjini Chatterjee *Courtesy*: Delhi Commons

COME OUT AND PLAY !...

Illustration 1.7 *Artist*: Maithila Baindur *Courtesy*: Delhi Commons

2

The Indian Premier League and the Future of Indian Cricket

Boria Majumdar

In the contemporary sporting world, few would doubt that India is the new cricketing superpower. More often than not, Indians lead, while other nations follow. Without exaggeration, Indian cricket is a mirror in which the nation, communities, men and women now see themselves. That reflection is sometimes bright, sometimes dark, sometimes distorted, sometimes magnified. Cricket for a billion-plus Indians is a source of mass exhilaration and depression, security and insecurity, pride and humiliation, bonding and alienation.

India's position as the new nerve centre of world cricket has been strengthened in recent times thanks to the impact of the Indian Premier League. The IPL, played for seven weeks between April–May for five seasons now has been a success by most yardsticks, so much so that there was talk of a withdrawal syndrome among cricket fans once the spectacle was over in Seasons I and II. In most metropolitan cities across India, as also in many cities across the world with large Indian diasporas, watching the IPL action has become a craze. As the clock strikes 8.00 IST, it is IPL time. Spread over a month and a half, the tournament has been full of moments of drama, spectacle, ecstasy and agony. At the cost of giving favourite soaps and serials a miss, entire Indian families have been converted to the heady mix of cricket and entertainment on offer, a package unprecedented and one that transformed the face of Indian cricket for all time to come.

Yet Brand IPL, many argued during IPL Season V, is no longer what it used to be in 2008–9. The argument was premised on the fact that some advertisement spots on Set Max were unsold, advertisement rates in 2012 had fallen in comparison to 2011, some stadiums were half full in the initial stages of the tournament and the buzz associated with the tournament was missing. The number of dedicated IPL shows on news channels, helping to add to the buzz, was also limited and the tournament, critics pointed out, was facing a 'midlife crisis'. The truth, however, is that a correction was only expected. After five years in existence, the tournament has indeed become a part of Indian households and is no longer the innovation it was in 2008 or 2009. But that does not mean the brand is in crisis. In fact, it is unfair to compare brand IPL with the EPL or the La Liga. While the latter have a hundred year old history, the IPL, in that sense is a toddler. More importantly even the EPL and the La Liga have faced a series of existential crises in their course of existence. The entire 1980s was a period of turmoil for the English Football league. Continental competitions had stolen a march over the English variant and the competition was badly in need of innovation. Stadium disasters like the Hillsborough tragedy added to the gloom and the FA had to carve out the premiership (in the avatar we know it now) in 1992–93 to give the league a new lease of life. Against such a backdrop it is far more pertinent to compare brand IPL with some of its other T-20 counterparts from around the world, the Big Bash League in Australia, the Bangladesh Premier League or the T-20 competition in England to better analyse the issue of the sustainability of the IPL brand.

By comparison with the first Big Bash league game at the Melbourne Cricket Ground in December 2011 between the Melbourne Stars and the Sydney Thunder, the IPL is on a firm footing. Despite all the novelty surrounding the Big Bash League and the tremendous brand building exercise done to promote the tournament, the MCG was more than two thirds empty on the opening night with some 24,000 people making it to the stadium to watch Shane Warne and team in action. However, the television audience, 858,000, the highest in Australian television history for cricket, made the start a successful one. While many of the later games were well attended, it was the TV audience that sustained the competition in its first year. Compare it with the IPL and the resilience of the Indian brand is evident. Despite being in its fifth year and despite being played in rather adverse weather conditions most of the games were eventually played before sellout crowds. Eden Gardens for example was full for most of the Kolkata Knight Riders' games and an unprecedented 70,000 plus attended the celebrations after KKR's maiden IPL triumph. More importantly, television ratings, in comparison to other soaps and serials, continue to remain vibrant.

The IPL has also resulted in an unprecedented windfall for the Board of Control for Cricket in India and some franchise owners of the competing teams, a number currently steady at nine. Except the Sahara Pune Warriors franchise, which continues to sustain a loss of over a 100 crores every year against the high franchise fee paid, most of the other franchises have broken even. Contrary to fears, the BCCI too earned Rs. 350 crore from the inaugural edition in 2008 and 118 crores from the fourth edition in 2011. Several franchise owners like Shah Rukh Khan had broken even in year one itself. It is this unprecedented success of the IPL, repeated in 2012, that helped consolidate India's position as world cricket's centre of gravity and completed the process of Indian cricket's 'decolonisation'.

Pre-Tournament Fears

The IPL administrators' decision to put the cricketers under the commercial hammer met with vociferous opposition from more than one quarter. Moralists and politicians throughout India were up in arms against this public auctioning in February 2008, even threatening to raise the issue in Parliament. The Communist Party of India claimed that the auction had sounded the 'death knell' of the gentleman's game. In Mumbai, the Shiv Sena castigated then BCCI President for turning cricketers into 'commodities'.

Other key questions that confronted organisers before the start of the IPL was whether the benefits of monetisation would truly filter down to the grassroots and contribute to improving the domestic cricket superstructure? Would fans come out to spend their hard-earned money to watch games in the oppressive heat of April and May? Indeed, the question of fan participation was pertinent because in India fans generally only ever attend international cricket contests, pitting countries against each other. Nationalism, in other words, has been at the core of cricket-watching in India. Meanwhile,

Indian domestic contests such as the Ranji or Duleep Trophy, even when major Indian stars like Rahul Dravid or Saurav Ganguly are playing, hardly attract more than a 1000 spectators per match.[1] It was also conjectured that faced with teams made up of random conglomerations of players, the draw for most spectators was less the game and more the entertainment on offer. But will fans really want to be merely 'entertained' for seven straight weeks?[2] Even in terms of television viewership, the IPL—pitted against soaps and reality-television shows—faced stiff competition. Finally, it was hotly debated whether the benefits of the new league would trickle down to the grassroots and whether the tournament could ultimately serve as a supply line for future national stars.

Post Tournament Reality

When the legendary Arthur Morris, key member of Don Bradman's invincible team of the 1940s, was asked what he got out of playing cricket, his answer was startling. Morris negotiated the question with a single-word retort, 'Poverty'.[3] With the onset of a cricketing revolution courtesy the Indian Premier League, contemporary cricketers will have a radically different answer to a similar question. Most, it can be conjectured, will respond with a satisfied smile, 'We became millionaires'.[4] One billion dollars in TV rights for a ten year period, hitherto unthinkable player-earnings, $5 million in prize money, $5 million for title sponsorship rights for five years, unprecedented television ratings and huge crowds in practically all the games in its five years of existence: what the IPL has unequivocally driven home is that the shift of the nerve centre of cricket to the subcontinent is now complete.

Modelled on Major League Baseball and the National Football League, IPL has come at a time when the Indian economy has opened itself to global riches and the big corporate houses trying to make India their home, are in search of lucrative investment platforms across the country.[5] IPL, for many, is the ideal answer. At one go, it has given them a foothold in a market of a billion plus and has generated eyeballs that millions spent on advertisements won't garner. Add to this the fact that for a billion plus cricket fans, filling stadiums was hardly difficult with proper marketing and hype. With celebrity owners like Shah Rukh Khan and Preity Zinta doing their bit in earnest, fans had more than cricket on offer for a couple of hundred rupees. The IPL was, and continues to be, a great evening out at a reasonable price. And with fans thronging the grounds or picking their seat in front of the TV set, sponsors queued up and paid millions for 10-second slots on Set Max, on in-stadia hoardings and team apparel.

IPL Impact

With IPL 2012 also a reasonable success, and with national cricket boards seemingly making room for it already, it will be of interest to note if the International Cricket Council soon creates a window for the billion dollar league despite its aversion to doing so. So far the ICC has been against creating a window citing its inability to offer preferential treatment to one domestic league.[6] The one time the ICC clashed with innovative private entrepreneurship in the 1970s, it was humiliated at the hands of Australian media tycoon Kerry Packer. If the IPL continues to humiliate it in the years moving forward, control of the game's most lucrative version may well slip from the ICC's hands. Interestingly, even when the league had to move to South Africa in 2009 at short notice because of its clash with India's national elections,[7] its popularity hardly waned. Half-full grounds or less than animated spectators in Durban or Cape Town could be perceived as blips only when IPL season two was compared to packed stands and wild spectators back home in IPL's inaugural edition.

For South Africa, however, the tournament was a success. Anyone with reasonable knowledge of South African sport will agree that the IPL, a foreign import, did much to present South Africa as a perfect sporting destination before the 2010 FIFA World Cup. Social integration, still far from complete in mainstream South Africa, received a significant boost thanks to the IPL. And sports organisers, fearing a western backlash citing under-preparedness for the FIFA event, had their hands hugely strengthened. IPL season two was also a successful experiment with globalisation. It was India's first truly global sporting export and helped create India's first international sporting brand. Unlike most sports still controlled and dominated by the West, the IPL is an example of 'atypical' globalisation, where the West has to look to the East. It has led to the possibility wherein Indian administrators can justly claim that in cricket at least, an Indian hegemony is finally about to commence. Unifying the global cricket world under its aegis, India has successfully consolidated its commercial hold atop cricket's global hierarchy. With leading exponents of the game like Shane Warne, Chris Gayle and others urging the International Cricket Council to create a window for the IPL, it is expected that this 'grip' over world cricket will grow stronger in years to come.

Also, the lasting gain from IPL's second edition was evident once the tournament returned home in March 2010.[8] The IPL came back to its home base having established itself as a leading global sports brand with multiple global enclaves and constituencies, carefully created and nurtured in the course of the second edition of the tournament. At a time when the irresponsible actions of some global sports administrators like the Australian Tennis Federation tried to identify India as an unsafe sports destination,[9] the IPL was India's best bet in reversing this unfortunate trend. Having received rave reviews in South Africa and having done much to woo the world's best, IPL 2010 continued to bring together the most impressive assemblage of the world's leading cricketers. And with resolute government support coming to its help in 2010, it did much to strengthen India's claim to being a safe sporting destination months before the controversy ridden New Delhi Commonwealth Games in October 2010.[10]

IPL and the Race Question

Besides consolidating India's position as world cricket's financial capital, the IPL also played its part in countering the racial problem, one that continues to plague international sports contests. The discourse on 'race' in India has been historically predicated upon a position of relative under-privilege. India, considered a 'white man's burden',[11] during its colonial conditioning fought for nearly two centuries to free itself of this position of inferiority. While discrimination based on conditions of colour and economic pre-eminence was a regular practice in colonial India, its vestiges continued for decades after independence. Hence, every time an Indian is questioned by an immigration official on entering a western country, it is immediately perceived as a deliberate act of racial discrimination. To go a step further—most Indians settled in the West, were, till a couple of decades earlier, expected to be living in a ghettoised urban space, hardly ever integrated into the mainstream of western society. This understanding of the West as 'superior' made for divisions between the occident and the orient and allowed for the perpetuation of the doctrine of 'orientalism'.

This kind of understanding of race has been substantively transformed in recent times and the Indian Premier League, a successful Indian innovation, has certainly helped mediate this change. Race, in contemporary India, is no longer a discourse predicated upon notions of inferiority. Rather, of late at least, it is built upon a notion of privilege, which has largely to do with India's new found status as a world player in an era of globalisation. At no point am I trying to claim that the IPL is a singular mover in heralding this transformation. Rather, it is my contention that the IPL has significantly enhanced the process, which, in the sporting domain, was spearheaded by India's takeover of world cricket's finances from the middle of the 1990s.[12] With the nerve centre of cricket moving to India, a process the IPL has finally completed, there occurred three significant changes:

1. The West was much better co-opted and appropriated within the Indian imaginary.
2. The tournament brought to light the complex and also exceptional nature of India's racialised modernity.
3. Finally, an aggressive hyper-jingoistic nationalist sentiment has emerged in India and this often results in a complete overturning of the conventional racial ideology.

This transformed race reality is borne out by an ethnography of spectator behaviour across IPL matches in South Africa in 2009. For example, when Shane Warne rushed to congratulate Yusuf Pathan after his super-over heroics for the Rajasthan Royals (Pathan now plays for the Kolkata Knight Riders franchise), the large Indian diasporic crowd was spontaneous in applauding Warne for his gesture. The Australian superhero, taken out of his nationalist context, had suddenly been appropriated and indigenised and was a key member of the Rajasthan Royals side. In the first edition of the IPL too this feature was prominent. David Hussey (who now plays for the Kings XI Punjab), the most consistent batsman for the Kolkata team in IPL season one, had soon become 'Hussey da', meaning elder brother in the vernacular. However, this co-option rests on unstable foundations, a fact evident from the venom spat at coach John Buchanan each time the Kolkata Knight Riders failed to deliver. Each failure was been greeted with murmurs of a 'white man here in India just for the money.'

This behaviour, it needs to be stated, is an exact throwback to a century earlier, when the British reacted in an exactly similar manner to Ranji, Indian cricket's first superhero. Ranji, a native chief who had no rightful claim to the throne of his principality finally became *Jamsaheb* thanks to the British support that came his way.[13] This support, it can be argued, was largely a product of Ranji's cricketing prowess. Educated at Cambridge, Ranji went on to represent England against Australia with distinction and thus captured the public imagination of his people back home. When Ranji scored a century on debut for England against Australia in 1896, his performance had a multi-layered impact. In England he became the people's darling and roused a 'Ranji fever'. In India, contrastingly, Ranji's batting was declared a triumph of nationalism on the sporting field disregarding the fact that Ranji was playing for Britain, the 'white master'. For the colonial Indian imagination, the political reality of colonialism was relegated to a lower rung in the hierarchy, below the cardinal question of 'race'.[14]

British administrators in India also tried to bail Ranji out of his financial difficulties on grounds that it was unworthy of a great cricketer to suffer such ignominy. For the British in India, Ranji was a hero having performed well against arch rivals Australia. The British rulers saw him as proto-British and used him as a trump card in sports contests against Australia. However, every time he failed, it didn't take much time for the spectators to label him a 'dirty nigger', displaying how sports as a social practice has always been used to signify far deeper and more significant cultural attitudes and political contours.[15] Another thing is certain. Post-colonial studies for more than two decades have been focussing on answering a cardinal question raised by Gayatri Chakraborty Spivak, "Can the subaltern speak?" The evidence from the IPL makes it possible to raise a counter-question: Is the subaltern a subaltern any more?

Controlling the Cricket Economy

Once the second edition of the IPL was over on 24 May 2009, action shifted to the UK for the world T-20, which was played out in June 2009.[16] Unlike the domestic T-20 circuit in the UK, which is gradually falling by the wayside, an international competition like the ICC T-20, which is rooted in nationalism and nationalist sensibilities, it was argued, will always thrive in multicultural London and its surrounds. And this is where the sub-continent comes into the equation. Put bluntly, the huge Indian and Pakistani cricket markets, both at home and in the British South Asian Diaspora, held the key to the organisers making substantial profits from the competition. In fact, soon after ESPN-Star sports, the host broadcaster, acquired the ICC telecast rights for a staggering billion plus dollars in early 2007, then ESS Managing Director Jamie Davis had declared, 'This acquisition affirms our commitment to the Indian sub-continent and the world and we are absolutely delighted to bring the exciting line-up of ICC events to millions of cricket fans globally.'

Inherent in this statement is the root of the problem. For the recovery of more than 80% of the $1.1bn spent, ESPN was and is banking on the cricket craze in India. Intrinsic to Mr Davis' statement is the notion that cricket continues to be the license to print money for broadcasters in the sub-continent. However, the reality, as Peter Hutton former boss of rival sports channel Ten Sports and one who had just taken over as Managing Director of ESPN, suggested is that 'the price being paid is linked to equity valuations, mergers and acquisitions. It is a dangerous time, when advertising income doesn't cover the rights fees being paid and there is every danger of the cricketing bubble economy going bust.'[17] With the economic downturn continuing to seriously affect the Western world, the cricket economy too, it is expected, will take a hit. With people's spending powers limited and with companies shutting down every month, in stadia advertisers are counting their pounds before agreeing to be a part of the spectacle. Even advertising rates are being tailored to suit the downturn and this is where the reliance on the sub-continent, relatively stable in comparison, increases.

In effect, this means that India and Pakistan need to play well all the time if the huge amounts invested by the broadcasters are to be recovered. In fact, if India or Pakistan crash out at group stage, as had happened in the Caribbean in the 2007 World Cup, advertisers' interest in the tournament nosedives.[18] The exact opposite happened in world cup 2011 with the India Pakistan semi-final at Mohali garnering an unprecedented television rating of 35.2. In fact, it can also be argued that the World Cups in 1999 and 2003, in England and South Africa respectively, were economic success stories because Pakistan (1999) and India (2003) made it to the finals. During the 2003 World Cup, market consultants in India had estimated a total advertising spending over the six weeks as something like $222m—more than the net profit that India's largest private sector company Reliance Industries posted in the first quarter of the financial year 2002–03.

Interestingly, in a time scale less than the length of Sachin Tendulkar's career,[19] the nature and economy of world cricket has fundamentally changed. In 1992, the Indian cricket board (BCCI), now the richest cricket body in the world, had a deficit of $150,000. And in 1997, the ICC, cricket's apex body, had a little more than $25,000 in its coffers.[20] Once cricket administrators decided to marry cricket with television, the game changed. The cricket market became an Indian monopoly and within months the schedule of cricket worldwide was driven by the needs of multiple television players each wanting a share of the Indian pie.

Indian Cricket and the Satellite Television Revolution

Cricket's emergence as a prime driver of entertainment television in India is a relatively new phenomenon. Until 2002, at the time when Sony television first made its mark with the telecast of the ICC Champions Trophy played in Colombo, cricket was hardly ever covered by non-news and non-sports channels in India. Till then cricket was not entertainment; it was sport, which was profoundly different and had a distinctive sphere of its own. Then came what can justifiably be termed the *broadcast* revolution. Just like most things novel, the first attempt to promote cricket with star divas as anchors in September 2002 was a failure.[21]

Unlike most novel Indian experiments, however, the plan was persisted with. And the biggest surprise of World Cup 2003, an even bigger surprise perhaps than India's qualification for the final, was the runaway success of the Mandira Bedi[22] phenomenon. The success was such that during the world cup Max showed a 24% growth while rivals like Star lost out on 47% of its viewers. Many ask whether this unique blending of entertainment with sport dilutes the essence of cricket. In other words, whether such a blending, which for some is an anathema for the cricket purist, can ever take the game forward. Such questions, I wish to suggest, are missing the point completely. As Amartya Sen had mentioned in an interview soon after winning the Nobel Prize, it is not relevant whether one likes globalisation or not, it is the defining feature of our age and we have to live with it. It is only pertinent how far we are able to tame it to suit our needs. Similarly, after the success of the *Set Max* brand of IPL cricket coverage with Archana Vijaya and Shivani Dandekar as the faces of the coverage, the important question is no longer whether this form of coverage is proper.

Rather, the question is, or should be, how the nature of coverage can be made more interactive—thus widening the ambit of cricket spectatorship. One simple statistic is enough to substantiate the above point. In 2003, most cricket magazines and portals had rallied against the 'invasion of the dumb belles' but by the end of the World Cup, Sony's managers themselves were surprised by the ratings: 2.2 crore women had tuned in and amounted to a massive 46% of the total viewership. Set Max had successfully become the 'voice of the cricket-widows'. At the same time the die-hard cricket purist had not condemned the Max brand of coverage. As Rajat Jain, a senior *Max* official had suggested, 'A purist is someone who will watch cricket regardless of whether or not India is playing. And remember even before India had played its first match Extra Innings had reached out to 25.1 million individuals. We believe that a majority of them were purists.'

Another interesting IPL innovation was the unique blending of Bollywood with cricket, something that has significantly advanced with the IPL. Given that cricket and Bollywood have been crucial in fashioning people's identification with a consumerist ethos within a liberalising society and economy, this was a masterstroke. The best evidence of this blending is the KKR celebration at the Eden Gardens on 29 May 2012, which was watched by close to 100,000 people inside and outside the stadium. What has helped the new brand of cricket broadcast is cricket's newest avatar, Twenty20 cricket. The similarities are indeed palpable—both have raised the eyebrows of the purists; both have proved to be runaway successes and both, to go a step further, seem defining aspects of the game's future.

In April 2003 the *Daily Telegraph*, London, had published a poignant picture the day after the start of the English domestic cricket season. A six-column, almost half-page picture, it showed a solitary spectator watching county cricket in an otherwise empty stand. The bottomline was clear. English cricket needed new infusion of oxygen to survive with the very existence of county cricket in peril. This oxygen was first supplied on June 13, 2003 at the Rose Bowl in Hampshire when Sussex Sharks played Hampshire Hawks. Nearly 15,000 people enjoyed the action and a new phenomenon in Twenty20 cricket was born. Present at the Rose Bowl on that eventful day, I was amazed to see the high percentage of children who had come along with their parents to enjoy the action. Not many, I must confess, watched cricket. However, they did have a good time. With games, toys and a concert to follow it was a perfect summer evening out for the family. Having just watched a few baseball games at Wrigley Field in Chicago, home of the Chicago Cubs, it all seemed familiar—the music, short duration, loud drawling announcements, a little break between innings, two-word alliterating names, frenzied action and, above all, non-stop fun. Anathema for the cricket purist, it was, simply put, the 'baseballisation' of cricket. If asked to describe the origins of Twenty20 cricket in a single sentence, the best answer would be: it was a survival mechanism. The unique blending of cricket and entertainment achieved by the IPL in the Indian context is yet another survival mechanism.

Most cricket fanatics, leave alone the occasional ones, are saturated by the amount of one-day cricket played each year. In such a situation it is almost imperative for television broadcasters to introduce new innovations, newer techniques of coverage that will continue to attract eyeballs to the nation's most perceptible passion. More than making profits, it may be suggested, the broadcaster is entrusted with the duty to ensure that Indians don't get bored with one-day cricket. And women anchors, noodle straps, tarot cards, models amidst the fans are all such innovations, which have successfully made cricket coverage more viewer friendly and more interactive.

The success of entertainment-focused cricket programming has led other Indian news and even global sports channels to replicate the same model. In fact, the strategy—special programming with women anchors and other innovative attractions have become the standard way of covering the IPL in India and also in some other countries like the UK. In England for example the ITV coverage of the fifth season of the IPL was fronted among others by Isa Guha, former England fast bowler and someone who can easily pass off as a model.

The Future

Brand IPL, some say is in danger. The spate of controversies that marred IPL season V, players caught spot fixing and accepting black money, molesting women at late night parties, were the reasons given in support of the argument. Lalit Modi, the banished IPL Czar, currently in London, continuously added fuel to this controversy. With the ongoing spat between the BCCI and Lalit Modi showing no signs of settling, Modi is every bit intent on sullying the image of the IPL in its current form. However, once we delve deep, there is little doubt that the IPL, the property itself, goes far beyond an individual's whim and that the institution of Indian cricket is surely much more resilient and capable than we hold it to be at moments of crisis. Even when the Modi-BCCI spat was spouting lava by the minute, the fans, the single most important constituent in making the IPL successful, continued to embrace it and throng the grounds in thousands. D. Y. Patil stadium in Navi Mumbai was full on the day of the final between the Super Kings and the Mumbai Indians on 25 April 2010 even though the head honchos of the BCCI decided to give it a miss and were intent in getting rid of Modi as their topmost priority.

Brand IPL, it was suggested following India's disastrous tour of the UK in July–August 2011 and Australia in January–February 2012, would need correctives to keep up its popularity. India's slump in England, it was argued, should be used as an opportunity to clean up the faults in the competition and ensure that it continues to help strengthen the foundations of Indian cricket. The problem with the Modi dispensation was that in their burning desire to bring in as much money as possible, they were even intent on sacrificing the game. By not ensuring that leading Indian stars get enough rest, the current dispensation too is misusing the IPL brand. There's little doubt that in the long term India has to prioritise Test cricket, which, despite assurances from the BCCI, isn't always the case. Clive Lloyd put it best at the Oval in August 2011, 'Why should your players value Test cricket when they get ten times the amount of money by playing the IPL? You need to make them understand that Test cricket is the pinnacle of all formats and the only way you can do so is by bringing Test cricket at par with other lucrative T-20 leagues. If a player knows and feels that he will get many times more money in the IPL than what he will earn by playing a year of Test cricket, it is only natural that a youngster will opt for the former. But if Test match remunerations are at par youngsters will want to work harder to make cricket's most acclaimed format their own.'[23]

To place Lloyd's thoughts in context: Sanjay Bangar and Akash Chopra have both played Test cricket for India. Yet they have less than half the bank balance or brand value of Yusuf Pathan, who has only excelled in the IPL not to forget his fantastic one day hundred against South Africa in South Africa in December 2010.[24] Bangar, to his credit, was instrumental in winning India one of its best test matches overseas, against England at Headingley in 2002. Chopra too was crucial to India's success in Australia in 2003–4 having blunted the new ball on more than one occasion. In India's cricket history, Chopra and Bangar have had far greater roles to play than Pathan. Yet, Pathan is a celebrity while the other two are almost forgotten.

While it is easy to say that players need to withdraw from the IPL or the Champions League to prioritise Test cricket, it is not always feasible for the players to do so on their own after having received substantial monies from their franchises. The best case study in this context relates to Zaheer Khan. Just like his cohorts, Zaheer, it is expected, will want to make the most of the IPL opportunity, knowing full well that as a fast bowler he has a shorter career span compared to others. It is natural that he will want to safeguard his future by earning as much as he can in the limited time available to him at the peak of his prowess. Also important to take into consideration is the interest of his franchisee, in this case the Royal Challengers from Bangalore. Having spent a substantial purse on Khan in the auction it is difficult to expect that RCB will agree to not playing Khan in the IPL or even the Champions League. This is where the persuasive powers of the BCCI will need to come into effect. They will first need to compensate Zaheer for his losses so that he doesn't feel let down for not being allowed to play in the T-20 league and second the BCCI has to convince Vijay Mallya about the need to preserve Zaheer for forthcoming important test series. RCB's spending on Zaheer will have to be returned and the team allowed to opt for a suitable replacement even if that means opting for an international signing. If doing this means tweaking the rules of the IPL to accommodate the needs of the Indian team so be it. In the long run the popularity of the IPL is directly proportional to India's performances at the international realm, a reality that is often forgotten by the powers that be driving India's cricket.

Finally, it is also upon the IPL team owners to safeguard the interests of Indian cricket going forward. As Indian businessmen who also have an interest in cricket, they need to understand that for the sake of the IPL and the Champions League India's test cricket needs to be in good health. In fact, it is now upon the BCCI to live up to its promise of transparency and ensure that the fans don't lose confidence in the property itself and continue to support it in season five in ways they have done in seasons one, two, three and four. Frankly, the fan isn't worried about whether the telecast deal rakes in the 1.64 billion that it is doing or it goes back to its original figure of 918 million, the amount for which the rights were sold in season one. These absurd amounts of money have little relevance for the viewer who wishes to watch the best players play and the best men and women commentate. It is the Wayne Rooneys and Didier Drogbas who make the EPL, they are the ones we watch rather than the individual team owners and administrators. In fact, one simple quiz question is enough to demonstrate the problem with the IPL— how many readers know the names of the leading administrators of the EPL and how many know the name of Lalit Modi? The answer is a given. Modi and the current

BCCI bosses are getting bigger than the brand or put more aptly bigger than the game of cricket. For the sake of the game itself, this has to change. Despite the autonomy, the BCCI, it must be acknowledged discharges a public function and it is the billion plus Indian cricket fans who are the custodians of the IPL. They have given their favourite soaps and serials a miss in supporting the tournament. They are the ones who have spent their last rupee in trying to catch a glimpse of the action and they are the one who have made IPL Season V a success.

Conclusion

The hubbub generated by the recent crisis in Indian cricket demonstrates that balancing between the needs of the market and the needs of the fan base will undoubtedly decide how well the IPL is able to sustain the hype it has generated. And until a final verdict can be made on that score, observers of cricket as a phenomenon would do well to support this incarnation and agree that it has converted the game into a multi-billion dollar enterprise and India into the real nerve centre of the game.

However, that is not to say there is no need for innovation. There always is. To go a step further, the more the tournament matures the more it will feel the need to innovate to keep the novelty factor alive. And one such opportunity has presented itself to the organisers in the form of Saurav Ganguly signing for the Pune Warriors. Ganguly's signing has ensured that the match between the Pune Warriors and the Kolkata Knight Riders at the Eden Gardens on 5 May 2012 was a blockbuster. The demand for tickets was huge and Eden Gardens on the night was buzzing with excitement. Kolkata was split down the middle in terms of fan loyalty and the excitement was palpable. This, for the IPL organisers, should be an eye opener. With a slight tweak in the schedule in Season VI they can ensure many more blockbuster matches.

The Ranchi stadium for example has already been given the nod by the BCCI to host international cricket in the forthcoming season. Ranchi, it can be surmised, can very well serve as another home base for the Knight Riders. Starved for cricket action, Ranchi fans, it can be expected, will be out in droves to soak in the excitement when the

IPL bandwagon reaches the city. And when M. S. Dhoni, the home boy leads his Chennai Super Kings to play the Knights in Ranchi, it will be an encore of the KKR-Pune situation at the Eden Gardens. You need not be a brand expert to suggest that a CSK-KKR match at Ranchi with Dhoni leading one of the teams will be a sellout affair. Finally, it is time for the IPL to tap into the newer mediums of fan engagement to give the brand a further fillip. Simple 'out of the box' thinking in the internet/mobile realm with offerings of new age digital programming will help to drive hitherto untapped traffic to the IPL and build value much beyond the current confines of the IPL's current fan base. The fact that India's mobile universe of over 800 million is far larger than the 150 million odd satellite and TV households means the IPL can become a far bigger property with these new mechanisms of fan engagement in 2013 and onwards.

All of these draw attention to two cardinal truths centering the IPL. First, the brand is already fairly robust and second there are significant opportunities moving forward to strengthen the brand even further. It is now up to the BCCI to exploit these opportunities.

Notes

1. This is despite the fact that attendance is free for most of these games.
2. In 2011 the tournament was played out for 51 days. In 2012 it was played for 54 days.
3. Interview with Arthur Morris, Sydney, 4 January 2008.
4. Manoj Tiwary, who has hardly played an international fixture for India, earned 675,000 USD in the first IPL auction.
5. Even when the world was in the throes of economic depression the Indian economy grew by over 6%.
6. The ICC is yet inclined not to because the IPL, it holds, is a domestic tournament. However, in the most recent FTP announced by the ICC in June 2011 April and May have been left relatively empty, unofficially sanctioning the IPL.
7. The move was prompted by the government's inability to provide necessary security for the IPL games.
8. The third edition of the tournament was once again played to good crowds between 12 March and 25 April 2010.
9. The Australian Davis Cup team refused to tour India in May 2009 citing security concerns. This was a strange decision because the Australian cricket team toured India for a 7 match one day series in October-November 2009.

10. India played host to the Commonwealth Games between 3–14 October 2010.
11. Coined by Rudyard Kipling it is still a much used term to describe India's colonial conditioning.
12. This happened in earnest from the middle of the 1990s after the Indian economy was opened up to global investment under then finance minister Manmohan Singh in 1991.
13. For details see 'Ranji's leg glance to the throne', in Boria Majumdar, *Lost Histories of Indian Cricket* (London: Routledge, 2005).
14. Ibid.
15. Ibid.
16. The tournament was played between 5–21 June 2009.
17. Interview with Peter Hutton, 8 March 2008.
18. India and Pakistan crashed out in the first round of the 2007 world cup with India losing to Bangladesh and Pakistan losing to Ireland.
19. Tendulkar debuted against Pakistan in 1989.
20. Interview with Jagmohan Dalmiya on 10 March 2011, President of the ICC between 1997–2000.
21. The first experiment was with Ruby Bhatia, the former Miss India winner. It was tried out during the ICC Champions Trophy in Sri Lanka in 2002 but did not succeed.
22. Bedi, a relatively unsuccessful Bollywood star, had never before done cricket commentary. Since then her career has undergone a complete turnaround and she now earns in millions as a cricket show host.
23. Interview with Clive Lloyd, London, 23 August 2011.
24. While this is conjecture it is a more than likely scenario with Yusuf Pathan getting 11 crores per year from his IPL contract between 2011–13.

3

Sporting Legacies in India: Mohun Bagan's 1911 Football Victory *versus* Olympic Hockey Medals

Novy Kapadia

Pre-Independence Sporting Successes

During British colonial rule, India's greatest sporting successes were the three successive gold medals won by the Indian hockey team: in the 1928 Amsterdam Olympics, the 1932 Los Angeles Olympics and the 1936 Berlin Olympics. On all three occasions, India won emphatically, beating Netherlands 3–0 in the 1928 final, Japan 11–1 and USA 24–1 (at the round robin league stage) in 1932, and Germany 8–1 in the 1936 final. The other major sporting success of the colonial period came in football, in the form of Mohun Bagan's epochal victory in the 1911 IFA Shield final.

Surprisingly, the national hockey team's victories have never been the subject of serious academic research. There is no existing historiography of these victories, exploring their significance in terms of nationalism or racism. Great Britain's hockey team, gold medalists in the 1908 (London) and 1912 (Antwerp) Olympics, withdrew from the Olympic hockey event in 1928, 1932 and 1936 as the colonisers did not want to be humiliated by the colonised. By the time of the 1928 Olympics, the British were well aware of the prowess of the Indian hockey team, with nine Anglo-Indian players in their ranks, and so thought it prudent to withdraw. The skill and brilliance of the Indian hockey players had been witnessed in the annual Beighton Cup (Calcutta) and Aga Khan Trophy (Bombay). Incidentally the Beighton Cup is India's oldest hockey tournament, commencing as early as 1895.

The Aga Khan trophy tournament began two years later in 1897. The National Championships for the Rangaswamy Cup started in 1928, the year India first participated in the Olympics. There has been only limited academic research on the socio-cultural significance of the predominance of Anglo-Indians in the national hockey team (nine in 1928, eight in 1932, seven in 1936), and India's hockey victories have rarely been viewed in a proper historical perspective.

It is quite remarkable that the sixteen-member Indian hockey team in 1928 consisted of nine Anglo-Indians and four Muslims and only three members were from the Hindu majority community. What were the factors which led to such a dominance of minorities in the national hockey team in 1928? The Anglo-Indian community in pre-partition India worked mostly in the railways, police, port trust, or British-run commercial firms, and as school teachers. Was it the nature of such employment which gave them time to practice? Or was it their proximity to the British, which enabled them to excel in hockey? Commander G. Nandy Singh (retd.), a member of the victorious 1948 London Olympics team, who played for the Calcutta Port Trust in pre-independence days, feels that 'the Anglo Indians were a privileged class during the British regime'[1] and this enabled them to excel in sports. Even after Independence, in the 1948 London Olympics, there were five Anglo-Indians in the Indian hockey team which beat Netherlands 2–1 in the semi-final and Britain 4–0 in the final. A remarkable Anglo-Indian member of this squad was centre-forward Reggie Rodrigues, who during his playing days was an active sports journalist with the *Times of India* (Bombay). Rodrigues, who later migrated to Canada, is probably the only active journalist who ever played in the Olympics.

The number of Anglo-Indians in the national squad declined as members of the community started migrating to Australia, England and Canada in the 1950s. The last Anglo-Indian to play for India in the Olympics was goalkeeper Mark Peterson in the 1988 Seoul Olympics. The subsequent rise to prominence of Sikh players is also a phenomenon worth analysing. The victories of the Indian hockey team in the Olympics, before independence, were as much a nationalist response to British cultural imperialism, as Mohun Bagan's historic 1911 IFA Shield triumph. Yet the composition of these teams makes

Illustration 3.1 1936 Berlin Olympics Gold Winning Indian Hockey Team *Photo*: Mohammed Shafiq

for a remarkable contrast. Mohun Bagan's playing eleven consisted entirely of Bengali Hindus, with the exception of the Reverend Sudhir Chatterjee, a Christian. In contrast the playing eleven of the Indian hockey team, which defeated Netherlands 3–0 in the 1928 Amsterdam Olympics final, included eight Anglo-Indians besides the legendary Dhyan Chand, Feroze Khan and Shaukat Ali. The impact and causes of these hockey triumphs and the remarkable social phenomenon of the Anglo-Indians dominance in Indian hockey has not been fully analysed.[2] The role of minority communities like the Anglo-Indians, Sikhs and Muslims in the rise and success of Indian hockey (winning eight gold medals in the Olympics and a World Cup title in 1975) deserves closer sociological analysis. The marginalised status of the community today may be one reason why its contribution has been neglected.

The Legacy of Mohun Bagan's 1911 Football Victory

By contrast, scholars have done a lot of historical and academic research on Mohun Bagan's 1911 triumph, which is often hailed as the most glorious sporting success of an Indian team under colonial rule.[3] There are contrasting Eurocentric and nationalist interpretations of Bagan's run of successes, especially the 2–1 win over the East Yorkshire regiment in the IFA Final on 29 July 1911. Soumen Mitra viewed the 1911 IFA Shield victory both as a Bengali martial reaction against the British charge of physical effeminacy and as a nationalist response to British cultural imperialism.[4] Sumit Mukherjee also sees this victory as a medium for the deconstruction of the image of the Bengalis as an effeminate race and the reconstruction of a more masculine and vigorous image.[5] Boria Majumdar echoes similar sentiments and sees the victory in a broader political context as having the potential to inspire similar acts of triumph in other spheres of life.[6] Tony Mason admits the political significance of the event but focuses more on the British imperial mission to promote sports for the moral training of the natives.[7] Paul Dimeo also offers a Eurocentric view. Though he admits the 1911 victory was a moment of national resistance, he declares that the celebration of this sporting success implied an acceptance of the British moral system introduced through Anglo-Indian colleges.[8]

Dwaipayan Sen says that each newspaper report of the 1911 victory was influenced by the writer's ideological commitments.[9] In his meticulously researched book *Stories from Indian Football*, the sports journalist Jaydeep Basu analyses this victory as a triumph of football expertise and Bagan's ability to field a team with a professional outlook.[10] For an excellent survey of existing historical literature on the 1911 victory and the difference between European and Indian scholarship one might read Kausik Bandyopadhyay's prologue to his book *Playing for Freedom: A Historic Sports Victory*.[11]

After the triumph of 1911, it took Mohun Bagan another thirty-six years to win this same tournament again. Bagan next won the IFA Shield in 1947, ironically the year of India's independence, when they beat East Bengal 1–0 in the final. Sarat Das was the Bagan skipper on that occasion and Selim scored the match-winner. The nationalist 'timing' of the victory might simply be a coincidence, as during this period Bagan did not win either the Durand tournament in Simla/Delhi or the Rovers Cup in Bombay. In fact Bagan's first victory in the Rovers Cup was in 1955 when they beat Mohammedan Sporting 2–0 in the final. Veteran defender Sailen Manna was Mohun Bagan's captain, and Samar 'Badru' Banerjee and Daljit Singh were the goal scorers. Bagan's first triumph in the Durand tournament was in 1953 when, under Manna's captaincy, they routed National Defence Academy (NDA) 4–0 in the final, with a brace by both S. Raman and Samar 'Badru' Banerjee. However, Sumit Mukherjee has blamed Bagan's indifferent record on 'motivated refereeing [which] saw to it that Mohun Bagan was always deprived of its due and the opponent gained undue advantage.'[12] Reference is also made to the slushy surface on which the barefoot Bagan players were forced to play in the 1923 IFA Shield final against Calcutta FC, losing 0–3.

What was the impact of Mohun Bagan's 1911 win on football clubs in the rest of the country? Kausik Bandyopadhyay has shown that newspapers all over the country and abroad gave wide coverage to this event.[13] The win obviously had a galvanising effect on football clubs in other cities. But there is little record of whether this win sparked off increased participation in football or improvement in standards. The late Captain Harnam Singh, the first Indian to officiate in the Durand final (in 1940, when Mohammedan Sporting won) spoke of

Illustration 3.2 Mohun Bagan 1911 Team *Photo*: Mohammed Shafiq

two occasions when the 1911 victory was seen as quite inspirational. It may be recalled that in 1911, the British shifted the capital from Calcutta to Delhi. King George V had ascended the throne in 1911 and in December that year held a Grand Durbar in Delhi to commemorate the occasion. For years afterwards on the anniversary of the Great Durbar, the 12th of December, an exhibition football match was staged in Delhi between a leading British regimental team and a leading club team, either the Mughals or Young Men. As a promising winger, Harnam Singh represented Young Men in this annual exhibition match from 1919 onwards. He recalled that days prior to the match people in Chandni Chowk, where he lived would tell him to be inspired by Bagan's victory in the 1911 IFA Shield and try to emulate the feat of beating a British team on the football field. '*Mohun Bagan jaise khelna aur Mohun Bagan jaise jeetna*' used to be the advice to the Delhi players before any match against a British regimental team. Football was seen as a symbol of manliness and resilience. Recalling those days, Harnam Singh said that the Young Men management would also harp on Bagan's sensational victory and ask the players to be inspired by it. He said that after 1911, for all local footballers, Mohun Bagan was a source of inspiration and the club acquired many followers in Delhi.[14]

The first Durand final was held in Delhi in 1940, since because of the Second World War, the summer capital of the British Raj had not shifted to Simla. This venue and match became historic for several reasons. In 1940, Mohammedan Sporting became the first Indian team to win the prestigious Durand tournament when they beat the Royal Warwickshire Regiment 2–1 in Delhi. Centre-forward Hafiz Rashid and inside-left Saboo scored the goals for the winners. It was also the first Durand final that was supervised by an Indian referee, Captain Harnam Singh. In those days he was a civilian sergeant in the Army Office in the Delhi Cantonment. An estimated crowd of 100,000 people in an amphitheatre-like stadium (now the site of the National Stadium built as the venue for the first Asian Games, 1951, and renamed the Major Dhyan Chand National Stadium), witnessed this final. There was seating on only one side: eminent Muslim politicians flew in from distant cities like Calcutta, Dacca, Hyderabad and Bhopal for the match and people came in trains from far-off cities.

This victory by a team consisting of eleven Muslim players was a massive boost to the Muslim national movement.[15]

There was considerable tension before the match, as the English linesmen, Sergeant Officers Oliphant and Greene, refused to officiate with Harnam Singh as the referee. They cited technical reasons, stating that Harnam Singh was a junior referee, but the boycott had clear racist overtones. The matter was only resolved when Lord Linlithgow, the Viceroy of India, intervened.[16] Whilst this furore was taking place, Harnam Singh went to the Mohammedan Sporting dressing room to tell the players that the match might be delayed. He recalls that when he entered the dressing room, senior players like goalkeeper Usman Jan and defender Jumma Khan were urging their teammates to be inspired by Mohun Bagan's 1911 IFA Shield victory and not to be overawed by the British team. Harnam Singh also recalled that all the morning newspapers, whilst previewing the final, and in their match reports next day, referred to Mohun Bagan's 1911 IFA Shield victory.[17]

Mohammedan Sporting's centre forward Hafiz Rashid, who scored a goal in the final, started his career in Ajmer. He then came to Delhi to play for the capital's oldest club, Young Men (formed in 1885). During his stay in Delhi, Hafiz Rashid became friendly with former international referee, K. G. Kakkar, who in those days played for Simla Youngs and later for Companion Club. Years later Kakkar's favourite anecdote was about Hafiz Rashid's dedication and how he trained twice a day. The training included running on the sand on the banks of the river Yamuna (to improve strength and stamina), sprints to develop sudden acceleration, and kicking the ball on the volley and from a stationary position at a target on a wall to improve his shooting. K. G. Kakkar recalled that Rashid used to say that he was motivated by Mohun Bagan's 1911 IFA Shield triumph and wanted to play in Calcutta, which was why he trained so hard. Rashid reportedly said that ever since he started playing football, he wanted to become a complete centre-forward like the burly Abhilash Ghosh who had scored the match-winner for Bagan in the 1911 IFA Shield final. Rashid had never seen Abhilash Ghosh play but whilst growing up in Ajmer had heard stories about his stamina and goal-scoring prowess. Ghosh thus became Rashid's childhood hero. It was by word of mouth that the glories of Bagan's 1911 IFA Shield win spread all over India, with senior players and coaches using it as a reference point of excellence to be achieved by any young aspiring footballer. So it can be seen that about two decades after their historic triumph, several of Bagan's players had become iconic figures in Indian football.[18]

K. G. Kakkar had another interesting anecdote, which also featured Mohun Bagan's 1911 IFA Shield victory. This anecdote is about Delhi's only triumph in the Santosh Trophy when they scored a memorable 2–0 win over Bengal in the 1944 final. Of many tales about Delhi's victory, one was that the Delhi management paid for the Bengal team to see the historic ruins of Mehrauli on the day of the final. The Bengal players, who had climbed the steep and narrow steps of Qutb Minar that morning, were exhausted by the closing stages of the final and lost the match.[19] However Kakkar also recalls that Delhi skipper Usman Jan, who had played as a goalkeeper for Mohammedan Sporting in the 1930s, frequently referred to Mohun Bagan's 1911 IFA Shield victory as a motivational factor in his team-talks. Bengal had a formidable team, including defenders Sarat Das and Sailen Manna (who was making his Santosh Trophy debut), midfielder Anil Dey and forwards Noor Mohammed (Jr.) and Apparao. To overcome such a formidable adversary on the football field was like achieving what Mohun Bagan did in the 1911 final! Hence Mohun Bagan's 1911 IFA Shield win became a symbol of inspiration for the underdog on the football fields of India.[20]

Delhi's left winger Bhabani Banerjee, who scored the second goal in the final against Bengal aptly summed up the atmosphere in the capital in the 1930s and 40s. He said that football was a passion but just a pastime and not a career. Many Bengali boys in Delhi took to football because of the stories they had heard about Mohun Bagan's 1911 IFA Shield triumph. For the football fans of Delhi, Mohun Bagan could do no wrong and their players were feted like demi-gods.

> But yes, football was the pastime, a common passion. And Mohun Bagan the social sentiment. Probably it had something to do with the 1911 IFA Shield triumph. The green-and-maroon could do no wrong. They could lose no match. Whenever they lost, people mourned just like they do when the cricket team loses nowadays.[21]

The Mohun Bagan impact was seen in Hyderabad football as well. The famous Nizam College popularised football by hosting two popular tournaments, one for educational institutions and another for clubs and regimental teams. Before Mohun Bagan's 1911 IFA Shield victory, these local football tournaments were low-key affairs. In the tournament meant only for the educational institutions, Nizam College was generally victorious. N. Ganesan, the chronicler of football in Hyderabad, has written that as news and the impact of Bagan's famous 1911 victory filtered through, other schools and colleges in Hyderabad and Secunderabad, such as St. George's High School, Asafia High School, and Darool-Ul-Uloom High School, took to football seriously. The All Saints High School trained diligently and won the tournament for educational institutions in 1911 and 1912 when it had requisitioned the services of the members of the Merry-Go-Round team, which had been formed some years earlier by Vilayat Hussein.[22]

So football in Hyderabad also took off after 1911. The Nawab of Tarbund became a great patron of the game. Various clubs began to be formed. The Merry-Go-Round (MGR), the most famous of the clubs in existence, was then regarded as one of the top teams in the country. It had the services of Mohammed Ali Khan, Ghulam Mahmood, Mohamed Usman and Qader Khan, all eminent players of the day. The Nizam College also fielded strong teams. In 1917, a match between MGR and the Nizam College was watched by over 20,000 people. Played at the Fateh Maidan, it was considered by many as one of the most exciting encounters of that era. It ended in a draw thrice and when replayed on the morning of the fourth day, the MGR won by a solitary goal.[23]

Besides Merry-Go-Round, another prominent club of that era was Qamar Club, which included some of the first well-known players of Hyderabad. The Qamar Club shot into prominence with players like S. A. Rahim (who later became the legendary coach who guided India to two gold medals in the 1951 and 1962 Asian Games), Sharifuddin, Aga Mahmood Ali and Quddus, turning out for them. In the initial decades of the 20th century, the Hyderabad clubs struggled against the well-trained and experienced regimental teams like Gordon Highlanders (winners of the IFA Shield from 1908 to 1910 and Rovers Cup runners-up in 1926), Wiltshire Regiment, Machine Gun Company and Royal Horse Artillery in the well-known All-India

Majeed tournament. The Qamar club became the first Hyderabad team to beat a British regimental team. In a Majeed tournament match they upset the 18th Hussars, which till then had remained an almost unbeatable British team. According to N. Ganesan, those who saw that match recall with relish the heroic display of Qader Khan, the Qamar Club goalkeeper. This famous victory by Qamar Club was compared in the local media to Bagan's 1911 IFA Shield triumph.[24]

The first All-India football tournament was staged at Hyderabad in 1910. Called the Majeed tournament, it was run successfully for three years before it was abandoned because of differences between the City Police and the Hyderabad Army. However, after 1911, the game's popularity had increased so rapidly in Hyderabad that other organisations came forward to fill the vacuum and new tournaments were started. Nearly a lakh of rupees was contributed to the First World War Fund by organising football tournaments in the twin cities of Hyderabad and Secunderabad. When the war ended in 1918, a peace tournament was held which the Merry-Go-Round team won. The glittering cup won by MGR was then auctioned for Rs. 35,000, a substantial amount of money in the early decades of the 20th century. The amount was donated to the Wounded Soldiers' Fund. The Majeed tournament was revived in 1915 and gained in popularity. Soon teams from Hyderabad started visiting cities in the Madras Presidency to take part in local tournaments held there. Thus in more ways than one, it can be seen that Mohun Bagan's famous 1911 IFA Shield victory was a take-off point for Indian football. Its impact on Bengal football was immense, with many socio-political and socio-cultural ramifications as well. Newspaper reports and testimonies of players of that generation reveal that even in other parts of the country the popularity of football increased and the local population took to the game with greater enthusiasm.

The Story of Hockey: Glory and Obscurity

By contrast, as we have noted, India's hockey triumphs in the 1928, 1932 and 1936 Olympics did not get a lot of media coverage and except for the legendary Dhyan Chand, none of the players became sporting icons. In Europe people were dazzled by his mesmeric dribbling skills. A statue of Dhyan Chand was erected in Vienna, as a token of appreciation of his exemplary skills. India's crisp, short passing game and dribbling flair was appreciated by the crowds both at home and abroad. The players were reasonably popular and were certainly fêted on their return from the Olympics. So it is difficult to fathom why in the pre-independence era, India's three successive Olympic triumphs did not get the mileage they deserved. One reason might be that owing to colonial rule, the Olympic hockey triumphs were denied prominence. Further, during that period hockey was popular amongst minority communities in India, like the Anglo-Indians and Muslims, and this could also be a reason for limited media attention.

Illustration 3.3 Dhyan Chand *Photo*: Mohammed Shafiq

The players in domestic hockey tournaments represented institutions, and not clubs, as in football. For instance the 1932 Los Angeles Olympics captain, Lal Shah Bokhari, was a member of the Punjab Provincial Service and goalkeeper Richard Allen worked for the Port Commissioners in Kolkata. Centre-half Eric Penniger and Arthur Charles Hind were employed by the North Western Railway. Other Olympians employed in the railways were Carlysle Tapsell (Bengal Nagpur Railway), William Sullivan (Central India Railway) and Richard John Carr (East India Railway). Dhyan Chand was a lance naik in the British Indian Army. Shaukat Ali, who could play in any position in the forward line, represented Calcutta Customs. Several others like Rup Singh, left winger Mohammed Jaffer, Gurmit Singh, Masud Minhas and Aslam Bagga were either studying in college or had just finished their bachelor's degrees.

Hence in domestic hockey there was no great rivalry, like that of East Bengal vs Mohun Bagan, or other major regional rivalries, which excited both the media and partisan crowds. Institutional teams never inspire the same level of loyalty and fan following as club teams. In the major domestic hockey tournaments like the Aga Khan Cup in Bombay which started in 1896, and Beighton Cup in Calcutta which commenced in 1895, the competitors were largely institutional teams, and the rivalry was not intense. Again (unlike their practice in football) British regimental units rarely fielded hockey teams in local tournaments. So there was no coloniser versus colonised rivalry in local hockey tournaments. By contrast, Mohun Bagan's 1911 IFA Shield victory over the East Yorkshire Regiment is seen not just as a sporting but a nationalist milestone. It was only after independence that the Olympic hockey victories became a symbol of nationalist sentiment.

There was also a strong regional bias in the coverage of domestic football. Vernacular newspapers in Bengal followed football passionately after Bagan's 1911 IFA Shield victory. Later the club's bitter rivalry with East Bengal, which started in the 1920s, was a focus of media attention. Hockey mainly got prominence in the media when the national team played in either the Olympics or went on foreign tours. The Olympic hockey players were admired and treated as heroes but there was little serious analysis of their victories or of the composition of the national team. After the victory in the 1928 Amsterdam Olympics, the team returned home via London. Expatriate Indians in London hailed the victory as an occasion for nationalist celebrations. A tea party and luncheon was organised in their honour.

When the team returned to Bombay they were welcomed by a large, cheering multitude of fans. The team also got a civic reception from the mayor of Bombay when they landed there. Non-resident Indians were thrilled at the victory of the Indian hockey team, as it gave them a sense of status amongst other migrants. After the comfortable victory in the 1932 Olympics, the Indian community in Los Angeles raised the considerable sum of $400 to enable the victorious squad to travel around USA and exhibit their skills. Yet despite these accolades, hockey was not backed by a huge grassroots following in India, and the celebrations were temporary.

Post-Independence Hockey and National Identity

After independence, India's hockey victories in the Olympics were newly seen as a symbol of national pride and a signifier of our status in the international sporting fraternity. The success of the hockey team in beating western nations was looked upon as evidence that India could compete on equal terms with the West. At this point, media interest in hockey and crowd support was abundant. The 4–0 victory over England in the 1948 London Olympics final was seen in a nationalistic perspective, the colonised dealing a blow to the legacy of colonialism. There were no live cameras to record this landmark hockey victory for future generations, but contemporary press reports noted that the few thousands of Indian supporters who saw this final enthusiastically celebrated India's win. The overwhelming Indian superiority was front page news in all Indian newspapers. There were scenes of jubilation in London. The Indian High Commissioner, V. K. Krishna Menon ran on to the ground to join the celebrations and joined the team for a group photograph. There was also a brief reception at India House where many sport lovers had assembled. After a fortnight's tour of some European countries, the team returned to India; victory celebrations continued for several days and were widely reported in the press. The jubilation culminated in the capital Delhi, where President Rajendra Prasad and Prime Minister Jawaharlal Nehru attended an exhibition match in which the Olympic team played the Rest of India at a crowded National Stadium.[25]

The captain of the 1956 Melbourne Olympics gold medal winning team Balbir Singh, in his book *The Golden Hat Trick,* wrote about the popularity of the team after each major triumph. There was frenzied jubilation when the team returned home after winning the gold medal in the 1952 Helsinki Olympics, beating Holland 6–1 in the final. In his book Balbir recalled:

> Back in India, our victorious team was received with endearing enthusiasm by our countrymen. We were given a host of receptions at a number of towns. At the official function in Delhi we played a match against the Rest of India XI. Present among a huge crowd were President Rajendra Prasad and the ever-cheerful Nehru. The train by which we travelled was literally mobbed by enthusiastic hockey fans—people surged around our compartment.[26]

The same scenes were seen when India won the gold medal at the 1956 Melbourne Olympics. So in the first decade after independence, the Indian hockey team received official patronage, enthusiastic crowd support and ample newspaper coverage. In a nation where sporting legends are rare, members of the Indian hockey team which won three successive Olympic gold medals became sporting heroes. Domestic hockey tournaments were also well covered by Indian newspapers. Excessive coverage of cricket and neglect of other sports was not characteristic of the Indian media for three decades after independence. Domestic hockey tournaments (still mostly played by institutional teams like Punjab Police, Northern Railways, Central Railway, Sikh Regimental Centre, Indian Air Force, Corps of Signals and Tatas and so on) did not arouse much spectator interest, and Indian hockey did not have a thriving club culture and rivalry as in football, yet because the national team were perceived as world champions, there were always packed crowds and ample media coverage whenever they played. Crowd interest also increased when the Olympians were representing their state in the National Championships. Further, jubilant scenes were witnessed when India won the World Cup title in Kuala Lumpur in 1975. The team was felicitated by the State Governments of Punjab, Uttar Pradesh, Madhya Pradesh, Andhra Pradesh, Karnataka, Kerala and Tamil Nadu. The players were given cash awards and gifts and were allotted flats. The team was also greeted by President Fakhruddin Ali Ahmed and Prime Minister Mrs. Indira Gandhi at a special reception.[27] In this post-independence period,

Illustration 3.4 1956 Melbourne Olympics Gold Winning Indian Hockey Team *Photo*: Mohammed Shafiq

the international triumphs of the national hockey team were widely publicised and the players were seen as heroes.

Illustration 3.5 Balbir Singh, Captain, Melbourne Team
Photo: Mohammed Shafiq

Global Media and the Decline of Hockey Spectatorship

The scenario changed in the early eighties. From the 1980s, hockey's popularity and media coverage declined rapidly, as cricket assumed centre stage in India. Cricket's emergence as a popular sport in India stems from social factors. The Indian hockey team won the World Cup in 1975, when only black and white television was available in India. Television sets were mostly confined to the metro cities. Until the 1982 Asian Games in Delhi, Indians had never seen sporting events on colour television. When colour television came to India, the Indian hockey failed in the showpiece event, losing 1–7 to Pakistan in the final of the 1982 Asian Games at the National Stadium in Delhi. As television in India expanded, the national hockey team's performances declined. Spectator interest and thereby media involvement with the game also decreased. By contrast, when Kapil Dev led India to victory in the 1983 World Cup in England, the match was telecast live in colour . The creation of a national network of transmitters linked with satellite technology had spread television and the national channel, Doordarshan, all over the country. Economic reforms had also made television sets cheaper. Millions of people all over the country watched the 1983 cricket semi-finals and final and the mass appeal of the cricketers was magnified. The 1983 victory was followed by another triumph in 1985 in the Benson and Hedges Champion of Champions trophy in Australia. It was also telecast live and in colour. Indian cricket's two major triumphs in the 20th century coincided with the expansion of the television network which became a key governmental priority. So the Indian cricketers of that era, such as Kapil Dev, Sunil Gavaskar and Ravi Shastri became the first brand names among Indian sportsmen. This also changed the balance of power between cricket and other sports in India.

There are other reasons too for cricket's rising popularity and hockey's decline, as Boria Majumdar and Nalin Mehta explain in their book on India at the Olympics:

> Cricket's emergence as the new Indian 'national' game does not necessarily stem from some peculiar Indian affinity for the game but is inextricably linked to the expansion of Indian television and a confluence of factors that came together: the creation of a large middle class, the economic reforms, the birth of the satellite television industry and a whole gamut of forces that fall under the broad rubric of globalisation.[28]

Cricket also dominated television as its administrators adapted best to the forces of television and globalisation as they took shape in India. Hockey lost out because their administrators refused to change. Television enabled the circulation of cricketers as commodity images in a way that was not possible before. Hockey, with a combination of bad performances, lack of administrative foresight and short-sighted planning, languished in the 1980s and got replaced in the national imagination by cricket.

In the last decade of the 20th century, the chasm between cricket and Olympic sports in the country widened. It became a vicious circle. The more TV promoted cricket, the more popular the game became amongst young people. The prevailing feeling was that the public was losing interest in Olympic sports, as India's performances were quite dismal. The hockey team's international stature further diminished, finishing 7th in the 1992 Barcelona Olympics, 8th in the 1996 Atlanta Olympics and 7th in the 2000 Sydney Olympics. So television coverage of Indian hockey, especially on satellite TV declined. There were also business reasons. Satellite TV deliberately glamourised Indian cricketers in the 1990s and regularly telecast India's matches. This set the trend for excessive media coverage. The print media tried to compete with the electronic media, giving even more prominence to cricket. As cricketers became richer, more people wanted to be associated with them, and even the most trivial incidents involving them became big news.

This problem persists even today. The media feels that cricket is the only sport that sells, and can bring in advertising support and revenue. This is then reflected in the choice of sports news. News anchors on major national channels such as NDTV/CNN-IBN/Times Now/Star News/Zee News, want cricket news because they feel it makes their programmes popular. If other games are not given an equal chance, they can never compete. There are no level playing fields. It is a classic chicken and egg situation.

In the post-Babri Masjid and early liberalisation days, India went through a very nationalistic phase. Cricket, especially one-day cricket and T-20 matches, became a convenient outlet for this jingoism. As a limited number of countries were seriously playing the game, a win against world champions did become possible. Increasingly, especially on electronic media, cricket tours and matches got portrayed in terms of banal nationalism, battles, and personality clashes. Class bias also influenced the neglect of hockey and the support for cricket. Hockey players do not get the support of the middle class urban media, for a variety of reasons including poor management and marketing by the Indian Hockey Federation (IHF). Unlike cricketers, hockey players often do not come from middle-class backgrounds, and cannot easily sell themselves to the media . They are not yet in the mobile phone, Facebook using, cocktail party, HT City/Times Now glamour circuit. Hence no personality-based articles, extensive interviews, or extra-hockey stories can be filed. Media barons with scant knowledge of the development of hockey all over the world do not realise that the game has changed radically and keep harping on India's past successes, preferring to ignore its present needs.

Temporary Revivals, Media Interest and Disinterest

Evidence of the lack of media interest in hockey was revealed in March 2003. The national team had just concluded their last training session at the Major Dhyan Chand National Stadium, New Delhi. It was a morning practice session as the team was to leave for Kuala Lumpur the same night. The media presence was limited except for a television crew, filming the practice session. After taking shots of some others in the team, the Zee News anchor approached skipper Dhanraj Pillay for a sound-byte. Dhanraj flatly refused. In the entire week that the team was in Delhi for training, Dhanraj had shunned the media and so he made no exceptions for the Zee News anchor. A verbal duel seemed inevitable as the anchor persisted, but Harendra Singh, a former international player and assistant to chief coach Rajender Singh intervened and sorted out the matter. This was quite unlike Dhanraj. But it probably stemmed from his belief that the media was neglecting hockey. During the entire week of practice sessions in Delhi, he was simmering with resentment at the media's neglect of hockey. It hurt him that the press ignored the news of his being reinstated as captain after a five-year gap. 'Isn't it a significant development? Our Azlan Shah news comes in five sentences whereas the papers have allotted full five pages for the World Cup (Cricket)'.[29]

Two months later, Dhanraj led India to victory in the Hockey Australia Men's Challenge Trophy at Sydney after missing victory in the Perth leg final by the proverbial whisker. Weeks later, the Indian hockey team, brimming with confidence, emerged triumphant in the Hamburg Masters' Cup in Germany. This was a competition in which India had never won a single match, let alone the title, in its six previous appearances. The double title triumphs in Australia and Germany caught the imagination of the people back home. It also jolted the national press into action. Hockey was back in the limelight on the scale of the 50s and 60s. Dhanraj Pillay's birthday, which he celebrated with his team at Barog in Himachal Pradesh, became a national event. Besides the print media, all major television crews visited the mountain resort to capture the moment live. Cinema stars appeared on television to congratulate him. The president of India, A. P. J. Abdul Kalam, and many ministers interacted with the hockey team. Marketing agents signed contracts with leading hockey stars like Dhanraj Pillay, Gagan Ajit Singh and Jugraj Singh. Schools in several states invited the heroes to conduct clinics for children. Dhanraj's hockey heroes lived up to national expectations in 2003. In September India won the Asia Cup beating Pakistan 4–2 in the final at Kuala Lumpur. Next month, India won the Afro-Asian Games title in Hyderabad again beating Pakistan in the final.

Victory over arch rivals Pakistan in two successive finals led to the expected media frenzy. Yet hockey did not get sustained media coverage because of the archaic policies of the IHF. On two occasions it was the IHF, with its old fashioned attitudes of management, which floundered just as the media had started to showcase hockey. In December 1998, India won the Asian Games gold medal in hockey after 32 years. In a closely fought final, in Bangkok, they beat South Korea 5–3 on penalties. The national hockey team, led by Dhanraj Pillay were feted and lauded by politicians, chief ministers and the media when they returned to India. Yet two months later when the test series with Pakistan was about to begin, there was internal discord between the administrators and players. After the success in Bangkok, Pillay and some senior players asked the IHF for monetary incentives and even asked for graded payment for playing international matches for India. During that period, the president of the IHF was KPS Gill, former IG Police of Punjab and the secretary was K. Jothikumaran of Tamil Nadu. Gill tended to be autocratic in his dealings with players and got the support of other IHF officials. The request for money and graded payment was seen as a players' revolt and Pillay and several other members of the victorious 1998 squad were suspended for the test series against Pakistan.

At a stroke, the momentum that hockey had gained after the 1998 Bangkok Asian Games victory was lost. India lost the series against Pakistan and media interest faded as the star players were not in action. Four years later a similar situation was repeated. After the victories in the Asia Cup and Afro-Asian Games, the interest in both the print and electronic media had reached a peak. By 2003, several news channels in both Hindi and English were flourishing, the internet was becoming increasingly popular and so the profile of hockey players was becoming bigger. However the IHF blundered again. They imposed a ban, and national team players were not allowed to speak to the press. When the team reported for training at the National Stadium, Delhi, the gates were locked and the journalists were prevented from covering even the training session. Security officials forced the sports journalists and TV cameramen to retreat from the gates and wait on the pavements near the stadium. Such high-handed behaviour reflected the feudal nature of national sports federations in India, where the focus is on officials rather than players. The excessive media coverage of hockey players, especially the volatile Pillay and young stars like Deepak Thakur and Gagan Ajit Singh upset the IHF officials. For a couple of days the national media gathered near the National Stadium but the ban was strictly enforced. In sheer frustration the media retreated from hockey and the coverage for the national team, the game and the players rapidly declined, as drab and terse official handouts were the only source of news. Thus on two occasions in the recent past when media interest in hockey peaked, the arbitrary policies of the IHF led to either negative or limited coverage. So the media is not entirely to blame for the insufficient coverage of hockey in the country.

Conclusion

Certain lessons can be learnt from these paired histories of sport. Though Indian football did achieve some notable successes in the pre-independence era, its achievements cannot be compared to those of the Indian hockey team. Yet football always had a strong support base, fostered by club rivalry and nationalist sentiment, following the 1911

Shield victory. The vernacular press have always supported football. That support base declined in the post-1980s era of globalisation, perhaps because the deficiencies of the national side, and even of club teams, became more apparent by contrast with the superiority of world football. Nevertheless, at the regional level football has retained at least something of its hold on the national imagination.

On the other hand hockey, with genuine international achievements to its credit, gradually lost both its international standing and its national popularity. The decline of hockey was very largely due to organisational faults and the failure to modernise (including the shocking lack of Astroturf practice grounds). Media neglect was part of the problem, but by no means the only reason for hockey's decline in public esteem. The story of Indian hockey is a complicated web of ethnic histories, extraordinary talent, class affiliations, national pride, bureaucratic inefficiency and media waywardness, which needs to be documented as serious academic study.

Notes

1. Cdr. G. Nandy Singh (retd.) 'Future Goal of Indian Hockey', in *45th Nehru Hockey Tournament Annual Souvenir*, 2008, pp. 54–7.
2. Boria Majumdar and Nalin Khanna *India and the Olympics* (New Delhi: Harper Collins, 2008). This is the only book which has some detailed analysis of India's Olympic hockey players and past victories.
3. Kausik Bandyopadhyay, *Playing For Freedom: A Historic Sports Victory* (New Delhi: Standard Publishers (India), 2008), p. 15.
4. Soumen Mitra, 'Babu at Play: Sporting Nationalism in Bengal: A Study of Football in Bengal, 1880–1911', in *Bengal: Yesterday and Today*, eds Nisith Roy and Ranjit Roy (Calcutta: Papyrus, 1991).
5. Sumit Mukherjee, 'Football in Colonial Bengal in Nationalist Perspective' *90 Minutes*, volume 1, issue 4 (Oct.–Dec. 2009), pp. 36–42.
6. Boria Majumdar, 'The Vernacular in Sports History', *Economic and Political Weekly* XXXVII, 29 (July 20, 2002), pp. 3069–75.
7. Tony Mason, 'Football on the Maidan: Cultural Imperialism in Calcutta,' in *The Cultural Bond: Sport, Empire, Society*, ed. J. A. Mangan (London: Frank Cass, 1992), pp. 142–53.
8. Paul Dimeo, 'Football and Politics in Bengal: Colonialism, Nationalism, Communalism,' in *Soccer in South Asia: Empire, Nation, Diaspora*, eds Paul Dimeo and James Mills (London: Frank Cass, 2001), pp. 57–74.

9. Dwaipayan Sen, 'Wiping the Stain off the Field of Plassey: Mohun Bagan in 1911,' *Soccer and Society* 7.2.-3 (London, 2006), pp. 208–32.
10. Jaydeep Basu, *Stories from Indian Football* (New Delhi: UBSPD, 2003), pp. 1–16.
11. Kausik Bandyopadhyay, *Playing for Freedom: A Historic Sports Victory* (New Delhi: Standard Publishers, 2008), pp. 13–19.
12. Sumit Mukherjee, 'Football in Colonial Bengal in Nationalist Perspective', *90 Minutes*, volume 1, issue 4 (Oct.-Dec. 2009), pp. 36–37.
13. 'The Exhausting Newsprint: Journalistic Enterprise at the Victory,' in Kausik Bandyopadhyay *Playing For Freedom: A Historic Sports Victory* (New Delhi: Standard Publishers (India), 2008), pp. 61–84.
14. Conversations with late captain Harnam Singh, first Indian referee to supervise a Durand final in 1940.
15. For more details on this match read Novy Kapadia, 'Witness to an era, a profile of Harnam Singh' *The Telegraph* (Kolkata) 11 February 1983, p. 16.
16. Ibid., p. 16.
17. Conversations with late captain Harnam Singh, first Indian referee to supervise a Durand final in 1940.
18. Conversations with late K. G. Kakkar, member of the Delhi team which won the Santosh trophy in 1940 and later an international football referee and hockey umpire.
19. K. N. K. Menon, 'Vintage Soccer', in *Souvenir* of 59th IOC-Senior National football Championship Delhi, 2004, ed. Novy Kapadia, pp. 47–9.
20. Conversations with late K. G. Kakkar, member of the Delhi team which won the Santosh trophy in 1940 and later an international football referee and hockey umpire.
21. Nilanjan Datta, 'Bhabani Banerjee: Delhi football's last action hero' in *Souvenir* of 59th IOC—Senior National football Championship Delhi, 2004, ed. Novy Kapadia, p. 7.
22. N. Ganesan 'Hyderabad Football,' *Sport and Pastime Magazine* (Madras: 9 July 1964), pp. 18–19.
23. Ibid., pp. 18–9.
24. Ibid., pp. 18–9.
25. Boria Majumdar and Nalin Khanna, *India and the Olympics* (New Delhi: Harper Collins, 2008), p. 107.
26. Balbir Singh, *The Golden Hat Trick: My Hockey Days* (New Delhi: Vikas Publishing House, 1977), p. 129.
27. Ibid., p. 193.
28. Boria Majumdar and Nalin Khanna, *India and the Olympics* (New Delhi: Harper Collins, 2008), p. 215.
29. K. Arumugam, 'Dhanraj Pillay, the Face of Indian Hockey', in *Top Hockey Stars*, ed. K. Arumugam (New Delhi: Field Hockey Publications, 2004), p. 142.

Part II

Sport and Literature

4

Other Histories: Modernity, Literature and Football in India

Supriya Chaudhuri

Modern competitive sport was brought to India in the wake of colonialism, although some sporting disciplines—such as wrestling, for example—have a long indigenous history. It is generally recognised that organised sports were an instrument of empire, and that the 'games ethic' cultivated in British Victorian boarding schools contributed to the formation of a kind of muscular Christianity appropriate to empire-builders and colonial administrators. In a famous lecture, Pierre Bourdieu argued that modern sport itself (as distinct from *play*, or the *games* common to all cultures), was very much a product of the nineteenth-century rationalisation and re-organisation of the public sphere in the technologically advanced West.[1] The historical situation within which this emergence took place was ideologically formed by nation, empire, race, class, and gender. Associated with public school education (for boys) and viewed as an apt instrument for toughening the fibre of future soldiers, imperial servants and colonial administrators, sport also acquired rules and associations that produced it as a spectacle for mass audiences and permitted the emergence of the professional sportsperson. What resulted, then, was a simultaneous restriction and democratisation of the sporting field, visible in the anxious distinction between *amateur* and *professional*, preserved in the interest of social class, and influencing the regulations of the early Olympics as well as many other sporting competitions. Yet modern sport, as a variant of the 'culture industry', was built on economically viable specialisations supported not just by popular enthusiasm but by public, that is State, money. It is closely linked to the phenomenon of modernity itself, insofar as it converted the labour of the sportsperson to a commodity that could be marketed for profit, while at the same time preserving the illusion of 'free time', or leisure. In creating a disjunction between production and consumption, participant and spectator, it enabled the emergence of a huge industry dedicated not just to sports practice but also to sports goods and training. Yet by its nature as sport, by its origin in the game, it was founded on a real ambivalence regarding the status of the sportsperson, engaged, so it seemed, simultaneously in work and in play. This ambivalence may be seen to extend to the whole field of culture, but modern sport certainly belongs to what Guy Debord described as 'the society of the spectacle.'[2]

Subaltern Sport

What was the role of the subaltern—both as nameless foot-soldier and as voiceless subject—in the public practice of sport in the subcontinent? The tension within these two senses of the term, barely acknowledged in its rapid assimilation into postcolonial historiography, but always present in Gramsci's use of it, is critical to our understanding of the complicated histories of colonial sport.[3] If the emergence of sport, as distinct from games, is characteristic of modernity in its implicit democratisation of the field of cultural practice, unequal power-relations and structures of control obviously persist and indeed become more mechanical and systematic. For Bourdieu, the contemporary field of sporting practices is 'the site of struggles in which what is at stake, *inter alia,* is the power to impose the legitimate definition of sporting practice and of the legitimate function of sporting activity.'[4] In this double context of domination, the figure of the subaltern combines, perhaps rather disturbingly, the attributes of the conquering army on the one hand and the oppressed masses on the other. In Indian modernity, football, rather than cricket, is the vehicle of these subaltern narratives, narratives of struggle and suffering that also reflect cultural conquest and oppression. These narratives of modernity are also linked to the endeavour of literary modernism to find an aesthetic idiom for a time of crisis and anguish.

Illustration 4.1 Tenement housing in Kolkata painted in Mohun Bagan colours to commemorate the 1911 victory *Photo*: Supriya Chaudhuri

The field of sporting practice is thus produced as a complex hierarchical structure regulated on the one hand by class distinctions and on the other hand by market forces determining the investment of leisure capital. By the early twentieth century, sport comes to be adopted as a form of *mimetic* capital, a resource for displaying, in the agonistic spirit of Pierre de Coubertin's Olympic Games, the strength, health and self-discipline of individual nation-states. Characteristically, this mimesis involves a form of cultural self-reproduction: classical Greece and imperial Rome supply the models for a modern European invention of the sporting body. The disciplines of modern athletics formalised through the Olympic Games (running, discus, javelin), were derived from the athletic contests of classical Greece, as celebrated, for example, in the Pindaric Odes and memorialised as instances of perfect male physique in the statuary and vase-paintings that survive from the classical period. At the same time, modern sport could equally well be linked to the gladiatorial combats of imperial Rome, public spectacles regulated on the one hand by a rigid authoritarian discipline and on the other by an unregulated appetite for cruelty and pain, which produced the male *agôn* as a violent, brutal show of strength in life-or-death contests before a huge mass of spectators. The pedagogic, aristocratic, military, masculine and contestatory nature of athletic cultures in antiquity is attested also by the athletic training of young warriors in pre-modern India as in other ancient cultures. In the context of a global history of sport, it would be interesting to note the tensions—in the East as in the West—between *survival* and *renewal*; between the continued existence of athletic disciplines with ancient roots (wrestling, sword-play, stick-fights, archery) and the re-invention of disciplines based on ancient exemplars in order to suit the altered requirements of modernity (boxing, judo, karate and other 'modern' martial arts).

C. L. R. James, acknowledging the divisions of race and class that run through the practice of colonial sport, nevertheless viewed the emergence of popular sport and mass spectatorship in a positive spirit in his classic work *Beyond a Boundary* (1963). There are insoluble contradictions in his account, especially in his evoking of the athletic ideals of classical Greece to the neglect of that culture's actual foundation on a slave economy and its aristocratic and militaristic bias. The value James attached to the egalitarianism of sport, if corroborated by the rise to greatness of the West Indian cricket team and the success of South American football, is clearly undercut by histories of prejudice and in the South African instance, of apartheid. But James saw the sporting disciplines as levelling influences in themselves: 'Even as I write some little Spanish boys in a little Spanish village are kicking a ball in a rough open space and shouting "*Gol*", "*Penalti*", and "*Corni*"'.[5] Though modern sport is obviously not the liberating influence James's own sporting loyalties sought to make it, others too, like the Marxist football commentator Eduardo Galeano, have chosen to view it as a resource of the underclass.

Colonial Histories of Sport

These uncertainties attend India's adoption of modern—that is to say colonial—sport, part of its uneven transition to modernity itself. The extraordinary success with which cricket has imposed itself upon the global imagination as India's national game (which it never was) has obscured the histories of other sports with a larger initial following: hockey, wrestling, volleyball, kabbadi, badminton, swimming, and above all, football. With the partial exception of wrestling and kabbadi, each of these sports gained its modern character in the colonial period, and was carried to every quarter of India by regimental teams. Each acquired a popular regional following in villages and small towns as well as in large urban settlements, and came to be practised according to a seasonal calendar which was identified with the sporting cycle itself. Since indoor practice facilities were largely unavailable, even for regimental teams in cantonment towns, volleyball and badminton were played outdoors under lights, in the late evening, when the air was relatively still. All over India, local involvement in these imported pastimes was through clubs and associations, many of which could trace their histories back to the nineteenth century. In the fractured, non-homogeneous space of cultural 'modernisation' as it affected not just the urban bourgeoisie but the rural poor and lower middle-classes, the new sports of colonial India existed alongside indigenous forms of physical culture like wrestling, body-building and stick-fighting, which had always enjoyed a degree of aristocratic patronage, but were re-invented in the nationalist discourse of the early twentieth century. The *akharas* [gymnasia] and *samitis* [associations] set up in the wake of the nationalist upsurge of 1905–06 in Bengal became hotbeds of radical politics advocating a new kind of *swadeshi* [homelandist] physical culture. Many of these organisations were inspired by the ideals of bodily cultivation (*anushilan*) celebrated in Bankimchandra Chattopadhyay's classic novels *Anandamath* (1882) and *Debi Chaudhurani* (1884).[6] In such works, indigenous sports are largely confined to wrestling and stick-play (*lathikhela*), and it is these, together with *yogasanas*, that came to constitute the core of *akhara* training, and to inspire generations of rebel nationalists. Yet they were also compelled to share the stage of nationalism with *subaltern* (in both senses) sports like football and hockey.

Partha Chatterjee argues for the intimate links between football, politics and collective identity in colonial Calcutta, especially in the period leading up to, and immediately following, Mohun Bagan Club's historic victory in the 1911 Indian Football Association Shield final, beating the East Yorkshire Regiment by two goals to one.[7] Ten Mohun Bagan players (all excepting the full-back Sudhir Chatterjee) played barefoot, the practice in Indian football well into the 1940s, and not felt as a disadvantage except when the ground was soggy. On the 29th of July, the day of the final, it did not rain, owing no doubt to the prayers of thousands at the Thanthaniya Kali Temple in Cornwallis Street. Ahindra Chaudhuri, who went to the ground as a ten-year old, wrote of the incredible scenes in his reminiscences, recalling how a fellow-spectator lifted him on his shoulders to catch a glimpse of the players.[8] Mohun Bagan's extraordinary run of matches, culminating in a final attended by eighty to a hundred thousand people, most of whom had no chance of seeing any of the action (the capacity of the Calcutta Football Club ground was roughly five thousand) but were informed of the state of the game by messages inscribed on kites flown in the sky, has been exhaustively commented upon by football historians and analysts. The coaching tactics of Sailen Basu, formerly a junior officer in the British Indian Army, who became secretary of the club in 1900 and introduced a strict physical regimen and strategic drills, the heroism of the goalkeeper, Hiralal Mukherjee, who saved three penalties in the game with Rangers, and the exploits of the captain, Shibdas Bhaduri (with his near-identical brother Bijaydas), have become part of Mohun Bagan legend. It is no longer necessary to argue this early connection between football and nationalism, documented by Novy Kapadia, Kausik Bandyopadhyay, Boria Majumdar, Tony Mason and Paul Dimeo among others.[9]

Yet one of the many paradoxes that the historian—even the subaltern historian—encounters in attempting to trace a nationalist history of Indian sport is that sport never came to carry the full burden of nationalist aspiration. This is true of the later history of football in the decades before Independence, despite the patriotic fervour with which the Shield victory of 1911 was greeted. The historian Dipesh Chakraborty contrasts sport, as a symbolic token at the heart of the nation, with salt, so effectively used by Gandhi in his salt *satyagraha*, the Dandi march of 1930.[10] This is why Asutosh Gowariker's extraordinarily successful postmodern film *Lagaan*—even setting aside the obvious anachronism of its use of cricket as a vehicle of rural protest—is so deeply inauthentic.[11] Football historians, struggling to find an explanation both for the decline of nationalist investment in the game through the 1930s and 1940s, and the tragedy of failed sporting aspirations in a global context, have justly noted the petty rivalries between regions and clubs, administrative corruption, the invidiousness of colonial sports policies, the myth of the feeble, unathletic Bengali male, and the marginalisation of Bengal in national politics. These observations are undoubtedly correct. Nevertheless, I would like to suggest that there was always, from inception, a difficulty related to the subaltern character of football in its adoption, in India, by the dispossessed (even disenfranchised) masses at a critical moment of nation-formation.

As a colonial sport with a global following, football was one of the most immediate means of social modernisation. In practice it inaugurated new kinds of interaction between castes and communities, new sites for patriotic enthusiasm, and new forms of patronage. Indeed, Nagendra Prasad Sarbadhikari is said to have formed the Shobhabazar Club in 1889 after a lower-caste protégé, a potter's son, was denied entry to the Wellington Club.[12] At the same time, as a global product of modernity—that is, as Bourdieu argues, not a game, but a sport, involving a high degree of official control and commoditisation—football also required Indians to keep up with the latest international developments, to continue the processes of public investment and training, in short to feed into a hegemonic global discourse of sport. Modern sport had already acquired this global character by the early twentieth century, moving beyond the public school ethic to the staging of competitive nationalisms, as in the modern Olympic Games. In India, however, while football may have initially offered itself for transformation in this way, its prestige as a colonial pastime was relatively short-lived. The early histories of the top Calcutta clubs suggest a fair degree of aristocratic and middle-class patronage. The 1911 Shield victory was undoubtedly seen as a kind of nationalist triumph. Yet by the 1930s, football on the Maidan (literally the Field, the major open space in the heart of colonial Calcutta) had become divided between the bitter communal and regional loyalties of religious and ethnic groups, and could no longer carry the hopes of a nation. Brought to India by the inferior foot-soldier, adopted by the impoverished commoner, football came instead to bear the burden of the struggles and disappointments of labour and the working poor, who queued for match-day tickets and crowded the stands, bringing to the game passion, indiscipline and sectarian violence.

Another History of the Nation

Football narratives are, therefore, at the heart of another history of the nation, a subaltern history compounded of marginalisation and loss, but also of deep cultural identification and loyalty. To understand the symptomatic character of this history is perhaps to make sense of the anxieties and failures of our present. The football historian of the 1920s and 1930s, documenting the ethnic and communal rivalries of the top Calcutta clubs, Mohun Bagan, East Bengal, and Mohammedan Sporting, the emergence of gifted players from other parts of India, and a degree of success even at international level by the late 1940s (appearances at the Olympics, with a fourth-place finish at Melbourne in 1956, World Cup qualification in 1950—though the team could not go—and Asiad gold medals) is also compelled to note the failure to modernise, the neglect of sports culture, and the lumpenisation of the sports public that effectively removes football from the national stage by the late 1960s. It is a story not of consolidation but of fracture, disruption and gradual impoverishment.

For eastern India, the defining event that accompanied Independence in 1947 was Partition, drawing the new boundary of the nation-state across the heart of Bengal. The trauma of this division, following upon the famine of 1943 in which about four million people were believed to have died, and the bloody Partition riots in Calcutta and Dhaka, was prolonged by repeated waves of migration across the border into India, creating 'colonies' of refugees for whom the state did little or nothing. It has been estimated that eight million refugees crossed the newly created border into India from what was now East Pakistan: two million went the other way. This enormous movement of populations, marked by violence, suffering, dispossession, and deep feelings of psychological alienation, left an unhealed wound in the fabric of the nation-state, and gave birth, in the city of Calcutta particularly, to a 'colony' subculture (rooted, that is, in the refugee colony) of struggle and resistance documented, for example, in the films of Ritwik Ghatak. Peasant revolts, from the Tebhaga movement of 1946 to the Naxalbari rebellion of 1967, were a measure of rural unrest. There were food riots in the 1960s, the period of my own Calcutta childhood, and the economic recession added millions to the state's poor, dispossessed and unemployed. In an essay on 'Football and Nationalism', the sports writer Moti Nandy, whose own family had lived in north Calcutta for generations, described the refugees in these terms:

> Searching for a roof over their heads in the city and its surrounds and a fistful of rice twice a day, they began their struggle for survival under conditions of unbearable hardship. Lost and impoverished in an unknown territory and hostile environment, faced with severe adversities, they would sometimes lose the battle and fall back, then return once more to dream of settling down to a secure and normal existence.[13]

Both before and after Partition, it was this shifting and uprooted population 'these ravaged and embittered masses', as Nandy calls them, which came to identify their own struggle for existence with the rivalries of the top Calcutta football clubs.[14]

Modernist Literature and Subaltern Suffering

Indian literary modernism was also formed against this harsh backdrop of migration, resettlement and suffering, for all that it may have commenced under the influence of international aesthetic movements in the 1920s. In form and expression, it never abandoned the language of social realism, and never sought to justify a formalist solution to problems of violence, disorder and mimetic lack. The project of modernity had been the principal concern of the Bengali novel from its inception in the nineteenth century, driving its search for subjects and its formal experiments. To some extent this project of representation follows the trajectory of desire, thus confirming Fredric Jameson's assessment of the novel's role in 'what can be called a properly bourgeois cultural revolution—that immense process of transformation whereby populations whose life habits were formed by other, now archaic, modes of production are now reprogrammed for life and work in the new world of market capitalism.' The novel then assumes 'the task of producing as though for the first time the very life world, that very "referent" ... of which the new narrative discourse will then claim to be the 'realistic' reflection'.[15] But at the same time, the form is a potent site for fantasy, its narrative materials not always amenable to the claims of reality. Though early historians of the novel in India repeatedly emphasise its commitment to realism, romance, that unacknowledged other of realist narrative in both Europe and India, remains one of its most powerful elements.

In the twentieth century, despite the hard-fought gains of the independence movement, the literary projects of modernity lose their aura of hope. A new kind of social realism, drawing upon modernist techniques of representation as well as upon the anger, confusion and despair of the rural poor and the urban unemployed, leaves its imprint in fiction. The great modernist writers of early and mid-twentieth century India, compelled to earn their livelihoods as journalists, schoolteachers, scriptwriters, or clerks, never experienced that break with the popular that is European modernism's most difficult legacy. The growth of mass entertainment, or what Adorno called the culture industry,[16] ubiquitous though it is today in India, in fact postdates the high period of literary modernism. In Bengal, the home both of a nascent modernism in all the arts and of a struggling football culture, there is a degree of coincidence between the ethics and aspirations of these apparently dissimilar forms of cultural self-expression. This is best seen in the novels and short stories of the sports writer Moti Nandy, who died in January 2010 at the age of seventy-nine. At his memorial, one of his contemporaries, himself among the most acclaimed of modern Bengali poets, spoke of Nandy's work as frightening in its pitilessness, its uncompromising 'cruelty'.[17] The term was used as a mark of admiration for a writer held in high regard by his fellows, despite the fact that he earned his living as a sports correspondent for a daily newspaper and wrote prolifically in the popular genres of adolescent sports fiction and reportage.

Moti Nandy and the Literature of Football

Nandy's fiction covers many sports, and an award-winning film was made from his novella *Kony*, about a young female swimmer. But he is probably best known for his short novels *Striker* (1973) and *Stopper* (1974), translated into French as well as twice, over thirty years apart, into English.[18] Football is everywhere in his writing, even in books that are not directly about a footballer, such as the unforgettable *Naran* (1990), set in the year of the Helsinki Olympics (1952) and the 10–2 drubbing of the barefooted Indian team by a formidable Yugoslavian side. Nandy knew the pulse of the Maidan as few have done before or since: the club rivalries, the fierce bargaining over prize players, the allegations of match-fixing, and, in the period about which he wrote, the vulnerability and exploitation of the players themselves, most of them from very deprived backgrounds, and the diseases, injuries and malnutrition that haunted the life of the athlete. This knowledge infuses all his sports fiction with a harsh, unblinking realism, a sense of the limitations and frustrations of the actual that runs counter to comic reassurance or sporting triumphalism. Even the novella *Dalbadaler Agey* (Before the Transfers, 1992), a relatively kind portrait of a successful footballer from a lower middleclass background, is made edgy and discomforting by its reflections on corruption, failure and incompetence. Nandy's sports fiction is technically categorised as being for young adults, though the 'serious' modernist novel that won him a major literary prize, *Nakshatrer Rat* (Night of Stars, 1959) and the 'refugee' novel *Dvadash Byakti* (Twelfth Man, 1969) chronicle similar histories of despair and impoverishment.[19]

The literature of sport repeatedly raises a question that academic discourse has never resolved, the question of the popular. Sports is perceived as belonging to the domain of the popular (though the majority of the very poor in a poor country cannot afford to follow sport) and writing about sport tends to be generically segregated from 'serious' literature. Yet it is modernism, with its existentialist ethic of gritty despair, that produces the most compelling philosophy of sport, and it was Albert Camus who was credited with the apocryphal statement 'All that I know most surely about morality and obligations I owe to football.' After the army, it is sport that offers the most unsparing contrast between a pitiless, mechanised, bureaucratic order that both produces and consumes the individual, and the ardours, desires, self-deceptions or self-denials of lonely contestants who struggle and fail. This is the world of Alan Sillitoe's *The Loneliness of the Long-Distance*

Runner, of Bernard Malamud's *The Natural*, and of Zinedine Zidane's World Cup tragedy. It is a world in which the dream or wish-fulfilment fantasy, the staple of popular imagination, co-exists with the inevitable disappointments of our hopes, the intractability of the system, the loss of talent, the harsh disaccommodation of the world to our desires. It is from being cast into a world of this kind, from *being-there*, that the philosophy of football is generated, a philosophy that places high value upon struggle and moral responsibility while recognising their general futility, a philosophy whose triumphalist public manifestations conceal deep feelings of alienation and cynicism. It is a philosophy rooted in the body and its pleasures, as in its inevitable decay.

Striker and *Stopper* represent two ends of a footballing career. The first is about a young forward, Prasun Bhattacharya, attempting to find a place in Calcutta's top football clubs, struggling against poverty and the disapproval of his father (a former star discredited and maligned after he missed a goal in a Shield final twenty years ago). The second is about a middle-aged fullback, Kamal Guha, playing the last game of his life, watched by a son who cares nothing for football. Both heroes come from deprived working-class backgrounds, and carry not just the expectations of their families but also the burden of past humiliations and present insecurities. Nandy's narratives also combine, in a remarkably modernist vein, the dreams and aspirations of their struggling heroes with the daily grind of work and training. *Striker*, in fact, commences with an entire chapter in which Prasun is dreaming of being sought out in his humble home in a dingy Calcutta lane by a talent scout from the Brazilian club Santos (Pele's club). But while these stories employ the well-worn formulas of sports writing, with their heroes facing failure and rejection before victory in a final, climactic match, they are also narratives of the lives that are lived in and around football, the inter-generational conflicts, the working-class fears and fantasies. Most strikingly, they convey the bitterness and anguish of working-class poverty at a time of labour unrest and lay-offs, with little to eat in most lower-middle class households, and nothing by way of extra nutrition for the struggling athlete. Nandy's powerful, intransigent evocation of the actual lives of footballers links his fiction to the modernist *angst* and alienation described in Sillitoe's *The Loneliness of the Long-Distance Runner*, though he does not replicate Sillitoe's characteristically modernist use of disappointment (*déception*, in the French *nouveau roman*) at the close.

It is worth recalling the remarkable body of modernist novels and films produced in Europe and America through the 1950s and 1960s which make use of sporting failure, refusal or tragedy as part of a vocabulary of everyday despair, making the modernist idiom itself an idiom of suffering. This is true of the substance of Nandy's writing as well, though *Striker* and *Stopper* also employ the classic tropes of sports writing by ending on a note of triumph. These works thus belong to the genre of the popular in their manipulation of crisis and tragedy, despair and ultimate victory: clichés, one might call them, of the sports narrative. Yet unlike the postmodern sporting fantasy—exemplified in India by films like *Lagaan*, *Iqbal*, and *Chak De! India*, it is not extraordinary success, but a moment of fulfillment grounded in the text of suffering, that Nandy's stories present.[20]

I would like to emphasise this difference, as I see it, between modernism and postmodernism in respect of the philosophy of sport and sports writing. Nandy's writing, and modernist writing generally, sees sport as a ground upon which the history of the suffering of the common man can be written. By contrast, the postmodern sports fantasy, though it does not deny the existence of pain and violence, is grounded in the magical simultaneity of desire and pleasure. Typically, its narratives are driven by exceptionalism, by a sense of fantastic possibility against all the odds, as for example in Danny Boyle's 2008 film *Slumdog Millionaire*. Ordinariness drives Nandy's fiction, as with the eponymous Naran in his novella *Naran*, a refugee football fan who is forced to conceal his East Bengal loyalties in his workplace, and becomes that loneliest of all athletes, a marathon runner. He ends by finishing a race, but finishes so late that he cannot meet his hero Emil Zatopek, brought to India in the wake of his exploits at Helsinki to give away the prizes.

Nandy's fiction chronicles, like little else in the period, the deep commitment to football among the urban poor as a vehicle of aspiration for its players and anguished pleasure for its spectators. In the Calcutta of the sixties, before middle-class homes acquired television, before satellite channels brought the best of world football to our living rooms, our lives were lived through the triumphs and disappointments of the Maidan, the fanaticism of East Bengal, Mohun Bagan, and Mohammedan Sporting fans. Young hopefuls, despite their talent, put on their first pair of boots when they were about nineteen—if they were lucky. The grounds, rock hard in summer, a sea of slippery mud in the monsoon, were unimaginably bad. The old wooden stands were rickety and dangerous; brawls and stampedes were common, such as the one at Eden Gardens in 1980 in which sixteen fans were killed. Starved of international success, individual neighbourhoods, while continuing to go to the league games, adopted Brazil or Argentina as 'their' teams. Football did make some players considerably richer, but it was also ruled by corruption and the despotism of trustees and managing bodies. It was a time of unfulfillment and despair, but it was also, I would suggest, the last significant period when sport and sporting narratives were at the centre of our perception of the everyday and its translation, in the texts of modernism, into literature. That perception of the everyday, in its banality and violence, its link with subaltern existence, has faded from our lives in the wake of globalisation. The pleasures of globalised sport, consumed through television and advertising, have turned an entire generation away from Calcutta football to support the superior skills of the English Premier League or the Spanish La Liga. The urban upper middle class has indeed rediscovered football, but as a spectator sport distributed by television channels, luring the young not so much through participatory enthusiasm as by the attractions of merchandise such as branded strips, scarves and pennants. During huge international events like the FIFA World Cup, Calcutta neighbourhoods still support Argentina, Germany or Brazil, but the energy of such support has lost some of its earlier, desperate edge. Despite many efforts to revive Indian football, most recently through the promotion of club competitions where international clubs, in their capacity as multinational corporates, are invited to put up teams, the national football team is ranked below 150 internationally. And club football in Calcutta continues to be locked into its subaltern state. Its followers come from the rank and file of the urban proletariat, and its promoters are still incompetent and corrupt. Football has not gained from international exposure, and the literature of sport has not acquired a sports writer to rival Nandy. He remains part of subaltern history, and what we knew about morality and obligations we owed to him.

Notes

An earlier version of this essay was published as 'Literary Modernism and Subaltern Sport' in *Moving Worlds: A Journal of Transcultural Writings* (University of Leeds), 12:1 (2012), 29–39. Some sections correspond to another published essay by me, 'Bodies at Risk: Gender and Sport', published in *Women Contesting Culture: Changing Frames of Gender Politics in India*, eds Kavita Panjabi and Paromita Chakravarti (Kolkata: Stree, 2012), pp. 181–98. Reprinted by courtesy.

1. See J. A. Mangan, *The Games Ethic and Imperialism: Aspects of the Diffusion of an Ideal* (Harmondsworth: Viking, 1986), and Pierre Bourdieu, 'How Can One be a Sportsman?' in *Sociology in Question*, trans. Richard Nice (London: Sage, 1993), p. 120.
2. See Guy Debord, *The Society of the Spectacle*, trans. Donald Nicholson-Smith (London: Zone Books, 1995).
3. See Antonio Gramsci, *Selections from the Prison Notebooks of Antonio Gramsci*, ed. and trans. Quintin Hoare and Geoffrey Nowell Smith (New York: International Publishers, 1971), pp. 52–3.
4. Bourdieu, 'How Can One be a Sportsman?', p. 122. Italics in original.
5. C. J. R. James, *Beyond a Boundary* (Durham: Duke University Press, 1993), p. 153.
6. For the Bengali texts, see Bankimchandra Chattopadhyay, *Bankim Rachanabali*, ed. J. C. Bagal, vol. 1 (Calcutta: Sahitya Samsad, 2003), pp. 653–726 and 727–808. For English translations, see Bankimchandra Chatterji, *Anandamath, or The Sacred Brotherhood*, trans. Julius J. Lipner (Oxford: Oxford University Press, 2005) and *Debi Chaudhurani, or The Wife Who Came Home*, trans. Julius J. Lipner (Oxford: Oxford University Press, 2009).
7. Partha Chatterjee, 'Football and Collective Identity in Colonial Calcutta', Paper given at International Leverhulme Network Conference on *Commodities and Culture in the Colonial World, 1851–1914*: 'Commodities and Affect', Jadavpur University, Kolkata, January 12, 2011; included in Partha Chatterjee, *The Black Hole of Empire: History of a Global Practice of Power* (Princeton: Princeton University Press, 2012).
8. See Ahindra Chaudhuri, *Nijere hārāye khunji* ('I Search for My Lost Self': Calcutta: Indian Associated Press, 1962), pp. 42–3; cited in Partha Chatterjee, 'Football and Collective Identity'.
9. See Boria Majumdar and Kausik Bandyopadhyay, *Goalless: The Story of a Unique Footballing Nation* (New Delhi: Penguin Viking, 2006), pp. 32–50;

Tony Mason, 'Football on the Maidan: Cultural Imperialism in Calcutta, in *The Cultural Bond: Sport, Empire, Society*, ed. J. A. Mangan (London: Frank Cass, 1992), pp. 142–53; Paul Dimeo, 'Football and Politics in Bengal: Colonialism, Nationalism, Communalism, in *Soccer in South Asia: Empire, Nation, Diaspora*, eds Paul Dimeo and James Mills (London: Frank Cass, 2001), pp. 57–74.

10. Dipesh Chakrabarty, 'The Rise and Fall of Indian Sports History', in *Sport in South Asian Society: Past and Present*, eds Boria Majumdar and J. A. Mangan (London: Routledge, 2005), p. 6.
11. Asutosh Gowariker, dir., *Lagaan*, Amir Khan Productions, 2001.
12. See Majumdar and Bandyopadhyay, *Goalless*, p. 22.
13. Moti Nandy, 'Football and Nationalism', in *The Calcutta Psyche*, ed. Geeti Sen (New Delhi: India International Centre, 1991), pp. 249–50. Cited in Majumdar and Bandyopadhyay, *Goalless*, p. 114.
14. Moti Nandy, 'Calcutta Soccer', in *Calcutta: The Living City*, vol. II, ed. Sukanta Chaudhuri (Delhi: Oxford University Press, 1990), p. 319. Cited in Majumdar and Bandyopadhyay, *Goalless*, p. 115.
15. Fredric Jameson, *The Political Unconscious: Narrative as a Socially Symbolic Act* (London: Routledge, 1989), p. 152.
16. Theodor W. Adorno, *The Culture Industry: Selected Essays on Mass Culture*, ed. J. M. Bernstein (London: Routledge, 2003).
17. Sarat Kumar Mukhopadhyay, speech at Moti Nandy's memorial meeting, January 2010; see his essay 'Chhoto Golpo o Moti Nandy' (Short Stories and Moti Nandy, in *Proma*: Special Moti Nandy Number, 29 (1415/2008), p. 12.
18. See Moti Nandy, *Striker/Stopper*, trans. Mihir K. Das (Calcutta: Orient Longman, 1994), and *Striker, Stopper*, trans. Arunava Sinha (Gurgaon: Hachette India, 2010)
19. Most of Nandy's novels have not been translated into English. His fiction for young adults, including *Naran* and *Dalbadaler Agey*, is available in the collection, Moti Nandy, *Dashti Kishor Upanyas* (Ten Novels for Young Adults, Calcutta: Ananda Publishers, 2010); some of his 'adult' novels are collected in Moti Nandy, *Dashti Upanyas* (Calcutta: Ananda Publishers, 2010).
20. See *Chak De! India* (Dir. Shimit Amin: Yash Raj Films, 2007) and *Iqbal* (Dir. Nagesh Kukunoor, Mukta Films, 2005).

5

Sport, Surveillance and Speed in *The Hunger Games* Trilogy

Sanam Khanna

Suzanne Collins published the first book of *The Hunger Games* trilogy in 2008, and since then the series, which includes *Catching Fire* (2009) and *Mockingjay* (2010), has gone on to attain cult status amongst young teens. *The Hunger Games,* released as a movie in 2012 has been described by the Guardian as 'a full-blown phenomenon'.[1]

The Hunger Games is the first novel of the trilogy, and it introduces readers to a futuristic, dystopian society where an overpowering government controls the lives and resources in twelve different districts. Sixteen-year-old Katniss Everdeen, of District 12, is the main character of the story. Each year, as punishment for the now demolished District 13's attempted rebellion, two children from each district, called 'tributes', are chosen by lottery to fight each other to death in an arena. The event is called the Hunger Games and is televised for everyone in the Capitol to see. The one simple goal, and rule, is to stay alive and, as Katniss observes, another unspoken rule is 'Don't eat each other'. The winning tribute is given food and a life of ease for themselves and their families, along with presents of food and resources for their district. The protagonist, Katniss ends up volunteering for the role of tribute to the Games after her little sister Prim is drawn in the lottery. Peeta, a baker's son who Katniss knows through school, is also drawn to fight in the Games. Katniss and Peeta are whisked away to the Capitol to fight other children in the artificial landscape created for the arena by the Gamemakers. In a twist of events, it is revealed that Peeta is in love with Katniss, which leads to their mentor, Haymitch, manipulating their image to the

Gamemakers who must change the rules of the game to accommodate the passionate fervour that the pair attract from the viewers. By the last book of the trilogy, Katniss has turned, unwillingly into a rebel leader against the Capitol, but realises that the rules of war are far too similar to the rules of the Hunger Games, and have the same compelling demand for narrativising and creating celebrities through selective telecasts.

Collins's aim is fairly clear; she leads her young (and not-so-young) readers to question their choices not only as spectators and fans but as citizens as well. She seems to suggest the dangers inherent in a society given to enjoyment of destructive ambition and brutal triumph, and uses the trope of sports, games and reality shows to drive home her point. The series is a biting indictment of surveillance societies, totalitarian regimes and celebrity culture.

Of course, Collins is not the first to suggest that an obsession with sports and celebrities is problematic. Increasingly, sports commentators and writers have addressed themselves to this issue. Commenting on the emphasis and pressure American parents place on young children to excel in sports, the well known sports culture writer Richard C. Crepeau notes that '...deeply imbedded in the society is the notion that somehow sport leads to the Holy Grail. If only one can succeed at sport the world will be at your feet. Fame, wealth, popularity, and self-fulfillment will be yours'. He observes that this notion has led to the 'objectification of children...exploited...by parents, coaches, and the fantasies of modern sport' and he terms this a 'malfunction in the values of sport.'[2]

I suggest that a critique of sports, success in the 'game' and spectatorship is visible in *The Hunger Games* trilogy. In order to examine the politics of media transmission and the role of spectatorship on sports, this paper draws on the concept of dromology and attempts to examine the 'malfunction in the value of sports' as one possible manifestation of a dromological, chronoscopic society. The term, from Dromos—the Greek word meaning 'to race'—has been coined by French hyper-modern theorist Paul Virilio, and it means the 'science or logic of speed'. Virilio speculates on the cultural implication of digital technologies, particularly in terms of a move from chronological to chronoscopic time.

The article seeks to examine the effects of chronoscopic time on viewership and its impact on sport as represented in the Hunger Games. It examines the values that sports represents or is made to represent, through its transmission and spectatorship, in the *Hunger Games*. I question the mediation, organisation and effect of spectatorship by technology, the technological effects of speed (dromology), and examine how the politics of speed affect our understanding of our 'lived reality'. The possible shift from a chronological to a chronoscopic society as a result of these is also explored.

This essay has four sections. The first section touches upon historical definitions of the concepts of games, sports, and sporting values. The second explores sports as 'media events', and the 'malfunction' in sporting values, as explored in the *Hunger Games*. The third introduces the concept of dromology and in the last section I elaborate on the 'sports as war' equation to question issues relating to sports transmission and spectatorship.

Working Definitions of Key Concepts—Games, Sports, Sporting Values

To begin with, it may be useful to define what is meant by the word game. Of the many possible definitions, I have chosen three, offered by renowned critics, Salen and Zimmerman, Costikyan and Sutton Smith, as representative. 'A game is a system in which players engage in an artificial conflict, defined by rules, that results in a quantifiable outcome.'[3] 'A game is an interactive structure of endogenous meaning that requires players to struggle towards goals.'[4] 'At its most elementary level then we can define game as an exercise of voluntary control systems in which there is an opposition between forces, confined by a procedure and rules in order to produce a disequilibrial outcome.'[5]

Similarly, when trying to define sports, one finds that the oldest definition of sport in English (1300) is of anything humans find amusing or entertaining. The European Sports Charter (2001) offers a more comprehensive definition whereby 'Sport means all forms of physical activity which, through casual or organised participation, aim at expressing or improving physical fitness and mental well-being, forming relationships or obtaining results in competitions at all levels.'

It also notes 'Ensuring and improving people's physical, social and mental well-being from one generation to the next requires...sporting activities.'[6] Central to the two concepts (of games and sports) is the idea that competition (and or conflict) is involved, either with self, or the (natural) elements, but usually with another competitor. Obviously then, control of the body (again of the self or the other, or even both) in order to achieve 'victory' is the goal. The unspoken agreement is that pleasure is part of the process (or the goal) for player(s) and spectators. Historically, these three key elements are valorised when a society or culture celebrates sport.

However, apart from the celebration of sports for these three key elements, in historical terms, the idea that participation in sport has some utility (other than being enjoyed for its own sake) can be traced to mid-nineteenth century Britain. Middle-class reformers in the areas of education and urban welfare began to develop the idea that sport participation, appropriately directed, could be involved in the development of certain values, individual and social. Amongst these were the development of a sound body and mind, the strengthening of moral character; the inculcation of work discipline, teamwork, fair play, and other socially approved characteristics. Sports also claimed social, community and national benefits, such as fostering national pride, integrated living and conflict resolution etc.[7]

As a result of this concept of positive value creation, political and commercial forces have competed to 'promote' sports and sports organisations, and ironically, the promotion of sports led to their commodification and packaging as entertainment.

So how does a game become a sport? And how does a sport become 'popular'? A codification of rules, stances, goals and objectives is only the primary level. To achieve popularity, it is well documented that the sport or game must necessarily engage public interest, even passion. Therefore the defining characteristic of sports as an activity seems to be its ability to become a spectacle—or to use a more modern phrase—a media event.

The rise of spectator sports to their present importance coincides historically with the rise of mass production, which intensifies the needs sport satisfies while at the same time creating the technical capacity to promote and market athletic contests to a vast audience.

But according to a common criticism of modern sport, these same developments have destroyed the value of athletics. Commercialised play has turned into work, subordinated the athlete's pleasure to the spectator's and reduced the spectator himself to a state of passivity—the very antithesis of the health and vigour sport is ideally meant to promote.

Media Events and the 'Malfunction in the Value of Sports'

In the *Hunger Games* trilogy, Collins combines the concepts of sport and war, and further complicates these by adding elements of the reality show, computer simulation games, concepts of celebrity creation, cult-hood, and the involvement of 'children' in the adult political game. She sardonically reveals the complete corruption of sporting values that follows when sports become media events, propelled by the need to satisfy demands for speed, and to construct imaginary narratives in the popular imagination. The 'objectification of children... exploited... by parents, coaches, and the fantasies of modern sport' which is noted earlier by Crepeau, is brought to life as it were, in this trilogy.

If we agree, at least for now, that sports becoming media events has led to a degradation of positive sporting values, we also need to question what is lost, and how. If the positives of teamwork and 'moral' character are the ones we address ourselves to, quite clearly, the cult of stardom, the rise of the individual is one factor. The other as many note, is the need to make the game faster, speedier, to accelerate it in order to make it attractive in a century where speed is a foremost value. These two factors, more than any other, have perhaps led to what, as quoted earlier, Crepeau terms 'malfunction in the values of sport'.

In the *Politics of Pleasure,* Rowe writes that for sport to be an event 'a conglomeration of interests must coincide', and asks the spectating public to recognize that 'media sport is actually made by humans' and 'somebody, somewhere, is making cold-hearted economic decisions about people's sporting passions.'[8]

In the *Hunger Games,* Collins displays the games as events which are very clearly mediated by a conglomerate of powers, political and capitalistic; the series is set in a dystopic future, but the parallel with our own time is clear: the current sporting events, the cult of celebrities, and the associated spectatorship. The Hunger Games, televised and broadcast over the country, are meant to entertain the over privileged citizens of the capitol, even as they suppress and control the twelve districts from which the tributes are drawn. A team of dedicated Gamemakers create the synthetic artifice of the games arena, encompassing any geographical and technological feature they wish to use, where every kind of camera and camera angle can be deployed.

In striking contrast to this mediated sporting event, Collins also presents another view of sport, of archery and game hunting, an activity that is companionable, healthy and pleasurable, precisely because it is private and unorganised (in the sense of spectatorship). In what is perhaps a reminder of the origin of sport—of game hunting by primitive man—the trilogy shows Katniss and her friend Gale at their happiest when they are alone together in the forest, free of cameras and surveillance, working as a team. In the final book, *Mockingjay*, the act of their hunting together causes Katniss to reminisce 'Here began countless days of hunting and snaring, fishing and gathering, roaming together through the woods, unloading our thoughts while we filled our game bags. This was the doorway to both sustenance and sanity'.[9] However the narrative makes it clear that this idyllic view of the forest is a creation of Katniss' selective memory, as even the woods are not totally free of surveillance. She feels alone, unobserved, and hence free, but this is not the reality of the text.

Mediascapes and Dromology

Collins sets up a complex circularity of history and politics, with the setting and the names (Seneca, Cinna, Plutarch etc.) leading readers back to the Imperial Roman past and Greek myths and she deploys these to critique the present at many levels. The first book seems to focus on society's obsession with achieving cult status in the media for sportspeople, and the oft publicised violent behaviour that gets media attention, as well as the idea of sports tourism. By the end of the trilogy the focus is on war and conflict as televised events, and politics as the arena of mass manipulation employing every technology ever created.

A rewarding approach to the *Hunger Games* series is through the prism of Arjun Appadurai's claim that the globalised post-industrial culture is governed and defined by five dimensions—ethnoscapes, ideoscapes, financescapes, and importantly for this paper, mediascapes and technoscapes, which I think are of primary importance in a reading of *Hunger Games*.

'Mediascapes are image centered, narrative-based accounts of strips of reality, and what they offer ...is a series of elements (such as characters, plots and textual forms) out of which scripts can be formed of imagined lives. Technoscape is the global configuration, ever fluid, of technology, both high and low...[which] now moves at high speeds...'[10] *Hunger Games* can be read to interrogate the creation and transmission of sports as mediascapes, its inextricable relationship to technoscape, and its undeniable impact on what can be normatively termed 'sporting values'.

In the trilogy, Collins brings together varied cultural phenomena, in order to critique concepts of gaming and sports culture. If we return to the various definitions and values suggested by examining the concepts of games and sports, a few certainly are fulfilled in the Hunger Games. The games are first and foremost a display of national (political) power, and perhaps even for the repressed districts they represent achievement and pride since at least a few districts seem to train children (called the careers) specifically for the Hunger Games. They do achieve a level of fitness for the athletes who must also display 'a skill' which may be useful in the arena. After being chosen and before the games begin, each contestant is given a complete 'make-over' at the Remake Center, and each district team is assigned a stylist who designs costumes and the look/presentation for the team. In a clear criticism of the cult of the sports celebrity, Collins lays bare the commercial instincts behind the modelling and beautification of athletes. In the scene where their mentor/coach Haymitch examines them, Katniss observes that:

> he circles us, prodding us like animals at times, checking our muscles, examining our faces. 'Well, you're not entirely hopeless. Seem fit enough. And once the stylists get hold of you, you'll be attractive enough.'
>
> Peeta and I don't question this. The Hunger Games aren't a beauty contest but the best looking tributes always seem to pull more sponsors.[11]

Sponsors are vital for the survival of the tributes in the Hunger Games, as they are vital for athletes in any sport, but here the analogy is made explicit. In the dystopian world of the Hunger Games, sponsors are the only ones who are allowed to provide food, tools or medicine to the contestants, at a huge financial cost, and so it is literally a matter of life and death for the tributes to attract, and hold, the collective gaze. In the third book of the trilogy, *Mockingjay*, Katniss continues to be styled and dressed for the cameras, albeit as a rebel leader, and is in fact told, 'You'll be the best dressed rebel in history'.[12] If wars are to be televised as carefully as games, both demand a high degree of presentability to keep viewers happy, it seems.

At the beginning of the games, many contestants team up together, working in dazzling displays of pooled skills and talents till the time they must turn on each other, and display individual talent and cunning to survive. Survival is the goal, obviously, since the one rule of the game is 'stay alive'. The prize is tangible—the benefits of staying alive—compounded by a life of luxury and ease for self and family, as well as food and material benefits for your district.

So, judging by the definitions of sports, and the values sport is meant to achieve, nominally, the Hunger Games are still a game, in the extended sense of the word. Overt sporting values are met, though certainly individual mental well being of the players is not achieved; through control of the spectacle, on the other hand, national stability and a putative 'integration 'is achieved. But if the games (and by implication sports) and spectatorship are fields of massive manipulation and mediation, then, perhaps at a deeper level this manipulation has an effect on a society's understanding of identity and reality. It is at this juncture that I suggest *Hunger Games* is critiquing the twenty-first century's use of technology to fulfil its need, its reliance, perhaps even addiction, to speed.

According to hyper-modern theorist Paul Virilio, 'we live in an era of accelerated culture. The world having reached the speed of light has thrown history in disarray and jumbles up the relation of the living towards the world'. Today, speed is power, and the effect of speed first perceived, according to Virilio, on vision has produced a state where in the late twentieth century, vision has completely lost its capacity to be 'objective,' it is, in fact, tele-objective. Thus, our concept of reality, our lived experience is a demand for a constant gratification of speed, creating a cognitive universe where there is 'a visible, instant present where immediacy, instantaneity and ubiquity rule'. He terms this a dromocratic society.[13] Steve Redhead takes this further while interpreting Virilio, and adds, 'Today speed, like power, is everywhere in the era of what I call mobile modernities and modern mobilities. This is especially evident in sporting culture and more specifically in mediatised sporting event ....'[14]

David Harvey and Baudrillard both share Virilio's concern for time-space compression and write about how 'society is now so given over to speed motion, cinematic images and technological fixes as to have created 'a crisis of explanatory logic'....and as Harvey notes, the irony is that 'The greater the ephemerality, the more pressing the need to manufacture some kind of eternal truth....'[15]

Virilio (1997; 1995; 1994; 1991) has gone to great lengths to show that the essence of postwar telematics involves the virtual elimination of both spatial and temporal distance between events' occurrences and their representations. Speed is no longer limited by moving across geographic distances by means of physical transport, or, movement through chronological time. Rather, speed is equated with real-time data transmission moving at the speed-of-light, giving rise to what is now understood as instantaneity. A key driver of chronoscopic time is the shift to an instantaneous mode of production and consumption. Virilio characterises this digitalised speed-up as a shift from chronological to chronoscopic time. He theorises that time-space compression has led to chronoscopic, rather than chronological society. In other words, we experience time through images, through vision, rather than any other ecological, biological or metabolic imperative.

Virilio writes 'I personally fear we are being confronted by a sort of pathology of immediate perception that owes everything, or very nearly everything, to the recent proliferation of photocinematographic and video infographic seeing machines. Machines that by mediatising everything ....end up destroying their credibility.'[16]

Virilio's contention is that with a proliferation of images directed at the viewer with speed and ferocity, we live in an era of 'eyelust', craving images, craving images at speed, unable to decode the symbols and logics of the image, to a point where the agency for telos is completely handed over to the mediatised narrativising process .

Eyelust also demands violence, as Virilio observes. Violence is action at high speed, a calculated high speed with immediate, visible consequences and rewards; and eventually, habituated by violence, the gaze demands more and more of it, at even greater speed. The disruption of speed, the freeze frame, is then a disjunct in the flow that draws attention to itself by dwelling on the moment of successful violence, creating the sensation of even greater violence by prolonging it in the gaze, imprinting it on memory.

The media fixation on speed and violence is most overtly the focus of Collins narrative. In fact, the narrative itself flirts with violence and plays with the speed of the narrative in what I perceive functions almost as a cognitive trick on the reader, alternating between seduction and disgust. At one point, Katniss has to watch another competitor being eaten alive, slow by slow bit, as cyborgian wild dogs manufactured by the Gamemakers gnaw away. Horrified but unable to act, she recognises that 'No viewer could turn away from the show now. From the Gamemakers' point of view, this is the final word in entertainment...' Like her, the reader is held captive, and it is at this point that we realise how complete is the hold of chronoscopic time over both her, and us. 'The horror holds us both captive,... it goes on and on.....blocking out memories and hopes of tomorrow, erasing everything but the present...'[17] In the Games, if speed is an essential factor in holding the viewer's attention, the lack of speed is equally a ploy, deliberately slowing the narrative, making the viewer of the Games (and therefore the reader of the book) linger at specific points, unable to skip forward. Gamemakers and game watchers are both implicated in prolonging of agony and violence.

Time–space compression, and selection, during transmission is precisely what we witness in the *Hunger Games*. The Games are televised and every moment is televised, but not every moment is telecast, as the narrative highlights. The control of the narrative occurs even in those very moments we 'see live', as camera angles are manipulated and scenes are censored by merely changing the angle.

In a key scene of *Hunger Games*, Katniss mourns the death of one of the competitors, Rue, who reminded her of her younger sister. She creates a memorial of flowers and leaves gathered from the artificial, simulated forest games arena they have been placed in. This is an act of rebellion and she thinks to herself "They'll have to show it. Or, even if they choose to turn the cameras elsewhere at this moment, they'll have to bring it back when they collect the bodies and everyone will see her then and know I did it.'[18] At the end of the games, during the closing ceremony, she again stresses 'whoever puts together the highlights has to choose what sort of story to tell....'[19] Lived reality then, is what is perceived to be real, what is shown to be real, leaving the viewer blind to what has been hidden.

The narrative highlights the fact that what is elided over and eclipsed is as important, though it may be hidden, as is that on which the screen lingers. Narrativity includes high speed, as well as the freeze frame, and while the spectator may feel (s)he has choices, ultimate control lies in other hands. In sports, the intervention, even penetration of technology—of the rewind, the replay and freeze frame—is presented by technology as sites and processes of repetitive, endless pleasure, selective pleasure, that seems to offer choice or independence, but blinds the viewer to the hegemonic social and cultural forces that guide and control both the view and the operation of choice.

Games as War

Giulianotti comments on the usage of surveillance technology in sports stadia, and elaborates on Virilio's linkage of war and sport.

> Compared to warfare, sport inhabits a secondary, albeit symbolic and strategic position in Virilio's framework...the instantaneous digital mediation of sports symbolises the high-tech potency of the white-dominated West's military-industrial complexes. Commodification of televised sport advances the material-speed divisions between the haves (who create and package content, and who buy instant televised rights) and the have-nots (who merely receive, and usually receive old, inferior highlights packages). Strategically, the surveillance and social control of sports spectators using advanced gadgetry, allow the military industrial complex to test its latest techniques in case of more overt political resistance. Thus Virilio promotes our general understanding of how time-space compression connects to technological exercises of power.[20]

In every sense, it is the games as war metaphor that is highlighted in *Hunger Games*. The selection of the players is a grim reminder if the power of the state and its absolute control over the body—of athlete and spectator alike. On the day of the 'Reaping' Katniss observes 'Taking the kids...forcing them to kill one another while we watch—this is the Capitol's way of reminding us how totally we are at their mercy.'[21]

The surveillance analogy is explicit as she also notes 'Attendance is mandatory....the camera crew [in the square] perched like buzzards.....the reaping is a good way for the Capitol to keep tabs on the population.'[22] The situation is almost that of a panopticon, within which two levels of control operate. At the level of the spectacle, the many watch the few, and at another level, the many are watched by the few, depending on which way the camera is turned. Who operates the camera and why, is the fundamental question.

The unstable image and the process of narrativity to construct 'fables of power' is critiqued at various points in the trilogy, in more overtly political ways as well. At the end of the second book, *Catching Fire*, we are made to realise that the Capitol has been using stock footage of the destroyed District23, which is being passed off as current and immediate. It is shown as a vast industrial desert, bombarded by Capitol aircrafts, when it has in fact resurrected itself and has been waging a steady covert war against the Capitol for the last seventy-five years. The Capitol has suppressed this fact from the larger population, and eventually in the third book *Mockingjay*, the battle for mindspace becomes a battle for airwaves—an acknowledgement that 'it's the power of that screen'[23] and that the control of the Capitol is based on '*Panem et Circenses*' or 'Bread and Circuses' (an obvious and loaded reference to Imperial Rome and the gladiatorial games).

Catching Fire stresses the fact that the control of the athletes' body is an act of control, of controlling the larger body politic, and that the Hunger Games are a reminder of the Capitol's control of every aspect of performance and viewership. In this book, the dictatorial President Snow recalls all former victors to fight in the Hunger Games, and expressly states that 'On the seventy-fifth anniversary, as a reminder to the rebels that even the strongest among them cannot overcome the power of the Capitol, the male and female tributes will be reaped from their existing pool of victors.'[24] At the opening ceremony, once again Katniss manages a symbolic act of rebellion against this control and forced competition, when in a spontaneous act she holds the amputated stump of a former victor standing next to her. Her triumph is the fact that the cameras transmit this act, and thus she wrests the narrative from the Capitol's control, into her own, even though it is not a planned act.

> And then it happened. Up and down the row, the victors begin to join hands......By the time the anthem plays its final strains, all twenty-four of us stand in one unbroken line in what must be the first public show of unity among the districts since the Dark Days. You can see the realisation of this as the screens begin to pop into blackness. It's too late, though. In the confusion they didn't cut us off in time. Everyone has seen.[25]

In *Mockingjay*, Katniss emerges as a successful rebel leader, though she is tortured and almost driven mad by the realisation that winning wars requires the same ruthlessness and ability to kill as was needed in the arena of the Hunger Games. Her arguments with Gale and other rebel leaders circle relentlessly around this point, and when the rebels justify their attack on certain districts, she bursts out 'But that kind of thinking...you could turn it into an argument for killing anyone at any time. You could justify sending kids into the Hunger Games to prevent the districts from getting out of line.'[26]

At one point during a raid on District Two, she is pursued by an assassin, who blames her for the destruction of his district. Helpless and at his mercy, Katniss throws down her bow and says, 'We've got every reason to kill each other. So do it. Make the Capitol happy. I'm done killing their slaves for them......It just goes around and around, and who wins? Not us. Not the districts. Always the Capitol. But I'm tired of being a piece in their Games.'[27] But even at this crucial moment, she is aware of the cameras trained on her, following her every move, as the rebels construct a narrative of their own in order to enlist and incite many more to revolt against the Capitol. Thus it is still a game of sorts, if we go by the three definitions suggested in the first part of this paper, but the conflict is real, and the quantifiable goal is a political victory. In fact, when she finally confronts the dictatorial President Snow, he turns the tables by reminding her that final bombing which killed her sister had not been ordered or televised by him, but by the rebel commander, Coin. The bombing was, he says 'So wasteful, so unnecessary. Anyone could see the game was over by that point....But I wasn't watching Coin... I'm afraid we've both been played for fools.'[28]

The narrative invites us to experience the Hunger Games, to confront the political and the personal as they play out in the arena of the games, and in the battle for air-time and mindspace, and to finally face the probability of sports as a mediated narrative which is intertwined with the processes of politics and capital, by the e-Empire (to use Rita Raley's phrase). Within this space then, sports cannot but function without loss of traditional values, and by accruing other values, that will produce (capital) value for the forces that promote, subsidise, and mediate their interaction across time and space. This e-Empire both creates and mediates the narrative and speed, to produce a disjunction of cognition, to induce cognitive damage, as it were; it functions by disrupting telos, or constructing it by forceful manipulation of images, and sport-arenas and sport spectatorship become a primary site of operation.

In the *Hunger Games* trilogy, the games present, in this scheme, the most rigidly controlled body of all—the site of control by state and spectator. The body of the athlete is under visible gaze, and control. The second less obvious control is on the viewer, sought to be controlled by media and technological forces and the capital they operate. Not only does Collins critique this in her trilogy, I suspect she is also playing an elaborate game with the readers; the narrative has an almost breathless pace, and many fanzines comment on this aspect. Thus, even as she lays bare the operation of speed in the games, she constructs a highly visual, spectacular narrative and forces a kind of narrative speed onto the reader, which she then disrupts because it is after all a trilogy, and one is forced to pause between each part of it.

The *Hunger Games* movie, released in 2012 has gone on to become a phenomenon, but fans of the *Hunger Games* books have been highly critical of its many deviations from the text. While this may be forgivable, it is interesting to comment on the 'pace' of the movie version. One would have thought that the visual media would bring in greater 'speed and immediacy', but the movie seems jumpy rather than edgy and fast paced. One reason may be that to make the movie suitable for all age groups, and to avoid the 'Adult' movie tag, the film removes all graphic violence from its narrative; in the book, twenty-two tributes die, in varied and violent ways. In fact, the scene wherein one of the competitors is gnawed to death is conspicuous by its absence, though it is a key scene in the novel. The emphasis on technology and its manipulation, the politics of hunger, control of the population, and surveillance, which are central issues in the book, are hardly touched upon in the Hollywood version of it, diluting the impact and complexity of the text greatly, in my opinion. In the book version, Katniss and Peeta are very aware of the aspect of spectatorship, of the fact that they too are constructing a 'story' for the viewers, and with it, combating the story the Capitol is creating. This awareness, crucial to the plot and theme of the trilogy, seems absent in the film.

At the end of the *Hunger Games* trilogy, Katniss, and the reader are forced back to the beginning, still haunted by the events that have happened in the past, to combat memory and guilt, even as a teleological 'success 'is obtained. The trilogy ends with the words, 'its like a game. Repetitive. Even a little tedious after more than twenty years. But there are much worse games to play.'[29] Given that the trilogy is rich with allusions to Greek and Roman history, these words leave us wondering, as readers and spectators, what these games are, or were, or will be.

Notes

1. 'Suzanne Collins: the queen of teen fiction for tomboys', http://www.guardian.co.uk/theobserver/2012/mar/18/suzanne-collins-the-hunger-games-profile (accessed July18, 2012).
2. Richard C. Crepeau, 'Sport and Society for Arete', January 22, 2009, http://www.uta.edu/english/sla/ss090122.html (accessed July 19, 2012).
3. Katie Salen and Eric Zimmerman, *Rules of Play: Game Design Fundamentals* (Massachusetts: MIT Press, 2003), p. 80.
4. Greg Costikyan, 'I have no words and I must design', http://www.costik.com/nowords2002.pdf (accessed on 12 December 2011).
5. Brian Sutton-Smith et al., 'Developmental structures in fantasy narratives', *Human Development* 19 (1976), pp. 1–20.
6. 'European Sports Charter', http://portal.unesco.org/education/en/ev.php-URL_ID=2221&URL_DO=DO_TOPIC&URL_SECTION=201.html (accessed July 15, 2012).

7. Jay Coakley and Peter Donnelly, *Inside Sports* (New York: Routledge, 1999), pp. 1–4.
8. David Rowe, *Popular Cultures: Rock Music, Sport and the Politics of Pleasure* (London: Sage, 1995), pp. 42–3.
9. Suzanne Collins, *Mockingjay* (New York: Scholastic, 2010), p. 127.
10. Arjun Appadurai, *Modernity at Large: Cultural Dimensions of Globalization* (Minneapolis: University of Minneapolis Press, 1996), pp. 33–4.
11. Suzanne Collins, *Hunger Games* (New York: Scholastic, 2008), p. 58.
12. Suzanne Collins, *Mockingjay*, p. 43.
13. Paul Virilio, *Speed and Politics: An Essay on Dromology*. Trans. Mark Polizzotti (New York: Semiotext(e), 1986), p. 47.
14. Steve Redhead,'Those absent from the Stadium are always right: Accelerated culture, sports media and theory at the speed of light', *Journal of Sport and Social Issues*, vol. 31, no. 3 (2007), p. 227.
15. David Harvey, *The Condition of Postmodernity* (Oxford: Blackwell, 1990), p. 6.
16. Paul Virilio, *Open Sky*, trans. Julie Rose (London: Verso, 1997), p. 90.
17. Suzanne Collins, *Hunger Games*, p. 339.
18. Ibid., p. 237.
19. Ibid., p. 362.
20. Richard Giulianotti, *Sport: A Critical Sociology* (Oxford: Polity, 2005), p. 177.
21. Suzanne Collins, *The Hunger Games*, p. 18.
22. Ibid., p. 16.
23. Suzanne Collins, *Mockingjay*, p. 257.
24. Suzanne Collins, *Catching Fire*, p. 43.
25. Suzanne Collins, *Catching Fire*, p. 258.
26. Suzanne Collins, *Mockingjay*, p. 222.
27. Ibid., p. 215.
28. Ibid., pp. 356–57.
29. Ibid., p. 390.

6

Quidditch Incorporated: Sport, Fantasy and the Consumer Child

Paromita Patranobish

J. K. Rowling's sporting invention in her *Harry Potter* series, Quidditch, has moved beyond its literary configurations to inhabit other semantic and cultural fields. This move has followed two identifiable and closely related trajectories that can be roughly summed as adaptation (cinema, fan-fiction and youth sports like 'muggle Quidditch' among others) and material reproduction (toys, souvenirs, costumes and collectibles). In this article my attempt shall be to place these three major configurations of the sport—as text, as a specific form of performative adaptation that brings Quidditch to the playing field, and as material reproduction in relation to the contested figure of the playing child—in conversation with each other, in order to bring out the complex life of a sport that originates outside the playing field and within a fictional landscape, and then enters the domain of performative and material culture. In staging this conversation I shall also attempt to highlight the ways in which the literary intertwines with the cultural, and how sport itself emerges as an endlessly adaptable phenomenon capable of mutating through different systems by both asserting a myth of universal currency (that allows a Rowling to marry a fantastical version of the British public school sport to the mythic and timeless archetype of the quest), even as it serves entirely different ideological and commercial ends in each of these (per)mutations.

As a part of the adaptation boom around Rowling's series, Quidditch too has moved through a large number of formats, from cinema to video games. Quidditch's status has shifted since the first *Harry Potter* novel from being a fictional sport to occupying the marketplace as consumer goods, and in a similar leap of boundaries, to emerging as sited events that transpose textual signs onto the performative context of competitive sports: the inter-university Quidditch matches that have taken American universities by storm. Recent years have witnessed a growing enthusiasm for Quidditch as a brand and symbol, for manufacturing, miniaturising and repackaging it as toys for children and young adults: Quidditch brooms, jerseys, board games, toy sets, Lego's latest do-it-yourself ensemble called the 'Harry Potter Quidditch Match' complete with a miniature pitch, mechanical contraptions, catapulting devices, balls and collectible figures of players.

The implications of reading Quidditch as a part of a fictional landscape are thus intertwined with the emergence of Quidditch as a product and a marketable brand. What makes Quidditch interesting is the convergence it embodies, of cultural narratives of childhood/adolescence, which project a depoliticised and potentially fluid space of childhood, its fantasies, desires and requirements, with contemporary systems of commerce.

In this article I wish to understand playing as a doubly encoded modality, as related to the instrumentalist discourse of skills, capacities and technologies of the self on the one hand, and to the socio-economic domain of childhood consumerism, on the other. My point of inquiry is Quidditch as a formation that is located at the intersection of these various discursive strands: of literature in its semiotic and mass mediated capacities, of playing as a component of childhood, of consumerist incursions into both childhood and play, and its more globalised intersection with professional sports.

Through examining Quidditch's complex mutations I shall attempt a reading of childhood and play that explores the interconnections among these diverse strands. The key themes in this reading will be the trope of fantasy on the one hand and contemporary forms of consumerism on the other. Some of the questions that this article will ask are: what is it in the nature of the fictional sport in particular and sport in general, that sustains such fascination and capacity for adaptation? What role does fantasy play in mobilising the discourse of consumerism, how does fantasy as a generic component of literature for children relate to the fantasies of fetishist recasting of objects, of ownership and role-playing, and the manipulation of such fantasies by the production of a certain material landscape of childhood? What are the burdens that sport as a represented topos comes to bear in the context of the book's own re-emergence as a commodity embedded in channels of marketing and publicity, and what relation does the 'Harry Potter phenomenon' as something closely associated with the book's own status as a bestseller bear to the dislocation of Quidditch from its narrative context and its subsequent transformation into various extra-literary formations, including toys and souvenirs? How do these two apparently dissociated fields of literature and objects collude in determining the texture of childhood consumption, and how does this collusion create a set of cultural values which then impinge upon the way in which playing as a generalised activity and sport as an organised, itself commoditised, phenomenon intersect with the child subject?

This article shall attempt to bridge these three concerns: a specific form of consumerist politics directed at the child in which books and readership play an important role, the phenomenology of games and playing as an aspect of childhood which is then targeted and brought within the ambit of a particular material culture of playing, and finally the issue of a sport as it intersects, through its occurrence as a part of the novelistic chronotope, with the site of childhood and its commercial destinies. Such a dual reading of Quidditch enables one to see texts, and texts for children in this case, as inseparable from patterns of consumption and underlying circuits of corporate power. The consumption of books, the pedagogic, moral and epistemological rubrics that facilitate and inform such consumption, are complicit in sustaining the assumptions and demands engendered by market forces, even though this complicity is not entirely indefensible.[1] Corporations like Lego and Warner Brothers that manufacture play objects for children in turn depend upon and exploit cultural notions regarding childhood as modes of legitimation and sale.[2]

Julia Mickenberg has recently analysed how the shift from 'a production-oriented economy to a consumer-oriented' one, from 'agricultural roots to an urban bureaucratised economy' led to changing perceptions about the child's status, which, now 'removed from the labour force, [was] sacralised: valued for sentimental rather than instrumental reasons.'[3] Apart from becoming an object of study and regulation by welfare organisations, child psychologists and paediatricians, advertising companies took an active interest in the child, attempting to cater to the newly emerging image of the child as a subject of needs and desires. The development of a market designed to benefit children exclusively was tied to changes in child-rearing philosophies, the emergence of developmental psychology and new norms of parenting, a shift from behaviourism with its focus on child management to 'permissiveness emphasising democracy within the family and cultivation of the child's natural impulses.'[4] The child had to be indulged in order to ensure proper physical and psychological development, but additionally, the child's unrestricted access to this specialised market meant the cultivation of certain necessary attributes, including that of autonomy and what Daniel Cook has described as the trait of 'personhood'.[5] In the merchandising discourse of the early part of the Twentieth Century, consumption was no longer a matter of material needs alone, but was bound up with questions of interiority and subjectivity. What sets the child consumer apart from her adult counterparts is the condition of childhood as an exemplary managerial site, at least in the context of Western modernity, an exemplarity constituted by the child's liminal, unstable status within social, legal, familial and economic structures, making childhood a potent ground for the realisation of the anxieties and tensions that pervade these very structures. Sandra Calvert has demonstrated, for instance, that the emergent debates in contemporary America around the issue of ethics in advertising for children is closely associated with broader political questions pertaining to marketing practices, internet security, media literacy and the regulation of the private sphere.[6]

It is at this conjuncture of the child's subjectivity and its material replenishment that the domain of games and playing becomes significant. Roland Barthes's essay on the place of toys in the cultural imaginary discusses the limitations of modern toys that are aimed at providing, through a universe of replicas, an authoritative and naturalised model of the normative roles and spaces that children are meant to inhabit as social beings. For Barthes modern toys, 'always entirely socialised, constituted by the myths or the techniques of modern adult life: the army, broadcasting, the post office, medicine (miniature instrument-cases, operating theatres for dolls), school, hair styling (driers for permanent-waving), the air force (parachutists), transport (trains, Citroens, Vedettes, Vespas, petrol stations), science (Martian toys)'[7] leave no scope for invention and are instead designed to make children into competent users. Barthes' phenomenological reading of toys and their role in engaging a child's perceptions is a critique of the industrially manufactured and mass produced synthetic toys which prevent children from developing meaningful haptic relationships with their textures and shapes.

Barthes' critique is not directed at the physical flaws of contemporary toys alone, but points to the doubleness of playthings: their status as symbolic goods within an experiential framework of use and pleasure, as well an economic one of production and exchange, bringing about in their construction as synecdochic extensions of childhood, a conflation of the two. Toys become crucial agents of consumer ideologies, creating ideological offshoots that target this very locus of association between children and playthings, a locus that is shaped around children's engagement with toys as objects of play. Fisher Price, a subsidiary of the business conglomerate Mattel Toys, exploits the ontological proximity of toys to children[8] in its marketing statements, thus promising to enhance through its 'age-based' toys and 'child-care products' the 'potential of children' and create 'supportive environments.'[9] Any understanding of the domain of childhood sports needs to, to my mind, negotiate this late capitalist disposit of consumerism and its material intervention into children's lives. Because the material coordinates that constitute and structure the activity of play have such operative and psychological currency in relation to the experience of childhood, play objects become determinants of identity. It is this identitarian composite: of the child and his plaything as a legitimate, psychosomatic and social extension, that gets employed in the consumerist narratives of 'products and services consumers can trust to improve their family lives.'[10]

Lego and Mattel Toys have capitalised upon this very narrative of agential determination in designing their range of Quidditch themed products (http://shop.lego.com/en-US/Harry-Potter-ByTheme), deriving an enduring cultural legitimacy from the books themselves and from the implied association thus created between the privileged act of reading, and the games (and their markets) that it references, even endorses. Priced at anything between nineteen and a hundred and fifty dollars and appended with such catchy instructions as '[C]atch the Golden Snitch™ and win the match for Gryffindor™! Marcus Flint and the Slytherin team are winning! Gryffindor's only chance to win is if Harry Potter is the first Seeker to catch the Golden Snitch! Beat the bludgers away, soar through goal posts, a tower or over the stands, fire catapults, catch the Snitch, then fly away through the Ravenclaw Tower with the trophy', Lego's building sets are premised on a vocabulary of childhood skill acquisition and developmental knowhow, into which the components of fantasy and competitive ethos engendered by the represented sport are incorporated, as also the interpellative possibilities of role-playing, itself informed by the mass mediated cult of the star persona embodied by Potter (and his screen avatar Daniel Radcliffe) himself. Despite Rowling's repeated disavowals of the commodity boom born out of her books and her refusal to endorse it, the plastic fantastic world of 'Harry Potter™' represents a form of modern childhood consumerism in which the lines between representation and production are continually bent to secure newer currencies of meaning and circulation, the mediatised life of children's narratives intersect with and sustain other material and cultural forms of mediation including those which inform the pragmatics of embodied playing and the psychodynamics of childhood development, and finally in which sport itself acquires a loose, malleable, discursively variable status invoking the values associated with playing as a situated, organised activity, alluding to its mythic archetypes and impinging upon the localised arena of children's play.

Quidditch as a part of the *Harry Potter* books acquires a new set of associations when read in the light of its proliferating parallel lives, a proliferation that can be read back and forth, into and out of the text itself, in its self-conscious response to commercial playing, its creation of an ambiguous excess of objects (and anti-objects like the self-destroying 'howler' itself a materialised emotion, or James Potter's cloak of invisibility) veering between the talismanic, the functional, the enchanted and the fetishistic (the Weasley brothers' prank objects which in many ways serve as the books' rallying point against commercialisation, raising it to a moral dilemma). It works through a double modality of both acknowledging the material lure of sporting paraphernalia (the Nimbus 2000 which is not a mere child's toy but a coveted signifier of sporting status) and then glossing the same with the moral and structural imperatives of the *bildungs* in which Harry must strive, so to speak, to 'deserve' being bestowed with the potent broom.

Quidditch and Other Games

> As the crowd's faces became flesh coloured pinpricks below and the horntail shrunk to the size of a dog he realised...he was back where he belonged. This was just another Quidditch match.[11]

Occurring as it does, in the midst of the first task of the Tri-wizard Tournament, this realisation that becomes instrumental in Harry's victory, serves to secure the symbolic significance of Quidditch in the scheme of the *Harry Potter* series. Quidditch is the only and official sport of the wizards, through which skills are acquired, animosities expressed and ethics tested. Located as it is within a public school narrative, Quidditch shares several ideological similarities with the role of sports in the British school story. As a controlled space for the formation of subjectivities, realisation of agency and exercise of choice, sports in the early Twentieth Century school story in Britain was deeply embedded in the discourses of pedagogy, serving as grounds for the building of moral and physical character.[12] Quidditch from its early appearance in *Harry Potter* takes on this ideological mantle and determines the ethical binaries that are developed through the rest of the series. Draco Malfoy, a prototype of what is designated as bad, is a bully, while Harry is naturally motivated to protest against and remedy his malevolence. Bullying, cheating, desire for supremacy in the field, egotism and violent play are demonstrated as trademark features of a homogeneously wicked Slytherin House, while Gryffindor to which all the three protagonists of the series belong, is known for its spirit of cooperation, skill and fair play. The game then becomes a schematic blueprint, guiding the reader's affiliations towards both the right characters as well as the right values. As a moral map of the novels, Quidditch sets the field for larger agonistic crises, becoming both a microcosm and a preparatory ground for the latter. The sport in as much as it serves to plot dichotomies and define values, is not an insulated site for simulated play. In Rowling's novels the school is not just a microcosm of social arrangements, but occupies the centre of her moral inquiry, and 'play' becomes a mode of negotiating with the dangers and ambivalences of the 'real'. It is at the end of a seemingly innocuous task at the Tri-wizard Tournament that Harry and his friend, instead of receiving the expected returns of having secured a victory, are brought into confrontation with mortality and loss, as Cedric Diggory, his fellow contender in the tournament succumbs to Lord Voldemort's death spell. Sport then takes on a dual role: as a moral compass of the novels, Quidditch inhabits a liminal site, played in an in-between aerial space, enacting through the symbolic terminologies of keeping, seeking and chasing, the physical and psychological conflicts of the players, while integrating the reader herself into this conflictual paradigm.

However, as a part of the narrative plot, sport takes on a functional dimension—the successful execution of a given game unlocking mysteries and imparting magical capacities, as is the case in *The Philosopher's Stone* (1997) where Harry has to mount on his Quidditch broom and deploy his skills as the 'seeker' of the snitch to locate the right key, and Ron offer himself up for demolition as a horse in a game of human chess. It is at this dual configuration of sport in *Harry Potter*, in which the British school story intersects with the fantasy and the quest, and the sociological connotations of sport intersect with its narratological deep structure, that Rowling locates her critique of sport as a cultural phenomenon.

The Goblet of Fire (2000) is in many ways the sporting book of the series, opening with the Quidditch World Cup and culminating in a contest between the polarised forces of Lord Voldemort and Harry. The preparations leading to the World Cup serve as a telling commentary on the culture of sporting events, with their intricate regimen of security and exclusivity, the phenomena of fandom and star personas, gambling, and the upsurge of commoditised advertising through posters, souvenirs and toys: 'salesmen were apparating every few feet, carrying trays and pushing carts full of extraordinary merchandise. There were luminous rosettes—green for Ireland, red for Bulgaria...pointed green hats, Bulgarian scarves...there were tiny models of firebolts...and collectible figures of famous players...'[13] The match itself becomes a site of multiple negotiations, even as the moral dubiousness of the event is underscored through the figures of the two mascots, the leprechaun and the 'veela', the latter a kind of seductress, putting up a display of deception and allurement. Ludo Bagman, significantly named, might embody the spirit of play 'with springs attached to the balls of his feet'[14] but he is also given to gambling. The eccentric and extravagant displays put up by the teams as Arthur Weasley recalls: '[n]ational teams bring creatures from their native lands, you know to put on a bit of a show',[15] serve as a critique of the spectacular, commodifying nature of institutionalised sporting events. Likewise the game itself is reduced to a vaunted theatrics, with aggression increasing the level of injury, the referee being seduced by the mascots and the supporters breaking into a ridiculous fight. Harry slips into a futile reverie at the end of the match fashioning himself as a celebrated Quidditch champion, which is deflated in turn by the entry of a veritable source of danger in the form of the Death-Eaters, the followers of Lord Voldemort. Sport is not a sanitised, regularised domain of athletic display alone, but is always in close proximity to danger, violence, and even death. The ludic is simultaneously pleasurable and sinister, and while the aerial space acts as a symbolic topography of temporary seclusion, of the taking on of alternative identities and formation of new communities and allegiances, it is also a space that is constantly threatened with disruptions, whether in the form of bodily harm or more frequently by encounters with alterity. In *Harry Potter and the Prisoner of Azkaban* (1999), while chasing the snitch in a Quidditch match, Harry is intercepted by a dementor, an amoral death-dealing creature acting solely on instruction, and incapable of distinguishing between innocents and criminals. Even as it allows for the creation of a playing community, Quidditch also isolates the individual, becoming a means for Harry as a prototype of the ephebic initiate, to encounter his subterranean fears and impulses.

If the domain of regularised professional sports constitutes one aspect of play in the *Harry Potter* novels, the paradigm of the quest constitutes the other. In *The Goblet of Fire*, the quest operates at two parallel levels, at the meta-level of the plot with Harry and his friends seeking to unravel the mystery of an initial cryptic dream and a series of subsequent inexplicable events at Hogwarts, and at the level of the Tri-wizard Tournament, a traditional inter-school sporting event. Unlike the team game of Quidditch, the Tri-wizard is a solitary affair, acting as a symbolic rite of passage for the coming of age participants. Although presented as a spectator sport, the spatial coordinates within which the tasks of the Tri-wizard are set also lead to the annihilation/undermining of the presence of the spectator. During his first challenge where Harry has to confront a dangerous dragon, his extreme concentration leads to a perceptual obscuring of the audience: 'Bagman was shouting something ...but Harry's ears were not working properly any more...listening wasn't important,'[16] while the other challenges take place underwater in the presence of the grotesque and hostile mer-people, a distorted mirror image of the spectatorial subjectivity: 'Mer-people were emerging on all sides now watching him eagerly, pointing at his webbed hands and gills, talking behind their hands to each other,'[17] and in the non-place of the labyrinth, where the opponent itself is no longer locatable and distinguishable from one's own terrors and delusions: 'But not one of the spells he had practiced had been designed to combat a sudden reversal of ground and sky. Did he dare move his foot...?'[18]

Johan Huizinga in his essay 'The Nature and Significance of Play' examines what he calls the 'profoundly aesthetic quality'[19] of play that prevents it from being analysed solely through the quantitative modes of 'psychology and physiology deal[ing] with the observation, description and explanation of the play of animals, children and grown-ups.'[20] He takes play as a 'significant form' that can be examined in terms of its structural peculiarities irrespective of its social significance or imperatives. Within this schema, play is 'based on the manipulation of certain images, on a certain imagination of reality (i.e. its conversion into images)'[21] and permeates the 'archetypal activities of human society' including communication, language being a paradigmatic form of 'playing with' the 'nominative faculty' that allows humans to 'distinguish, to establish, to state things...'[22] Similarly, for Gregory Bateson, the various modes of abstraction necessitated by forms of play make it in many ways similar to the functioning of linguistic systems with their connotative and denotative components.[23] For Bateson play is a mode of communication that involves the transmission and decoding of and tacit agreement regarding a certain message between interested parties. Like the Saussurean system of '*Langue*' and '*Parole*', play is structured by an implicit set of rules, which operate as 'meta-frames' as well as varied interpretations of the same in different local contexts which cause paradox and ambiguity, 'which necessitate[s] constant and consistent communication and interpretation for maintenance of the event'.[24] Rule-bound games in contrast negate this possibility of multiple interpretations, the 'paradoxical reference system' of play 'is embodied in a codified system of rules which organise the use of objects, space, time as well as player activities.'[25] Looking at theories of mimesis as a shared cultural activity, Carol Fleisher Feldman has drawn attention to the affinity between the natures of narrative and play. Play and narrative share a common operative mode of symbolic representation, and are analogous with respect to at least four features that Feldman identifies as 'construction, convention, artfulness, and interpretation'.[26] It is this affinity between the structural logic of aesthetics and ludic forms that enables play to take on the morphological features of narrative. In constructing the Tri-wizard Tournament, Rowling draws upon the structural components of the fairy tale, the hero-obstacle-helper-prize schema, and places it within and in perpetual exchange with the meta-narrative of the novel, which subverts this neat narrative progression through its deliberate foregrounding of ethical ambiguities. Thus even as Harry is chosen as a legitimate contender by the 'impartial' non-human agency of the magical goblet, he is shunned by the entire school, and his choice of ethical, affective action over adherence to rules in the underwater feat earns him particularly low points from a judge. The culturally embedded discourse of sports as spectatorial diversion, glamour and rule bound, and ruthless competition, continually disrupts other models, Rita Skeeter, the nosy, vituperative journalist is never too far away, and Harry is simultaneously the contemporary star and the archaic hero.

The play, in its multiple, contentious forms becomes a site of productive tension in the *Harry Potter* series. The debate over what is the right model or ideology of playing is a question that is asked and projected onto the issue of the ideal cultural attitude to sports in children's fiction. While a plea is made in favour of ethics over rules, self-improvement over winning and intrinsic merit over strategy, Rowling seems to suggest the difficulty of sustaining such a discursive structure of sporting ethics under the conditions of rapid commoditisation and professionalisation of sports. Rowling mobilises the generic resources of the fantastic as a device to instruct subjectivities and undercut the pure instrumental rationalism of rule-governed sports, to make space for human error, chance and ethical choice, even if it is at the cost of failure. Rowling's emphasis on the multiple meanings of sport and its symbolism in the *Harry Potter* novels has resonances in the theoretical associations that have been made between forms of playing and non-rational philosophies. Roger Caillois in his seminal work on games, has identified a four-fold typology of cultural systems of playing: competition or 'agon', chance or 'alea', simulation or 'mimicry', and vertigo or 'ilinx', each of which can be approached as either 'ludus' (regulated play) or 'paidia' (spontaneous play).[27] Extending the idea of the 'play form', Brian Sutton-Smith discusses the significance of 'fate' in various 'rhetorics of play', which counteract modern progressivist accounts of play as a kind of mastery of the self or control over circumstances.[28] Fate and chance come to occupy a central epistemological valence in such alternative theories of play. Taking the case of Hindu cosmology, Sutton-Smith delineates a model of play in which categories of mastery and winning as the teleological ends of a game are subordinated to a rhetoric of uncertainty and chance. Using Don Handelman's idea of the 'bottom-up play' that construes play as external to commonplace reality, either a non-serious deviation from normative experience or a mode of subversion/resistance, as opposed to 'top down play' that sees play as constituting another plane of reality and creating alternative kinds of knowledge from that which is made possible through rational epistemologies, Sutton-Smith demonstrates the limits of popular western conceptions of play as tied to an individual's behavioural aspects. 'Typical Western definitions', to quote him, 'make the player a more entrepreneurial kind of being.'[29]

Within this context then, is fantasy to be understood, as Rosemary Jackson does, as a 'secondary'[30] order which exists outside or in excess of what is the designated social real, or is it possible to view fantasy itself through this paradigm of play as constitutive of multiple and simultaneously existing planes of reality? In this sense, it becomes possible to construe fantasy as an epistemological resource enabling a redefinition of such concepts like the self, the other, authority and the unknown. Sutton-Smith, drawing on Richard Schechner's 'broad spectrum approach' and Handelman's analysis of Hindu mythology, suggests a rhetoric of 'broad play', one that 'encompasses all the mind materials of dreams, day dreams, tropes and active play forms...'[31] Working with this 'broad version'[32] makes it possible to posit children's play as a domain of resistance to and interrogation of commodified forms of playing that are sustained and popularised by consumerist discourses of play and sports, enabling in turn the possibility of viewing games as outside the skill and development oriented narratives through which market forces structure them. In *The Goblet of Fire*, the exteriorised and performance oriented objective rationality of Quidditch is replaced by a model of play as interiorised, affective engagement. If the heterogeneous nature of playing in *Harry Potter* acts as a resistance to a monolithic culture of sports, what is the relationship of such a model to the very paradoxical afterlife of the *Harry Potter* series, to its transmutation from literature to brand, or to what Jyotsna Kapur has called 'consumption webs?'[33]

The Commodified and the Fantastic

Quidditch is not just a fictional sport, operating within the strictly insular bounds of narrative fantasy, nor a purely diegetic representation of an actual sport; but without being either, fact or fiction, event or representation, it has come to occupy the space of both possibilities and embody the very process of osmosis between the two. In November 2007, inspired by the sport that the young witches and wizards of England (and elsewhere) play in the *Harry Potter* novels, Vermont's Middlebury College became host to a new inter-collegiate sport called 'muggle-Quidditch' or 'Quidditch for non-magical people'. The International Quidditch Association was formed in response to the growing popularity of this new sport to facilitate regular matches between colleges across the world, and in its own words 'promote Quidditch as a new sport and lead outreach programmes to increase athletic participation among children and young adults and bring magic to communities' (www.internationalquidditch.org).

The second part of this statement has become a major humanitarian credo of a number of American non-profit organisations that interpret and put to particular discursive usage the moral polemics of Rowling's novels. The Harry Potter Alliance is one such organisation that redefines 'magic' to stand for a range of cultural values and social activities based in charity and self-consciously configured in opposition to the dangers of a consumerist ethos. Its various campaigns include, the fund raising 'Helping Haiti Heal' which had as its grand prize a set of *Harry Potter* books signed by the author, the awareness fostering campaign in 2009 called 'what would Dumbledore do' that partnered with the social networking site twitter.com to collect and share ideas on social improvement, or the more recent 'Deathly Hallows campaign' which identifies in the wake of the final book of the *Harry Potter* series, real-life equivalents of the horcruxes, parts of Lord Voldemort's 'evil' soul stowed away in different parts of the world, thus starting a set of eradication drives against poverty, illiteracy, gender discrimination, unhealthy lifestyles and negative media influence. In its mission statement HPA describes itself as an organisation that 'takes an outside-of-the-box approach to civic engagement by using parallels from the *Harry Potter* books to educate and mobilise young people across the world toward issues of literacy, equality, and human rights'. (www.thehpalliance.org). In 2001 J. K. Rowling published a couple of books, fashioning them as extensions of the Potterian chronotope; thus *Quidditch Through the Ages* came out as a kind of sourcebook for Quidditch lovers written by the fictional sports enthusiast 'Kennilworthy Whisp' and housed in the library at Hogwarts, complete with a circulating index and names of students scribbled in it and an exhortation issued by the school librarian about the proper care of books. Both *QTTA* and its companion book *Fantastic Beasts and Where to Find Them*, were marketed in collaboration with Comic Relief, a charity organisation that used 20% of the retail sales price of each book sold for creating the 'Harry's Books Fund' aimed at sponsoring education for underprivileged children.

These three instances serve to underscore more than just a culturally enduring and discursively overdetermined afterlife of a literary text. They point towards a space of radical ambiguity produced by an emergent tension between what Philip Nel, Andrew Blake and Jack Zipes have identified as the capitalist overtake of cultural forms including literature and sports on the one hand,[34] and an attempt to rewrite this very landscape of consumerist fetishisation by imbuing it with a resistant vocabulary of the fantastic and the magical. It is this resistant vocabulary that legitimises, distinguishes and is circulated in the new discourses and practices of ethics, leisure and socialisation that the above examples point to. By examining the percolation of the literary into the everyday through the production of a new typology and discourse of youth sports, this paper seeks to argue that the relationship between these three domains, of literature, sports and culture, is marked by a process of constant exchange and renewal. My contention against critics like Nel and Zipes, who identify the success and multiple reproductions of the *Harry Potter* novels as a symptom of the 'instrumentalization of fantasy and the fantastic'[35] is that the so called 'Harry Potter phenomenon' cannot be dismissed solely through a myopic glance at the interpellative horizon of the commodity boom engendered by it, but needs to be understood as a more complex and transverse site of interaction. I do not wish to posit fantasy as the freewheeling and utopian other of the logic of commodification. Rather, this paper wishes to understand the fantastic as a cultural process both colluding in but also resisting the pressures of cultural homogenisation.

The creation of muggle Quidditch and a large scale investment in its popularisation is a part of this double process, in which a literary prototype of a magical sport serves to anchor the ideology of playing in an atemporal and infantile zone, where there is a deliberate eschewing of such notions of athletic propriety like fitness and discipline, and a sustained valorisation of a code of the bawdy and the carnivalesque. The muggle variant of Rowling's game is played on foot by running around a field bounded by three guarded poles through the hoops of which the 'chasers' try to pass a deflated football that stands for the 'quaffle.' The 'snitch', an elusive and rapid golden ball with wings, is a player in the muggle game, who enters the field midway and runs around trying to remain unintercepted by the designated seekers. The muggle 'beaters' meanwhile throw the 'bludgers', the heavy aggressive balls that fly through the Quidditch pitch in the novels, attempting to hit the chasers and throw them off course. The game of muggle Quidditch is not merely a rule bound game, but also an enactment of a sporting scenario, where the equipment doubles up as theatrical prop and spectators come dressed as characters from the book. As a play in both senses of the term, Quidditch enables a playing of both the readers' interpretation of the literary text as well as of the spectator's appropriation of the live sport, and creates a strategic collapse between the two modes, whereby the game becomes a hermeneutic process of rewriting its novelistic counterpart.

What are the implications of a crossover of sporting rules and tactics from literary representation to sited practice, and particularly in the context of a text that is already mediated through multiple expressive formats and cultural goods? What are the implications of the extrapolation and transposition of a sport from one ideological scheme to another? Does this transposition from a narrative component catering to a readership comprising children and young adults, to a full-fledged cultural event in which adults participate, symptomatise a shift in the social meaning of sport from being a key ingredient in the socialisation of the child and the construction of normative adults, to becoming a space for experimentation, parody and rejection of the very codes of normativity? That literature can engender sporting lexicons suggests more than just a whimsical propensity for adaptation; such crossovers also underscore shifting semantic lexicons through which sports is understood and legitimised. But that literature for children engenders cultural forms and commodities which become the site of contending economic and political forces also suggests that the child as the 'consumer' of certain cultural forms is perhaps becoming like Harry Potter, an empty and reified signifier, a unit of value rather than an active player in the cultural field.

Notes

1. When Coca-Cola wanted to use characters from the novel as brand endorsers, Rowling withheld consent, refusing to showcase her characters as supporting

the product. Instead Coca-Cola organised a reading-initiative programme 'Live the Magic,' providing '10,000 Classroom Library Collections for at-risk schools,' and 'Ingenuity Grants to help explore innovative ways to encourage children to embrace reading.'(Philip Nel, 'Is There a Text in This Advertising Campaign?: Literature, Marketing, and Harry Potter', *The Lion and the Unicorn*, vol. 29, no. 2 (Baltimore, Maryland: The John Hopkins University Press, 2005), 241 http://muse.jhu.edu/journals/lion_and_the_unicorn/v029/29.2nel.html (accessed on 25 March 2013). Rowling has also expressed discomfort with the *Harry Potter* range of action figures, and critiqued Mattel Toys for encouraging violence. Mattel has changed its marketing terminology and now calls these figures 'collectibles'.

2. The issue of children and globalisation has been explored in several recent works in the area. *See* Paula Fass, 'Children and Globalization', *Journal of Social History*, vol. 36, no. 4 (Virginia: George Mason University Press, 2003), 963–77. http://muse.jhu.edu/journals/journal_of_social_history/summary/v036/36.4fass.html (accessed on 25 March 2013); Daniel Thomas Cook, *The Commodification of Childhood: The Children's Clothing Industry and the Rise of The Child Consumer* (Durham: Duke University Press, 2004); Lisa Jacobson, *Raising Consumers: Children and the American Mass Market in the Early Twentieth Century* (New York: Columbia University Press, 2004); Sandra L Calvert, 'Children as Consumers: Advertising and Marketing', *Children and Electronic Media*, from *The Future of Children*, vol. 18, no. 1 (New Jersey: Trustees of the Princeton University, 2008). http://futureofchildren.org/futureofchildren/publications/docs/18_01_FullJournal.pdf (accessed on 25 March 2013); Nicholas Sammond, *Babes in Tomorrowland: Walt Disney and the Making of the American Child 1930–1960* (Durham: Duke University Press, 2005).
3. Julia L. Mickenberg, 'American Studies and Childhood Studies: Lessons from Consumer Culture' *American Quarterly*, vol. 58, number 4 (Maryland: The John Hopkins University Press, 2006), p. 1218.
4. Ibid., p. 1219.
5. David Thomas Cook, *The Commodification of Childhood: The Children's Clothing Industry and the Rise of the Child Consumer* (Durham: Duke University Press, 2004), p. 88.
6. Sandra Calvert, 'Children as Consumers: Advertising and Marketing', *Children and Electronic Media*, from *The Future of Children*, a collaboration of the Woodrow Wilson School of Public and International Affairs at Princeton University and the Brookings Institution, vol. 18, no. 1 (New Jersey: Trustees of the Princeton University, 2008), http://futureofchildren.org/futureofchildren/publications/docs/18_01_FullJournal.pdf (accessed on 25 March 2013).
7. Roland Barthes (tr. Annette Lavers), 'Toys' from *Mythologies* (New York: Jonathan Cape, 1972), p. 54.

8. On the question of objects as extensions of the body schema, see Andy Clark, *Supersizing the Mind: Embodiment, Action and Cognitive Extension* (Cambridge, Massachusetts: The MIT Press, 2008).
9. From the Fisher Price website: www.fisherprice.com (accessed on 25 March 2013).
10. www.fisherprice.com (accessed on 25 March 2013).
11. J. K. Rowling, *Harry Potter and the Goblet of Fire* (New York: Scholastic Publications, 2000), p. 204.
12. David K. Steege has analyzed the parallels between Thomas Hughes's *Tom Brown's School Days* and *Harry Potter* as working with the same prototype of the inexperienced and diffident boy who develops in the course of his public school education into a benevolent youth, an 'upholder of school values, the protector of the younger boys, and a leader largely through the guidance of the Doctor…the wise and kind headmaster' in 'Harry Potter, Tom Brown, and the British School Story: Lost in Transit?', in *The Ivory Tower and Harry Potter: Perspectives on a Literary Phenomenon*, ed. Lana A. Whited (Columbia, Missouri: University of Missouri Press, 2004), p. 143.
13. J. K. Rowling, *Harry Potter and the Goblet of Fire*, p. 85.
14. Ibid., p. 85.
15. Ibid., p. 91.
16. Ibid., p. 309.
17. Ibid., p. 432.
18. Ibid., p. 542.
19. Johan Huizinga, 'The Nature and Significance of Play as a Cultural Phenomenon,' in *The Performance Studies Reader*, ed. Henry Bial (New York: Routledge, 2004), p. 138.
20. Ibid., p. 137.
21. Ibid., p. 139.
22. Ibid., p. 139.
23. Gregory Bateson, 'A Theory of Play and Fantasy,' in *The Game Design Reader: A Rules of Play Anthology*, eds Katie Salen and Eric Zimmerman (Cambridge, Massachusetts: The MIT Press, 2005), pp. 314–28.
24. Helen B. Schwartzman, 'The Anthropological Study of Children's Play', *Annual Review of Anthropology*, vol. 5 (Sao Paolo, California: Annual Reviews, 1976), p. 302.
25. Ibid., p. 302.
26. Carol Fleisher Feldman, 'Mimesis: Where Play and Narrative Meet', *Cognitive Development*, vol. 20, issue 4, 'Play and Narrative in the Process of Development: Commonalities, Differences and Interrelations' (Amsterdam: Elsevier, 2005), p. 510.

27. Roger Caillois and Elaine P. Halperin (trans.) 'The Structure and Classification of Games', *Diogenes*, vol. 3, no. 12 (Thousand Oakes, California: Sage Publications, 1955), pp. 64–5.
28. Brian Sutton-Smith, *The Ambiguity of Play* (Cambridge, Massachusetts: Harvard University Press, 2001, first published 1997), p. 46.
29. Ibid., p. 57.
30. Rosemary Jackson, *Fantasy: The Literature of Subversion* (London: Methuen and Co., 1981), p. 1.
31. Brian Sutton-Smith, *The Ambiguity of Play*, p. 58.
32. Ibid., p. 58.
33. Jyotsna Kapur, 'Free Market, Branded Imagination—Harry Potter and The Commercialization of Children's Culture', *Jump Cut: A Review of Contemporary Media*. no. 46 (2003), 3, http://www.ejumpcut.org/archive/jc46.2003/kapur.potter/text.html (accessed on 25 March 2013).
34. See Jack Zipes, 'The Age of Commodified Fantasticism: Reflections on Children's Literature and The Fantastic' *Children's Literature Association Quarterly*, vol. 9, no. 4 (Baltimore, Maryland: The John Hopkins University Press, 1984–85), pp. 187–90. http://muse.jhu.edu/journals/childrens_literature_association_quarterly/v009/9.4.zipes.html (accessed on 25 March 2013); Andrew Blake, *The Irresistible Rise of Harry Potter*, London: Verso, 2002 and Philip Nel, 'Is There a Text in This Advertising Campaign?: Literature, Marketing, and Harry Potter', *The Lion and the Unicorn*, vol. 29, no. 2 (Baltimore, Maryland: The John Hopkins University Press, 2005). 236–67. http://muse.jhu.edu/journals/lion_and_the_unicorn/v029/29.2nel.html (accessed on 25 March 2013).
35. Jack Zipes, 'Why Fantasy Matters Too Much', *CLCWeb: Comparative Literature and Culture* vol. 10, no. 4 (2008), http://docs.lib.purdue.edu/clcweb/vol10/iss4/3 (accessed on 25 March 2013).

7

In the Long Run: The Modernist Experience as Long Distance Running

Sohini Banerjee

No matter how mundane some action might appear, keep at it long enough and it becomes a contemplative, even meditative act.[1]

I

The space that running occupies in a world of runners—divided between running for its own sake, for individual need, fitness, and health, and running as a professional sport, with the related paraphernalia of associations, nationalities, and fiscal rewards—is complicated. At the heart of this complication is the tension that arises from the simultaneous formation of this space by the personal as well as the recognisably public and political. The exact factors that make an individual run may or may not coincide exactly with either the personal or the political, but these invariably tend to accommodate both in varying degrees. To attempt, however, to homogenise all running as equal in import would be naïve. When a professional athlete runs, he ultimately represents the political realm of the nation. His decision to participate in the act of running might, on the surface, be a personal choice, but he is eventually a function of the context of that act of running; by virtue of belonging to an arena which pins itself on international competition, he is obligated to run for the nation. Running professionally, therefore, has implications which are far different from 'everyday' running, a category which cannot be tied down to the politics of professionalisation. What Alexis Tadié calls the 'ultimate individual occupation'[2] can also be in many cases an overwhelmingly communal act.

Game and Play

The realms of both the individual and the communal are characterised by the dual aspects of play (a free, uncertain and undirected instinct), and that of the game (a classified, organised activity, involving the fundamentals of play but further defined by a definite spatio-temporal element). However, sport as a modern phenomenon with the game as its unitary structure is marked wholly by what Roger Caillois, in his response to Johan Huizinga's *Homo Ludens*,[3] demarcates as one of the four ways to classify games: that is, the agonistic or competitive impulse:

> A whole group of games would seem to be competitive, that is to say, like a combat in which equality of chances is artificially created, in order that the adversaries should confront each other under ideal conditions, susceptible to giving precise and incontestable value to the winner's triumph. It is therefore always a question of a rivalry which hinges on a single quality (speed, endurance, strength, memory, skill, ingenuity, etc.) exercised, within defined limits and without outside assistance, in such a way that the winner appears better than the loser in a certain category of exploits.[4]

Viewing the realm of the game as 'combat' in which an 'equality of chances' is created artificially, so that adversaries confront each other in idealised situations and the winner's triumph is 'precise' and 'incontestable', Caillois defines the abstract structure on which the game is built in modernity. Sport, after its integration into professional practice, from merely connoting the free and unstructured human impulse to play, has gradually come to stand for a formal, well-defined, rule-bound activity which was once synonymous with the game. This 'constitution of a field of specific practices',[5] according to Pierre Bourdieu, is the essence of modern sport.

Modern sporting practice thus turns into an esoteric culture, which separates the professional from the amateur and transcends its identity as a rigidly structured rule-bound game-space to specifically favour the agonistic motive. This is a culture with its own rewards and rules, along with a dedicated spectatorship with stakes in the performance of the athlete (who must, in turn, depend on his game for his livelihood). The 'creation of a body of specialists living directly or indirectly off sport' operating as 'a system of agents and institutions functioning as a field of competition', to quote Bourdieu,[6] has turned modern sport into an intensely competitive domain. However, while being primarily agonistic, it is not devoid of either cultural or historical significance, so much so that our relationship with sport often defines aspects of our modernity; it is no exaggeration to claim that sport is one of modernity's fundamental cultural institutions. Modernist literature which makes use of running as a symbol or as a metaphorical process in its narrative allows us to reflect on the relationship between modernity and sport, enabling us not only to precisely articulate what constitutes the experience of running in a modernist context, but also to use that experience of running as a means of fathoming the position of the individual in a postmodern world.

The role of running in this correlation between sport and the agonistic drive is substantial. This role is inextricably linked to the notion of competitiveness. Anthropologically, the instinct to run has been equated with the need to fulfill basic functions of life such as hunting and foraging for food, finding shelter, and ensuring safety.[7] Running has played a crucial role in the evolutionary history of humankind, as exemplified by both the cultural and the scientific use of the term 'fight or flight'. In fact, the very action of running has been inseparable from the idea of survival and competition to the extent that, while many other forms of sport or games seem to mimetically use the motif of the 'quest' or the 'hunt' in varying degrees, the act of running is evocative of the hunt itself on a directly physical, individual level. Almost as a preordained condition, running as a sport is destined to be supremely agonistic.

Space and Time in the World of the Runner

What characterises the agonistic impulse in running as a sport is the space and time that form the fabric of the action. The nature of any competition is a function of the time and space that it is embedded in. If the two were to be stretched or compressed, it would result in a definite change in the agonistic principle that defines the competition.

If the element of time in a race, for instance, were to increase indefinitely, the inherent competitive nature of the race would arguably decline with the gradual onset of physical and mental exhaustion, following the 'hierarchy of needs'.[8]

The dichotomous conjunctions of the personal and the political, the communal and the individual, the professional and the amateur notwithstanding, time, space and the recurring motif of running as a means to an end unite running across cultures and largely disparate interests. Running both as a sport and as an activity which punctuates our lived experience—one in which we have all 'got to run' as the saying goes—acquires symbolic value by virtue of its universality. Literature and popular culture make use of the conduciveness of both the sense of achievement that the figure of the runner projects as well as the narrative of the process of running—the race, the sprint, the long-distance run. The basis for this trope is a broadly essentialised construct which projects the act of running as both self-referential and essentially mimetic in the same way that certain forms of literature are expected to act as a mirror to life. This is what Kipling's polemical 'If' sketches through the 'sixty seconds worth of distance run'[9] over the 'unforgiving minute' ('If', line 29). The combination of the ambient elements of space and time adds meaning to the race as a metaphor for life. These spatio-temporal unities form the basis of the universal symbol of the runner as well as the oft-encountered analogy between running and life itself.

With regard to this analogy of the race with life, the image that immediately comes to mind is that of the race track—the well-defined space that the race usually occupies. One can argue, in fact, that these well-defined limits and the resultant finitude of the race track are what impose on the race a sense of highly defined structure, making it conquerable, thereby defining the very principle of the race. The optimal combination of limited time and a well-marked, definite space makes the race the most iconic form of running. The sprint, as it is technically called, satisfies the basic human need to overtake and achieve victory. Intense, focused and brief, the sprint emphasises victory as its only goal. But if this well-defined, limited space of the track were to be expanded, to include an area beyond the sporting arena, or if it were to be run multiple times to fulfill the conditions of a greater distance, would that have an impact on the momentum of the agonistic impulse? More importantly, would that extension force the competitor to be subservient to non-competitive factors, in spite of the agonistic impulse? These are questions which are integral to an understanding of distance running.

It is important at this juncture to understand the process of running as a function of the space and distance needed to be run. Middle-distance and long-distance running occupying track space[10] already begin to show the effect that continual repetition of the space traversed might have on the agonistic charge. The competitive motive is still strong, but with an increase in time it begins to bear a more complicated relationship with the race, beyond the obvious equations underlying the sprint, where the time taken is much shorter. This is one motivation for what in running parlance is called 'pacing'; the pace of a sprint is demanding because it is covered in a shorter time. With the marathon and cross-country running, the extension of both time and space covered changes the pacing strategy. The changing of these parameters transforms the experience of running into one of endurance, rather than the exultation of the sprint. The athlete needs to both preserve his strength and use it continuously—the thrust is more on an optimum speed that can be sustained for most of the race, before the time comes to move in, idiomatically, for the kill. Thus, while the sprint also certainly has a psychological effect on the runner, its prioritisation of speed above all other skills ensures that this impact is briefer, more fleeting. This is the speed that is conventionally alluded to in literature and culture in terms of both brevity and levity. Browning's 'Pheidippides,' for example, recounts the mytho-historical narrative of the first marathon run in terms of fire, flight and sparks. The figure of the runner becomes fire running through a field, burning over the hills. The distance he has to run is trivialised as a field of stubble through which a fire runs. Pheidippides has no 'care for his limbs'[11] (line 23) which have the power of 'lightning' and fret like the 'fire frets, an inch from dry wood' (line 29). The 'blaze' (line 42) in his blood turns the distance into a landscape rushing past. Browning's treatment of the long-distance run is suitably romanticised and belies the grim physicality of the process, dismissing it only as 'racer's toil' (line 96) —escaping which becomes Pheidippides' promised reward.

Only the flight-like rush of the usual sprint runner is highlighted. After an encounter with Pan sets his mind at ease and warms him to his task, Pheidippides declares, 'If I ran hitherto, /Be sure that the rest of my journey, I ran no longer but flew. /Parnes to Athens, earth no more, the air was my road' (lines 84–86). Afterwards, he is made to run again and succumbs to the exhaustion, crying, in a tragic moment of irony, 'Rejoice, we conquer!' (line 111) at the moment of his death. The use of the word 'we' is remarkable: it underlines that Pheidippides' run is important not as a personal feat but for the service it does towards the salvation of the nation. The act of the run itself is immaterial; what is important is that he runs to save his nation. The Pheidippides incident is the fable to which, it is believed, the modern marathon owes its origins. Browning's poem suggests that even at its inception, the marathon was underscored by the same truth as the one it continues to be underscored by today; no matter the emotion that the runner feels, his run is a politicised event. In a polis marred by doubt, war and lethargy, the runner saves the nation by keeping faith in both Pan and Athens—conventional symbols of a political and religious awareness.[12]

The Tactics of Running

The format of running that Pheidippides engages in is verifiably long distance, but the emotional charge, for Browning's poetic needs, is immediate; Browning stresses less on the endurance required for the format than on the moment the threshold of this endurance snaps. While this seems at first to undermine the distinction made previously between different forms of running in terms of the time-space-experience scale, it actually reinforces it. The goal of sport is not the death of the player—which it only symbolically duplicates in the loss of the game—but victory. This victory is ultimately that of the nation; it leaves the runner isolated, tricking him into death. If the victory must be solely the runner's, and not (as in the case of Pheidippides) the nation's, the pace and style of running become key to navigating the space of the sport. This style and pace invite natural comparisons to different literary forms. As John Landy says, for instance, the mile has 'classic symmetry'[13] and is a 'play in four acts', 'theatrically just the right length', 'a story unfolding' with 'beginning, middle, end'.

> The mile is split into four laps with different tactical plans. The first lap is to get out comfortably fast and to stay out of trouble. The second lap is to maintain pace, evaluate your competitors and to relax mentally. The third lap is to pick off faltering runners, maintain good form and to get into position. The last lap is time to move when others show weakness, keep quick turnover and to use one's final sprint.[14]

The longer distances, by virtue of seeming like, to quote Sebastian Coe, 'lap after lap of waiting',[15] are not as easily reminiscent of narrative structures with a sense of well-measured unity. The rigid structure of the sprint or the race dissolves with the lack of temporal and spatial cohesion and this makes distance running a fundamentally different experience from the sprint. Thus, while the rise and fall of action in shorter distances like the mile and the sprint seem to parallel a conventional dramatic structure, the format of the long-distance narrative, with its special time-space continuum, is more suited to post-modern experiences; indeed, in these narratives, the motif of long-distance running often appears as a metaphor for the modernist experience. The crux of the difference between these different representations of the short and long formats lies in the difference in the promises each format makes to the runner. Emil Zatopek succinctly testifies to this from experience that validates the distinctive treatment that modernist literature accords to distance running:

> We [long distance runners] are different, in essence, from other men. If you want to win something, run 100 meters. If you want to experience something, run a marathon.[16]

It is this experience that the modernist literature of running aptly records. The metaphor of the long-distance run engages the structural disintegrations articulated by the postmodern; even when the narrative structure of the text is not in itself disjointed or concerned with structural unity or disunity, the thematic concerns of narrative time and space and the runner's existence in that narrative echo the disintegration and decentralisation of the postmodern world which moves away from a conventional 'central plot' with a linear narrative. The experience of distance running, therefore, becomes an extension of the postmodernist condition itself. The relaxation of the rigid space-time structure of the motivated race into the relatively relaxed and unstructured space-time corresponding to long-distance running becomes an area peculiarly suited to both the formal and thematic concerns of modernist and post-modern literature.

Modernism and Postmodernism

The post-modern narrative with its anti-'progressive historical' slant discards its objective to reach a finite certitude. In the realm of the post-modern, history becomes a myth, 'a lost referential'[17] as Baudrillard says in *Simulacra and Simulation*. The myth of order and referential progression transforms the 'pre-modern' and 'modern' into a culture lived in the 'march of history', in the 'euphoric or catastrophic expectation of revolution'. History has retreated, leaving behind it 'an indifferent nebula, traversed by currents, but emptied of references'.[18] This distrust of 'grand narratives',[19] to use Lyotard's term, and the rupture of meaning, is captured more clearly in the trope of distance running. Long-distance running delineates the experience of the individual in a postmodern world—characterised by 'a pure and random play of signifiers',[20] the 'rupture of the relationship between the sign and its referent'[21]—while lending a sense of positive direction to this experience. This further illustrates the natural human tendency to think in terms of a narrative even when faced with disorder—which in fact is the main criticism of Lyotard's theory. Even while breaking experience up into several meta-narratives, the commentary on this collection of meta-narratives itself is a grand narrative. This tension between the inclination to both disbelieve a grand narrative while at the same time not lose faith in the possibility of some underlying narrative, however haphazard and meaningless, is what Marshall Berman engages with in his book *All That Is Solid Melts Into Air: The Experience of Modernity*.

Berman critiques the concept of post-modernity by defining the 'modern' and 'modernity' in terms that strip the postmodern of any intrinsic value, by including the category of the postmodern within the reach of the modern. In Berman's formulation, the very concept of being postmodern is not a progression from the modern, but fundamentally a denial of it. While the 'modern' is a state of flux, the experience of modernity is the abstract desire for home in that flux, and the postmodern is a denial of both the home and the desire. Berman recognises the fragmentary post-modern as the realm of the soulless and the hopeless, but his conception of how the individual responds to the condition of the postmodern is in terms of modernity. If the long-distance runner's world is typically postmodern in landscape, structure and marked by the disbelief of grand narratives, the runner can reach into the modernist project of surviving in spite of the paranoia and apparent meaninglessness of the postmodern world. Berman's definition of modernity almost seems to describe the very process of long-distance running as captured in postmodern texts like Sillitoe's *The Loneliness of the Long Distance Runner* and Murakami's *What I Talk About when I Talk About Running*. Berman writes,

> To be modern, [I said], is to experience personal and social life as a maelstrom, to find one's world and oneself in perpetual disintegration and renewal, trouble and anguish, ambiguity and contradiction: to be part of a universe in which all that is solid melts into air. To be a modernist is to make oneself somehow at home in the maelstrom, to make its rhythms one's own, to move within its currents in search of the forms of reality, of beauty, of freedom, of justice, that its fervid and perilous flow allows.[22]

Berman's description of being a 'modernist' can be taken as a critical part of the definition of long-distance running: to optimise effort and to 'feel at home' with pain and exhaustion, to merge the rhythm of the run with the experience of time and space and set the pace, propelled forward at a speed through a disintegrating epistemological framework. It is as if in a world of shifting signification the only solace is the feeling of the body in motion; as if only through that motion can self-verification become possible.

The Lonely Runner

The desolate postmodern landscape that forms the domain of the experience of modernity encourages parallels between life and running, but denies the runner the comfort of a meaningful ending. The runner thinks the very act of running engenders in him the ability to predict an outcome—but it is the impossibility of causal relations that the narrative upholds in Sillitoe's *The Loneliness of the Long Distance Runner*.

> The long distance run of an early morning makes me think that every run like this is a life, a little life, I know—but a life as full of misery and happiness and things happening as you can ever really get around yourself—and I remember that after a lot of these runs I thought that I didn't need much know how to tell how a life was going to end once it had got well started. But as usual I was wrong, caught first by the cops and then by my own bad brain, I could never trust myself to fly scot-free over these traps, was always tripped up sooner or later no matter how many I got over to the good without even knowing it. Looking back I suppose them big trees put their branches to their snouts and gave each other the wink, and there I was whizzing down the bank and not seeing a bloody thing.[23]

So says Smith, the seventeen-year-old, disgruntled, angst-ridden, delinquent first-person narrator of Alan Sillitoe's short-fiction. Smith equates the act of running with life in a text that uses the recurring motif of a continuous sense of motion as a commentary on the difference between running and racing. The correctional 'public school' value attached to sport is explored through the itinerant physical being, forced to resemble a prized 'race horse',[24] a tool in the hands of the system. Correctional running makes Smith think while also irrevocably convincing him of the righteousness of his deviant behaviour, because he finds his claim to authenticity more legitimate than those who are 'In-lawed', which is what Smith collectively defines the administrators in power as. The governor wishes him to race for Borstal, where he is an inmate, and sends him out to practice alone (because it is a 'modern' correctional home), but for Smith, it is this very idea of racing for institutional glory and political empowerment that he is running against—a sentiment he gives voice to when he says:

> Because you see I never race at all; I just run, and somehow I know that if I forget I'm racing and only jogtrot along until I don't know I'm running I always win the race. For when my eyes recognise that I'm getting near the end of the course—by seeing a stile or cottage corner—I put on a spurt, and such a fast spurt it is because I feel that up till then I haven't been running and that I've used up no energy at all. And I've been able to do this because I've been thinking.[25]

There is also a marked analogy drawn by the governor between running and professional sport, a notion that Smith treats with the same disdain with which he treats anything that has the stamp of authorial power. It is interesting to note that, while both 'Pheidippides' and *The Loneliness of the Long Distance Runner* engage with the theme of long-distance running, Browning's poem, because it is recounted in a third person narrative, does not insist on the protagonist's own experience of the world. The evolution of the history of the long-distance runner from Browning to Sillitoe inhabits what Helen Small sees as 'two strikingly opposed kinds of political romanticism.'[26] For Browning this 'political romanticism' becomes a 'beleaguered but defiant nationalism';[27] for Sillitoe, 'an equally beleaguered and defiant class antagonism.'[28] Indeed, the highly politicised act of running for Smith is the closest he can get to the feeling of being on the run. His lack of a plan to break away while running is tied to his fear of getting caught and hence to be further tied down to the system he is trying to run away from. Smith's body internalises his pain, giving rise to an endurance that reflects the class struggle that he epitomises. While the sheer physical burden of his task is overwhelming, the rhythm of his run is characterised by ease. And yet, he does not run to win, for getting caught would have the same effect as winning the race he is being trained for; this is the reason for his purposeful deflection of victory. In a literal correspondence, life and running for the convict become one and the same, by virtue of the fact that his freedom to be himself is characterised by his being on the run.

But why does this grimly humorous, surreptitiously loathing delinquent subject himself, in the first place, to training and running for someone else's prize? This clearly cannot be explained by alluding to his sporting ambitions: he does not have any. He does not want to 'run for money, trot for wages on piece work at a bob a puff rising bit by bit to a guinea a gasp and retiring through old age at thirty-two because of lace-curtain lungs, a football heart, and legs like varicose beanstalks.' Success for him entails a situation in which 'winning meant that [he] was going to escape the coppers after doing the biggest bank job of [his] life.' He runs because the thought of not smelling the grass or tasting 'that dusty bark' or 'trotting this lovely path' makes him cry.[29] He runs because it makes him feel 'like the first and the last man on the world, both at once.'[30] He runs because feeling like the last man on earth makes all those who are asleep seem dead, and running like the first man on earth seems to thaw that feeling somewhat. And yet, because he is being forced to run, the extent of time he can now spend thinking still does not provide an outlet for his sense of confinement within a cloistered space. So overcoming is his desire to return to an unlimited space for running that he is often tempted to alter the usual course of his run. It is his immersion within his deep thoughts, however, that has the effect of contracting both time and distance. In this state of heightened self-awareness, the bonds that tie him to conscious reality, fray. This subversion itself is reflected not just in how he grapples with reality, but in his appropriation of the world as a subject of modernity, defined by loneliness. Running, rather than offering an escape from the maelstrom of his existence, seems to recoil on its initial purpose, as Smith cogitates:

> I passed the Gunthorpe runner whose shimmy was already black with sweat and I could just see the corner of the fenced up copse in front where the only man I had to pass to win the race was going all out to gain the half way mark. Then he turned into a tongue of trees and bushes where I couldn't see him anymore, and I couldn't see anybody, and I knew what the loneliness of the long distance runner running across country felt like, realising that as far as I was concerned this feeling was the only honesty and realness there was in the world and I knowing that it would be no different ever, no matter what I felt at odd times, and no matter what anybody else tried to tell me.[31]

The sense of immediacy inherent in the narrative structure and the experience it recounts reinforces the protagonist's awareness of his own existence in an ideologically postmodern world, and the political issues that the agonistic principle promotes. Smith's right to be deviant and to avoid the rules that bind the other inmates is thus conveyed on the one hand through the actual descriptions of running, and on the other through the narrative device of the rushed, slightly neurotic first-person account. The narrative is essentially a compendium of Smith's thoughts on running, as well as his thoughts while running. The simultaneity of these two kinds of thoughts in the narrative, in this instance, becomes what Alexis Tadié in his essay calls a form of 'thought-experiment'offered to the reader.[32] In Sillitoe's discussion of the background to the story, the idea of an individual entity fighting a hostile modernity is prominent, as he explains:

> The theme of the story [is] really [...] about a writer, but you can't write about a writer so I put my hero into a Borstal and all around him the Borstal attitudes were the attitudes of society and what they expected of him, and what they expected and hoped he would believe. But he fought against it. He knew, he realised, that the only value to keep is your own integrity. It was really an extended essay on the integrity of a person in prison, in Borstal, or if you like, the integrity of a writer.[33]

In another extract, he exemplifies:

> The story seemed to be dictated. I wasn't thinking, I was simply writing, the pen racing over the paper.[34]

Running and writing unite in the writer's quest for honesty and in his position as a rebel. The text itself shows a heightened thematic awareness of this fusion, all the while nudging the framework of the post-modern that it is embedded in. The author's writing process is likened to the smoothness of his protagonist's running; the 'pen racing over the paper', creating the harmonious union of form and content, is a perfect metaphor for the same act of running that the work is describing. Sillitoe is clearly aware of the essence of running without being an actual runner himself. He recaptures the narrative act 'in a field of energy, the rhythmical narration of a runner coming from hardly to be guessed where—except possibly from the beats of the printing presses'.[35] The text itself flows at a frenetic, urgent pace, with measured colloquial words, reflecting in a way the rhythm of Smith's run, even though it doesn't aspire to the poetic cadences that Browning structurally invests in his treatment of long-distance running. The individual in a race is not the dominant image of this modernity—this is not Kipling's runner, or Browning's Pheidippides. This runner more closely resembles Charles Sorley's 'ungirt runners'[36] who 'do not run for prize' (line 4). This is the runner whose experience of running is formed as a consequence of and in dialogue with the phenomenological world in which he finds himself, one in which he 'run[s] because he like[s] it/Through the broad bright land' (lines 23–24). 'We know not whom we trust/Nor whitherward we fare/But we run because we must/through the great wide air' (lines 5–8).

The act of running becomes an extension of one's situation, propelled by the awareness of the self as situated in the broader context of the world, which for Browning and Sillitoe is unavoidably political. Long distance running contradicts what we expect from sport as a spectacle, and becomes a metaphor for modernity. As a sport, running long distance might seem more of a challenge than running a sprint. But does that really ensure deeper fulfillment for the runner? Is the fatigued body not a constricting influence on the mind? Or is the psychological engagement with running itself the primary instructor of individual's urge to inhabit the space of modernity? The influence of the experience of running when it is democratised, to the extent where the runner fulfills no apparent political function while still being a part of a political system, is a theme that Haruki Murakami addresses in *What I Talk About When I Talk About Running*, his intensely personal engagement with the stylistic and narrative synonymy of literature and running.

The Postmodern Runner: Murakami

'Pain is inevitable. Suffering is optional',[37] says Murakami, remembering the mantra of a runner he once knew. It would seem from Murakami's words that the answer to why pain is necessary is that it is, simply put, inescapable. But while pain cannot be wholly eradicated, the experience of unbearable pain can be tackled. Learning to endure pain is what long distance running teaches, and in that, it becomes an allegory for the inherently painful journey of life itself.

> Say you're running and you start to think, Man this hurts, I can't take it anymore. The hurt part is an unavoidable reality, but whether or not you can stand any more is up to the runner himself.[38]

What makes Murakami a perfect commentator on running as a literary metaphor is the fact that he is a modernist writer and runner himself, and his book is a collection of 'life lessons'—personal lessons he learned through 'actually putting his own body in motion'.[39] While constantly drawing analogies between long distance running and the writing of his postmodern fiction, Murakami stresses the physical and mental exhaustion involved in both, and the importance of rhythm in any long term undertaking. Comparing the start of his running career with the start of his 'real' career as a novelist, the process of running, Murakami declares, is to him both an exercise and a metaphor. When he thinks of life, he often feels 'like a piece of driftwood washed upon a shore'; one of his reasons for running is in order to 'set the pace'; he writes, 'The problem is getting the flywheel to spin at a set speed—and to get to that point takes as much concentration and effort as [one] can manage'. His quest as an artist and a runner–is to give direction to an existence which is 'fundamentally meaningless', as a product of modernity.[40]

Connections between Sillitoe's narrative and Murakami's memoir abound and it is possible to find recurring motifs common to both. Crucially, it is almost impossible to miss the continual appearance of themes of solitude and contemplation, loneliness and reality. Although running entails very different things in Sillitoe and Murakami, neither believes in the idea of a race–Murakami cites himself as not 'totally uncompetitive'), but not too bothered about whether he gets ahead of others, being more interested in the goals he set for himself. Both runners try to understand what happens to the mind in terms of conscious thought while the body is in motion. For Smith, it is the overpowering force of thought that makes him forget his physical motion, pain and speed. For Murakami, running is a return to 'private time' and 'mental well-being':

> When I'm running I don't have to talk to anybody and don't have to listen to anybody. All I need to do is gaze at the scenery passing by. This is a part of my day I can't do without. I'm often asked what I think about as I run. Usually the people who ask this have never run long distances themselves. I always ponder the question. What exactly do I think about when I'm running? I don't have a clue.[41]

Both runners seem to want to beat something which refuses to yield easily to them–for Smith, it is the space of the race, which symbolises the 'In-laws'. For Murakami, it is his running time that he seeks to improve, although he progressively finds himself failing to do so. A third remarkable conjunction that Murakami and Sillitoe's texts share is the deep connection between running, loneliness and modernity. Murakami's thoughts while he runs echo Smith's, in that they are both underlined by a sense of solitude. The theme of being plunged headlong into an existential maelstrom keeps returning as Murakami recognises life as being 'basically unfair', where it is possible with concentrated time and effort to seek out a 'kind of fairness', even if at the end it feels like it wasn't 'worth all that'. The feeling of 'living in an unimaginable world', knowing that every experience is the first of its kind, and that nothing can be understood fully because it has no precedent in one's experience pushes the individual towards accepting things just as they are. Murakami sees the comical side to a life lived like this, and does not want to discard it completely; the temptation of a grand narrative and a search for meaning is denied by a postmodern world which insists that things are as they are, even if without meaning.

I just run. I run in a void. Or maybe I should put it the other way: I run in order to acquire a void. But as you might expect, an occasional thought will slip into this void. People's minds can't be a complete blank. Human beings' emotions are not strong or consistent enough to sustain a vacuum. What I mean is, the kinds of thoughts and ideas that invade my emotions as I run remain subordinate to that void. Lacking content, they are just random thoughts that gather around that central void.

Running becomes an almost unreal process in which the 'imagined' is heightened to make the runner realise that 'nothing in the real world is as beautiful as the illusions of a person about to lose consciousness' and that isolation, like 'acid spilling out of the bottle, can unconsciously eat away at a person's heart and dissolve it'. To endure this isolation, Murakami has 'had to constantly keep [his] body in motion, in some cases pushing [himself] to the limit, in order to heal the loneliness [he] feels inside—to put it in perspective—not so much as an intentional act, but as an instinctive reaction'. He writes,

When I'm criticised unjustly (from my viewpoint, at least), or when someone I'm sure will understand me doesn't, I go running for a little longer than usual. By running longer it's like I can physically exhaust that portion of my discontent. It also makes me realise again how weak I am, how limited my abilities are. I become aware, physically, of these low points. And one of the results of running a little farther than usual is that I become that much stronger. If I'm angry, I direct that anger toward myself. If I have a frustrating experience, I use that to improve myself. That's the way I've always lived. I quietly absorb the things I'm able to, releasing them later, and in as changed a form as possible, as part of the story line in a novel.

We are approaching an existence where the experience of time and space is such that the experience of running itself is unending. Smith is on the run both under and beyond the law, while Murakami's running influences his writing in fundamental ways. Finishing lines, therefore, no longer have any inherent meaning. Finishing a race, for Murakami, leaves him with no real sense of 'accomplishment'. Running becomes its own reward.

> And at the end I feel like a car that's run out of gas. But after I finish and some time has passed, I forget all the pain and misery and am already planning how I can run an even better time in the next race. The funny thing is, no matter how much experience I have under my belt, no matter how old I get, it's all just a repeat of what came before. I think certain types of processes don't allow for any variation. If you have to be part of that process, all you can do is transform—or perhaps distort—yourself through that persistent repetition, and make that process a part of your own personality.

In this endless repetition of action, the runner finds purpose. Murakami's meta-narration expands the metaphor of the runner-writer in modernity. His work does not actually attempt to encapsulate the rhythm of the running experience in the structure of the narrative (as in the works of Browning or—to a lesser degree—of Sillitoe). Its function is to comment on the process itself, from a non-fictive realm, in order to prove beyond doubt that not only does the structural co-relation of running with modernity and literary output exist, but that it is in fact fundamental to the structure of the entire body of his work, even when it does not engage explicitly with running and modernity. The shift from the realm of the political to that of the personal does not in any way diminish the grasp of the experience of modernity in a postmodern world. The suffering human subject, who runs 'in a void' or to 'fill a void' becomes, as Berman theorised, a critique as well as a definition of the postmodernist experience. Forrest Gump's running is an assertive action in the face of his personal turmoil in a postmodern world just as Amir's running in *The Kite Runner* is his personal, defiant rebellion towards finding a sense of freedom in a violent and politically charged Kabul. Indeed, the structural similarity between running and the texture of the dynamic world in post-modernity positions the post-modern subject as both a critic and the author of his condition.

The Suffering Subject and Postmodernist Recuperation

The position of the post-modern subject itself is marked by a sense of struggle. While Caillois uses the word *agon* in the traditional sense of a contest or a competition, the word *agon* in classical Greek also means 'to suffer'. In the figure of Forrest Gump the agony of the long distance runner and the experiential value of running is used as a cultural trope. For Forrest Gump, running becomes a way to break the shackles that physically bind him. Forrest's first run, being an effort to outrun a gang of bullies, implants in him the awareness of running as something which has no end. What becomes a pivotal point in Forrest's narrative is not the emotional release of running but the physical sensation of motion. Remembering the first time he ran he says, 'But I can run like the wind blows. From that day on, if I was going somewhere, I was running!'[42] Noticed by the coach of the college football team, he is offered a place and achieves distinction as a player. This distinction is based only on his ability to run and not so much on his skill at the game. Forrest continuously goes against the structure of the game, literally running beyond its boundaries. Running without a sense of definite purpose, with a complete lack of competition, becomes for Forrest a response to the disjuncture of a post-modern experience marked by uncertainty. When disturbed or unsure, as in the case of his relationship with Jenny, Forrest decides to run.

> That day, for no particular reason, I decided to go for a little run. So I ran to the end of the road, and when I got there, I thought maybe I'd run to the end of town. And when I got there...I thought maybe I'd just run across Greenbow County. And I figured since I run this far, maybe I'd just run across the great... state of Alabama. And that's what I did. I ran clear across Alabama. For no particular reason, I just kept on going. I ran clear to the ocean. And when I got there, I figured since I'd gone this far, I might as well turn around, just keep on going. When I got to another ocean, I figure since I've gone this far, I might as well just turn back, keep right on going.[43]

The very way in which Forrest undertakes this run is symptomatic of his conception of running. Running, having fulfilled its function as a physical liberation earlier, is for him a way of making sense of the world. He runs for over three years acquiring a large group of followers who run with him and view him as a messianic figure. His run is televised and publicised even though he is quite unaware of his fan following. People come to him for his endorsement, seeking to exploit his iconic value. Forrest, unaware of his own status, becomes an indirect creator of cultural value. Indeed, Forrest's encounter with his 'fan' following begins to simulate the demands made by professional sport on an athlete. Just as suddenly as he had started running, Forrest stops. The moment of cessation coincides with the moment of realisation. As Forrest tries to make sense of the world as he perceives it, his followers run to find meaning in their own lives. As space and time dissolve and Forrest runs, something in his struggle reaches out to others, who then set out to find the meaning of their existence, making sense of their modernity.

The grand narrative of running arches over the disjointed post-modern world. In fundamental ways Murakami, Smith and Forrest question and engage with the experience of the self in an uneasy world made up of conflicting signals. Culture, politics, authorship and personal freedom within the text exists in endless flux and the text itself becomes more of a process than an event. The experience of running in a postmodern world becomes, for the runner, an exploration of a culture marked by 'fragmentary situations, eclectic nostalgia, disposable simulacra, and promiscuous superficiality'.[44] The swirl of empty signals which engulfs the possibility of meaning and significance subverts claims to authenticity and linearity of narrative. For the post-modernist text, the need for artistic coherence is couched in a feeling of alienation, achieved either by disorienting techniques or the conscious, numbed, often flippant awareness of the self in the world. While Sillitoe's text articulates this modernity through the treatment of the postmodern protagonist, engaging in an exercise which imitates the cultural, individual experience of the postmodern world, Murakami theorises the very process of producing post-modern textual meaning through his own experience of running in a post-modern world. Long-distance running, in both works, becomes equivalent to the very experience of modernity—a metaphor for lived experience which simultaneously encourages and inhibits the possibility of closure. In the absence of closure, the only other reprieve is, perhaps, the sense of an ending.

Notes

1. Haruki Murakami, *What I Talk About When I Talk About Running* (New York: Alfred. A. Knopf, 2008), p. vi.
2. Alexis Tadié, 'Running for Freedom: The Politics of Long-Distance Running in Modern Fiction', Unpublished paper presented at the International Conference on Sport and the Nation. Jadavpur University, January 2012.
3. Johan Huizinga, *Homo Ludens: A Study of the Play-Element in Culture* (London, Boston and Henley: Routledge & Kegan Paul, 1949). In this work, Huizinga suggests that play is a primary, necessary, even if insufficient, condition through which culture and civilization develop. Huizinga's 'Play-Theory' defines a conceptual space in which play occurs. My definition of play is largely dependent on Huizinga's theorisation of the play element in culture. My definition of sport incorporates, to a large extent, his analysis of the contest vis-à-vis 'play' in culture as war and civilisation.
4. Roger Caillois, *Man, Play and Games* (University of Illinois Press: Simon and Schuster, 2001), p. 14. Caillois builds on Huizinga's sociological analysis of game and play by drawing a definite distinction between them and placing them on a continuum ranging from *ludus* (play) to *paidia* (game). In this paper I use primarily Caillois' definition of the *agon* and his analysis of the corruption that the *agon* seems susceptible to.
5. Pierre Bourdieu, 'How Can One be a Sportsman?', *Sociology in Question* (London: Sage Publications, 1993), p. 118. Bourdieu, in this essay, offers a complex argument about what constitutes the field of sports in terms of the social classes who are its patrons and use sport to express their aesthetic and distancing strategies. My argument is based on a linkage of Caillois' agonistic impulse and Bourdieu's field of 'modern' sport and its related professional quality.
6. Ibid., p. 118.
7. See: Deniss M. Bramble and Daniel E. Lieberman, 'Endurance Running and the Evolution of Homo', Nature Vol. 432(2004): 345–52. NATURE, http://www.fas.harvard.edu/~skeleton/pdfs/2004e.pdf (accessed 24 March, 2013). This paper assesses how well humans perform at sustained long distance running, and reviews the physiological and anatomical bases of endurance running capabilities in humans and other mammals arriving at the conclusion that judged by several criteria, humans perform remarkably well at Offering a biological interpretation of why humans are uniquely predisposed to long distance running, it throws light on the instinct and ability to run which I talk at length about in my discussion.
8. See Abraham Maslow, 'A Theory of Human Motivation', *Psychological Review,* 50(4)1943: 370–96, http://psychclassics.yorku.ca/Maslow/motivation.htm (accessed 1 Nov. 2012). Simply stated, Maslow forms a pyramid of human needs and draws a direct co-relation between the

motivation to fulfil a need based on the importance or relevance of that need to the individual. Maslow denotes five categories ranging from the most basic physiological to the more abstract intellectual. In ascending order these are physiological (breathing, food, air, water, sex), safety (of body, employment, family, property etc.), love/belonging (friendship, family, intimacy), esteem (confidence, achievement, respect for and by others), self-actualization (morality, creativity, spontaneity). This is to say that no matter what the extent of self actualization, if the run did not ensure any of the needs below this category the will to compete in an essentially meaningless run will naturally decline. The act of long distance running thus utilizes a meaningful space and time in that it fulfils a need of the higher order than a sprint.

9. Rudyard Kipling, 'If—', *The Collected Poems of Rudyard Kipling* (Kent: Wordsworth Editions, 1994), pp. 605, l. 29–30.
10. Here I'm making a distinction between the space enclosed by race tracks as opposed to the unmarked space the runner runs in. The latter is still theoretically a track if the concept of the track of a run is limited to the physically unmarked route the runner takes. I argue that there is a fundamental difference in the construction of these spaces—in the expectation that it offers to us as sport, as well as what it does to the psychology of those running.
11. Robert Browning, 'Pheidipiddes', *Selections from Robert Browning* (USA: Robert Morss Lovett, 1934), p. 33.
12. See Helen Small, 'The Loneliness of the Long-Distance Runner in Browning, Sillitoe, and Murakami', *Essays in Criticism*, 60:2 (2010) for a wonderful discussion of the politics of running in 'Pheidipiddes'.
13. John Landy, quoted in *The Gigantic Book of Running Quotations*, ed. Amby Burfoot and Hal Higdon (New York: Skyhorse Publishing, 2008), p. 253.
14. John Landy, in *The Quotable Runner*, ed. Mark Will-Weber (New York: Breakaway Books, 1995), p. 292.
15. Sebastian Coe, quoted in *The Quotable Runner*, ed. Mark Will-Weber (New York: Breakaway Books, 1995), p. 192.
16. Emil Zatopek, 'The Warm Up', *Runner's World*, 43:9 (2008), 27. Web. 7th November 2011.
17. Jean Baudrillard, *Simulacra and Simulation* (Ann Arbor: University of Michigan Press, 1994), p. 43.
18. Ibid.
19. Jean-Francois Lyotard, *The Postmodern Condition: A Report on Knowledge*. trans. Geoffrey Bennington and Brian Massumi (Manchester: Manchester University Press, 1984).
20. Fredric Jameson, *Postmodernism: Or, The Cultural Logic of Late Capitalism* (USA: Duke University Press, 1991), p. 96.
21. Ibid.

22. Marshall Berman, *All That is Solid Melts Into Air: The Experience of Modernity* (New York: Simon and Schuster, 1982), p. 345.
23. Alan Sillitoe, *The Loneliness of the Long Distance Runner* (London: Harper Collins, 2007), p. 18.
24. Ibid., p. 12.
25. Ibid., p. 37.
26. Helen Small, 'The Loneliness of the Long-Distance Runner in Browning, Sillitoe, and Murakami', *Essays in Criticism*, 60:2 (2010), p. 130.
27. Ibid.
28. Ibid.
29. Sillitoe, *The Loneliness of the Long Distance Runner*, p. 35.
30. Ibid., p. 8.
31. Ibid., pp. 38–9.
32. Alexis Tadié, 'Running for Freedom: The Politics of Long-Distance Running in Modern Fiction', International Conference on Sport and the Nation. Jadavpur University, 2012. [unpublished conference paper]
33. Alan Sillitoe, Voice commentary for *The Loneliness of the Long Distance Runner*, Dir. Tony Richardson. BFI, 1960. Film.
34. Ibid.
35. Alan Sillitoe, *Life without Armour: An Autobiography* (1995; repr. 2004), p. 244. .
36. Charles Hamilton Sorley, 'The Song of the Ungirt Runners', *Marlborough and other Poems* (Cambridge: CUP, 1916), p. 40.
37. Haruki Murakami, *What I Talk About When I Talk About Running*, trans. Philip Gabriel (New York: Alfred. A Knopf, 2008), p vii.
38. Ibid.
39. Ibid., p. viii.
40. Ibid., p. 6.
41. Ibid., p. 16.
42. *Forrest Gump*, Screenplay by Eric Roth. Dir. Robert Zemeckis. Perf. Tom Hanks, Sally Field, Robin Wright. Paramount Pictures,1994.
43. Ibid.
44. Jean Baudrillard, *Simulacra and Simulation* (USA: University of Michigan, 1994), p. 43.

8

The New Girl and the British School Story

Aishwarya Subramanian

In Sarah Fielding's *The Governess, or The Little Female Academy*, the students are urged to take exercise 'that they might not, by sitting constantly still, impair their Health.'[1] Though the exercise in question takes the form of a gentle walk to the nearby dairy, it is interesting that the importance of physical activity in education is being emphasised this early. Written in 1749, *The Governess* was the first novel to be written for children as well as the first school story. However, the school story as a genre did not really come into being for more than a century after its publication. It was Thomas Hughes' hugely successful *Tom Brown's School Days* that spawned the school story genre, and in this genre sport played a major role.

Athleticism developed in boys' public schools in the latter half of the nineteenth century. According to J. A. Mangan, G. E. L. Cotton (who appears as the young master in *Tom Brown's School Days*) encouraged organised sport primarily as a solution to the numerous disciplinary problems he found when he arrived at Rugby School as headmaster in 1852.[2] At a practical level, sports would give the students something to do and keep them from the wild behaviour and vandalism that made the schools so unpopular with the local populace. However, the policy was framed in terms of the moral development it would supposedly bring about—developing the spirit of co-operation, promoting unselfishness and building character. Thus from their introduction in the public schools games were used as a method of social control while couched in the language of moral virtue. 'Cotton's educational rationale disguised the nature of the enterprise and legitimated the action.'[3]

School Sports

Thomas Arnold was the headmaster of Rugby during Thomas Hughes' school days. Arnold was not particularly a supporter of games, and sport would not have been a major part of school life in Hughes' time. Mangan suggests that the muscular Christianity that influenced Hughes only after he had left Rugby is the driving force behind *Tom Brown's* focus on sports.[4] The huge success of the book, however, did much to associate sport with morality in the popular consciousness as well as within the genre itself. An entire vocabulary was built up around sporting morality in which one was exhorted to 'play up and play the game', 'be a sport', remember that certain things were 'not cricket'. The writers of girls' school stories would inherit this tradition.

Secondary education for girls developed rapidly through the end of the nineteenth century and the beginning of the twentieth. According to Ju Gosling, '[a]t the beginning of the twentieth century, less than a quarter of all British girls aged between twelve and eighteen attended any kind of school, but by 1920 the number receiving a secondary education had risen from 20,000 in 1897 to 185,000'[5] even though the vast majority of working-class girls still left school by the age of fourteen. Some girls' schools copied the general pattern of the boys' schools, though there were differences; as Quigly notes, since many upper class girls continued to be educated at home, the girls' school had of necessity a more middle class demographic.[6] Sports were by this point an ineradicable part of the public school structure and ethos. Writing of her time at Sherborne, E. Arnot Robertson remembers that 'we were terribly, terribly keen on games...I do not believe that sporting conjecture of this kind comes natural to one girl in twenty; but this was the tradition of the place (officially described as the High Moral Tone of the School).'[7]

In Victorian England, sports for girls, particularly upper-class girls, had been limited. While the deficiency in this area of women's education had been noted by a number of reports[8] very little could be suggested as a suitable form of exercise for young girls. Hockey had not yet become a formal game and football was thought to be unsuitable for girls[9] though there were accounts of young women who played cricket. Furthermore, the idea of young women indulging in strenuous exercise was often received with hostility. Some sections of the medical community, including women, wrote anxiously of the negative effects of exercise on the female body; particularly the potential damage to offspring. 'For Nature knows what are the faculties whence this new muscle-energy is born. She knows it is the birthright of the babies Clara and her sister athletes are squandering.'[10] Fletcher cites an article in *The Lancet* in 1885 which warned that injury caused by a cricket ball hitting a woman's breast might cause cancer and advised the wearing of a well-padded corset for female cricketers.[11] Victorian women's clothing was hardly conducive to strenuous activity, and the gym tunic (first worn by students of Madame Bergman-Österberg) was revolutionary in the freedom of movement it allowed the female body. In time the tunic came to be recognised as 'the uniform dress ...which symbolised the separate identity of the schoolgirl.'[12] The focus of the girls' schools on sports, the adoption of a practical costume that symbolised girlhood; these were part of a radical shift in what girlhood meant, and the 'new girl' was a far more active creature than her predecessors. Penny Summerfield feels that 'the strong ethos of competitive outdoor games, a development in all the schools including the convents...was part of the redefinition of femininity in which the schools were engaged.'[13]

The Girls' School Story

The writers of the girls' school story, while inheriting the basic structure of the story from the boy's version, were consciously engaging in this redefinition of femininity, often taking a direct stance on contemporary debates. In 1899, the *Girl's Realm* magazine published Isabel Orman's story 'The Strike of the Two Sisters' in which two teenaged girls protest against cleaning up after their brothers and present them with a 'bill of feminine rights'. Both girls excel at sports and use them as a way to express frustration at the double standard they face within the home.[14] *The Girl's Realm* also frequently published interviews with

'Girls Who Excel at Sports'.[15] In Angela Brazil's 1913 school story *The Youngest Girl in the Fifth*, the concept of an entirely new sort of girl is linked directly to sports. Brazil's heroine, Gwen Gascoyne assists in the rescue of a small boy, much to the surprise of her friend Dick who expects very different behaviour from a girl.

'Girls generally stand by and shriek'.

'Not modern girls', affirmed Gwen. 'They used to do the shrieking business in old-fashioned novels. It's gone out of fashion since hockey came in.'[16]

Rosemary Auchmuty feels that sports in the girls' school 'took on a radical significance since it gave women access to what were seen as 'masculine' values.'[17] These included leadership, discipline and loyalty, all of which women had presumably been previously incapable of. In a school story of 1944, *Second Form at St. Clare's*, Enid Blyton specifies exactly what values can be learnt from sport: 'We have to learn to work together as a team–each one for his side helping the others, not each one for himself.'[18] In the 1921 work *Dimsie goes to School* the headmistress of Dorita Fairlie Bruce's fictional school forbids her juniors to play hockey, believing that the teamwork they develop playing Rounders will prove more useful to them as future hockey players than actual hockey practice.

Already in Brazil's book we see a visible contempt for women who do not play sports and are therefore incapable of anything but standing by and shrieking. Enid Blyton shows nothing but disdain for her character Gwendoline, who in *Upper Fourth at Malory Towers* (1949) laments the lack of 'nice *feminine* girls...ones who like to talk and read quietly, and not always go pounding about the lacrosse field or splash in that horrible pool.'[19] From the first book in the series it becomes something of a class joke to push Gwendoline into the swimming pool–something that is never classified as bullying except on the one occasion when Gwendoline herself does it to another student. Blyton's heroines are always good at sports, though she seems suspicious of people who are prodigies in any field. Darrell Rivers is the youngest student on the lacrosse team in *Third Year at Malory Towers* (published in 1948) because she practises constantly–the ability to play a sport is less important than taking in all the moral lessons that supposedly come with it. Darrell's sister Felicity is allowed to play in a match in

In the Fifth at Malory Towers (1950) even though her friend June is the better player. The reasons for this are made clear: 'You've got team spirit all right. You play for your side all the time.'[20] June, however, does not 'pull her weight'. 'You practise and practise–and then in a game all you want to do is go your own way, and blow the others!'[21] Mere talent for the game is inadequate, and a character must show the enthusiasm to work at it constantly as well as to demonstrate acceptance of all the values Blyton associates with the game. The gym mistress was a figure of admiration in these books, and Fletcher suggests that this admiration extended beyond fiction. Students had 'confidence in the sense of justice and fair play of the Gymnastic Mistresses.'[22] Even a later (and considerably less generic) book like Antonia Forest's 1974 novel *The Cricket Term* contains traces of this link between sport and virtue. Nicola Marlow, the moral centre of Forest's books, triumphs over her enemy Lois Sanger in a cricket match, but only after subjecting her team to gruelling practice sessions.[23] And though Forest breaks radically with tradition in characterising most of the school authorities as incompetent and flawed, the games mistress, Miss Craven, is one of the few shown to be concerned with such values as justice and fair play.[24]

Masculinity and Sport

The link between masculine, 'superior' values and sports is perhaps never so clear as in Elinor M. Brent-Dyer's *Tom Tackles the Chalet School,* first published in 1955. Tom Gay (real name Lucinda Muriel), who has been raised as a boy by a conservative father, arrives at the Chalet School convinced that all girls (herself excluded) are sentimental, 'soppy' and not as honest or straightforward as boys. The other schoolgirls are naturally surprised to hear this. Tom is soon forced to admit that 'her father must have got a wrong idea of girls—modern girls, anyhow.'[25] Ironically, she herself immediately develops a crush on the games prefect, though the author goes to some lengths to assure us that this is not 'soppy' at all. Throughout the book 'sport' and 'gentleman' (the two are used interchangeably) are the highest possible compliments. Despite the masculinist vocabulary used here, there was a definite feminist impulse behind the constant insistence that girls could be as good as boys. Though it is doubtful whether any of these writers would have ever called themselves feminists, given that the authors seem to have uncritically accepted that traditionally 'masculine' values were superior to 'feminine' ones, their advocacy of sport was 'radical...in contrast to the Victorian girl's almost complete lack of physical freedom and her attenuated sense of self-worth.'[26]

If sports were a way of gaining access to masculine values, they were also a method of curing specifically feminine faults. Girls who played sports did not have the time to think of their appearance, of young men, or similar unhealthy topics. E. Arnot Robertson was told while at Sherborne school to 'run about, girls, *like* boys, and then you won't think *of* them.'[27] Miss Stansfeld, headmistress of Bedford College, wished that working class girls had more access to sports so that 'we should have less slobbering along the road with young men every night.'[28] In *A Problem for the Chalet School* the upper- and middle-class schoolgirls are shocked by Joan Baker, a working-class girl whose family has recently 'come into money'. The most shocking thing about Joan, apparently, is that 'well–she talks–about—*boys*!'[29] It is through Joan's latent talent for tennis that her peers eventually seek to reform her. 'I can see for myself that if I take an interest in Joan's tennis it's just possible it may make all the difference to her.'[30] This strategy works, even though in subsequent books Joan is seen to never quite fit in.

It seems likely that when Brent-Dyer introduced Tom Gay, she was unaware of the implications of the character's name. Similarly, Angela Brazil seems to have innocently named the heroine of *Loyal to the School* (1921) 'Lesbia', a fact that few commenters on the girls' school story are able to refrain from pointing out. Early school stories often depicted sentimental relationships between women that were frequently parodied. Citing Rosemary Auchmuty's study *A World of Girls*, Sheena Wilkinson suggests that the disapproval of these close female friendships had to do with a concern over how young women's energies were directed.

> Teachers would wish her to devote herself to work and sport; other authorities to maintaining her health, preparing to be a wife and homemaker or to religious experience. To none of these parties would too absorbing a friendship with another girl be considered a legitimate focus for the girl's energies.[31]

As mentioned above, sports were seen as a way of preventing girls from thinking too much about boys; often they were used to stop them from thinking too much about other girls as well. Later books in the genre seemed to be vigorously defending themselves against the charge of 'soppiness'. In Dorita Fairlie-Bruce's Dimsie series, the head-girl Sylvia Drummond suggests that the younger girls need to play sports frequently 'or you'll become soft and soppy'. This inspires the girls to form an 'Anti-Soppist League' to counter the dreaded scourge of sentimentality amongst themselves.[32] Alison O'Sullivan's various crushes in Blyton's St. Clare's series are seen with contempt, as are the Lower Fifth girls in Antonia Forest's 1959 novel *End of Term*, whose adoration of their seniors consisted of 'giving [them] roses in silver paper and sleeping with [their] kirbigrips under [one's] pillow.'[33]

However, it would be an error to see the schoolgirl 'crush' and the focus on sports completely in opposition to one another. Tom Gay, as I mention above, appears to have a crush on the school sports captain, and in a later book (*The Chalet School and Rosalie*, 1951) is the subject of one herself. Forest depicts Miranda West's feelings for an older girl, Jan Scott, as entirely positive. The critic Victoria Coulson suggests that the real 'queerness' in the girls' school story consists in the fact that these books deal with entirely self-sufficient homosocial worlds; 'there's gender difference amongst the girls so you don't need boys: the hetero is contained within the ostensibly homo.'[34] In a sense, the role of sports in the creation of new and extended gender roles for girls might have contributed to, rather than hindered, these ambiguous relationships between schoolgirl characters.

No Sports Republic for Girls?

In 1866 Miss Beale had advised against the playing of cricket in girls' schools, since 'the independent republican spirit of boys' schools... should not be fostered in those for girls.'[35] By the beginning of the twentieth century, most girls' schools had facilities for sports, but this does not mean that an 'independent, republican spirit' was being particularly encouraged. While Auchmuty and others are right to emphasise that sports allowed girls greater physical freedom than they had ever been given before, they could hardly be said to be free from gendered conditioning. The sporting traits that are emphasised in the girls' school story are all to do with unselfishness and subordination of individual desire, traits that women were expected to have anyway. Competition is rarely a factor. In Blyton's books, exciting matches between schools are frequently played but the losing team (invariably the other school) never seem to mind very much. In the later Chalet school books, once the school has removed to Switzerland there is no local competition and the students merely play friendly games among themselves. In *Last Term at Malory Towers* Amanda, a new girl, is competitive and plans to participate in the Olympic games. But she is consistently portrayed as aggressive and domineering as well as 'rather masculine'.[36] She is only redeemed when, too badly injured to compete in sporting events she decides to spend her time coaching the younger students, thus using her sporting talents to nurture, rather than to compete.

In the early decades of the twentieth century some educators, Sara Burstall among them, believed that the emphasis on sports had been carried to an extreme.[37] In the post-war period particularly, there was increasing pressure on women to conform to traditional domestic roles. Both Mirabel in the last St. Clare's book and Amanda in the last Malory Towers book are examples of sports mania taken too far. In *Dimsie goes to School,* the Jane Willard Foundation is a school whose interest in sports has severely compromised its academics. Both Fairlie Bruce and Brent-Dyer introduce courses in domestic science into the curricula of their fictional schools–a move paralleled by many real life schools at the time. However, none of these depictions quite rings true. If Blyton undermines the moral value of sport through her portrayal of Amanda, she simultaneously shows it to be redemptive in the case of June. The domestic science classes are barely mentioned in the Dimsie books, and in Brent-Dyer they only turn up as humorous interludes in which a character hilariously puts one wrong ingredient in the school dinner. Miss Yorke, the new headmistress of the Jane Willard Foundation, wants to wean off the school from its interest in sports but the students only really accept her when they learn that she previously played hockey for Cambridge. Thus the structure of the school story with its emphasis on sports remains largely intact in the *Girls' Own* genre, even while the treatment of sports within these texts is subject to differences in gendering, politics and educational policies.

Notes

1. Sarah Fielding, *The Governess, or The Little Female Academy*, ed. Mary Cadogan (London and New York: Pandora, 1987), p. 59.
2. J. A. Mangan, *Athleticism in the Victorian and Edwardian Public School: The Emergence and Consolidation of an Educational Ideology* (London and Portland, Oregon: Frank Cass, 1981), p. 22.
3. Ibid., p. 28.
4. Ibid., pp. 16–7.
5. Ju Gosling, 'Virtual World of Girls Index: The History of Girls' School Stories', http://www.ju90.co.uk/his.htm (accessed March 20, 2013), p. 1.
6. Isabel Quigly, *The Heirs of Tom Brown: The English School Story* (Oxford: OUP, 1984), p. 213.
7. E. Arnot Robertson, 'Potting Shed of the English Rose', in *The Old School*, ed. Graham Greene (Oxford: OUP, 1984), pp. 154–5.
8. Sheila Fletcher, *Women First: The Female Tradition in English Physical Education*, 1880–1980 (London and Dover, New Hampshire: Athlone, 1984), pp. 14–5.
9. Ibid., p. 15.
10. Dr Arabella Kenealy, quoted in Fletcher, *Women First*, p. 26.
11. Sheila Fletcher, *Women First: The Female Tradition in English Physical Education*, 1880–1980 (London and Dover, New Hampshire: Athlone, 1984), p. 26.
12. Ju Gosling, 'Virtual World of Girls Index: The History of Girls' School Stories', http://www.ju90.co.uk/his.htm (accessed March 20, 2013), p. 7.
13. Penny Summerfield, 'Cultural Reproduction in the Education of Girls: A Study of Girls' Secondary Schooling in Two Lancashire Towns, 1900–50', in *Lessons for Life: The Schooling of Girls and Women*, ed. Felicity Hunt (Oxford: Basil Blackwell, 1987), p. 168.
14. Mary Cadogan and Patricia Craig, *You're a Brick, Angela! The Girls' Story 1839–1985* (London: Victor Gollancz, 1986), p. 76.
15. Ibid., *Brick*, p. 78.
16. Angela Brazil, *The Angela Brazil Omnibus Book* (London and Glasgow: Blackie, 1937), p. 81.
17. Rosemary Auchmuty, *A World of Girls* (London: The Women's Press, 1992), p. 61.
18. Enid Blyton, *Second Form at St. Clare's* (London: Mammoth, 1991), p. 12.
19. Enid Blyton, *Three Great Malory Towers Stories* (London: Armada, 1990), p. 42.

20. Ibid., p. 274.
21. Ibid., p. 259.
22. Sheila Fletcher, *Women First: The Female Tradition in English Physical Education*, 1880–1980 (London and Dover, New Hampshire: Athlone, 1984), p. 80.
23. Antonia Forest, *The Cricket Term* (Harmondsworth: Puffin, 1979), p. 61.
24. Ibid., p. 101.
25. Elinor M. Brent-Dyer, *Tom Tackles the Chalet School* (London: Armada, 1987), p. 28.
26. Rosemary Auchmuty, *A World of Girls* (London: The Women's Press, 1992), p. 64.
27. E. Arnot Robertson, 'Potting Shed of the English Rose', in *The Old School*, ed. Graham Greene (Oxford: OUP, 1984), p. 153.
28. Quoted in Sheila Fletcher, *Women First: The Female Tradition in English Physical Education*, 1880–1980 (London and Dover, New Hampshire: Athlone, 1984), p. 78.
29. Elinor M. Brent-Dyer, *A Problem for the Chalet School* (London: Armada, 1987), p. 114.
30. Ibid., p. 116.
31. Sheena Wilkinson, *Friends in the Fourth* (London: Bettany Press, 2007), p. 17.
32. Dorita Fairlie-Bruce, *Dimsie Moves Up* (Melbourne: Geoffrey Cumberlege, Oxford University Press, 1947), p. 24.
33. Antonia Forest, *End of Term* (Harmondsworth: Puffin, 1978), p. 39.
34. Quoted in Caroline Gonda, 'Being Faithful', *Journal of Lesbian Studies* 11:1 (2007), p. 96.
35. Quoted in Sheila Fletcher, *Women First: The Female Tradition in English Physical Education*, 1880–1980 (London and Dover, New Hampshire: Athlone, 1984), p. 16.
36. Enid Blyton, *Three Great Malory Towers Stories* (London: Armada, 1990), p. 337.
37. Sheila Fletcher, *Women First: The Female Tradition in English Physical Education*, 1880–1980 (London and Dover, New Hampshire: Athlone, 1984), p. 3.

Part III

Sporting Bodies

9

The Expressive Body: Notes on Individualism and Solitude in Sport

Maitri Baruah

The expressive body in sport affords an image of extraordinary beauty and transcendence. Alternatively it points to a life of extreme routine that paradoxically co-exists with a life of extreme uncertainty. The sporting body is always aware of the ever-present prospect of failure, the prospect of sudden injury and the possibility of sudden, inexplicable disappearance of skills. The shortness of careers, the ephemeral nature of sporting performance, the fragility of skills are factors that lead to feelings of loss and emptiness that haunt the sporting body even during its moments of success and glory. My essay seeks to explore this feeling of loss that confronts the sporting body by drawing together complex relationships that exist between the negotiation of precarious bodily skills and solitude, obsessive routines and self-destruction, and the attainment of sporting glory and melancholy. I will begin my article with a detailed examination of the practice of spin bowling in cricket. Spin's template of mystery stages a range of critical debates about the sporting body, though it is not my suggestion here that this is by any means distinctive to spin. And it must be noted, further, that spin is distinctively used both in racquet sports (such as tennis and squash) and in soccer and rugby. But since spin bowling in cricket provides in many ways a revealing example, I will start with a discussion of spin bowling to study some of the attributes that mark out and confront the sporting body. What is at stake here is the negotiation of complex, more significantly precarious, skills; the spin bowler must subject his art to endless repetitive regimens, must confront the risk of loss, endure contingency, and engage with obsession and self-destruction.

This article will move between these issues, bringing in examples from other uses of the sporting body, such as goalkeeping in football and long-distance running.

Spin bowling in cricket relies on a set of skills and deft negotiations of fingers and wrist to give the ball a twist producing a curling movement in the air, and a turn off the pitch. Writing on Clarrie Grimmett, the Australian leg-spinner from the 1930s, Cardus provides the most evocative distillation of spin and an equally riveting portrait of the spinner. Cardus's highly literary and elaborate language provides a way of thinking about spin, shaping and establishing a set of conventions through which spin as a practice may be represented and understood. Cardus develops his metaphors to describe spin as a mysterious pursuit casting the spinner as an enigmatic artist, a craftsman and ambusher, embodying a practice that is both skillful and ambiguous. Cardus describes Grimmett as an 'unobtrusive little man', cat-foot on a 'wet pavement', hiding his skills, the 'master of surreptitious arts' who seemed to jump out of the shadows to catch the batsman unawares. 'Twist' and 'curl' were elements of his 'surreptitious' arts that he employed to 'ambush' the batsman. The wrist always perfectly sinewy, Grimmett, Cardus writes, went to work with a 'dark lantern'. There is a hint of something illegible and even dangerous. But there was supreme craftsmanship too, as Cardus recalls how Grimmett at Trent Bridge in 1930 took the wickets of Hammond, Woolley and Hendren in quick succession: his low arm flighted the ball or pushed a straighter one (the flipper that Grimmett is credited with). The batsman, shaken and half-relieved, is left pondering about what may have actually happened. Cardus writes, 'it is like an amputation done under an anaesthetic'. The final line in the portrait identifies Grimmett with the spirit of audacity, seeing in him the liveliness of an adventurer pursuing his own private booty: his wickets were 'swag', and Cardus sees him leave the field with a bag over his shoulder, his score 7 for 57. The spinner is never a defensive player but puts on his masks in pursuit of new possibilities and adventures.[1]

The ever expanding inventory of spin and an equally rich vocabulary that matches its infinite variations of flight, top-spin, side-spin, dip, drift embodies a practice, a distinctive body culture that in its texture is delicate, precarious and impenetrable, its practitioners represented as creatures of mystery and speculation. Spin's distinctive body culture therefore invites sustained consideration in any discussion of the expressive body in sport. It invites us to consider how we may apprehend and evaluate the relationship between body and specific body pedagogy: the question of bodily experience in relation to the embodied practice of a sport, the lived body of a sportsperson subject to a set of practices or specific body pedagogy.

Spin's Many Modernities

Amol Rajan's recently published *Twirlymen: The Unlikely History of Cricket's Greatest Spin Bowlers* discusses an interesting account of spin, dating from the eighteenth century, offered by John Nyren. Nyren's account of the peculiar revolutions of the ball achieved by Lamborn, who played for Hambledon between 1777 and 1781, is perhaps the earliest literary description of spin's imaginative appeal: the 'twist', the 'curl' and the exactness made possible by a playful intelligence bent on disguise and ingenuity.[2] Nearly two hundred years down the line two photographs, one of Bishan Singh Bedi, one of India's best left-arm orthodox bowlers, and the other of Subhash Gupte, arguably India's best leg-spin googly bowler offer a telling demonstration of the appealing tangle of exquisiteness, grace and unintelligibility that defines spin's distinctive features. Bedi's photograph shows him with his classic side-on action, body behind the bowling arm, one foot raised slightly, his hands moving together in perfect rhythm, the bowling arm high and making a graceful pose as it prepares to release the ball. The other equally compelling photograph of a small-built man (Gupte), eyes shut, wrist slightly uncoiled, captures spin's impenetrable language: both photographs—one suggestive of something ethereal in its grace and concentration, and the other ambiguous and full of mystery—are true to the imaginative powers of their represented objects.

The question of mystery comes sharply into focus when we are faced with bowlers who inhabit diametrically opposite conventions of spin: two kinds of break, variable pace and many pleasurable shades and variations in between. Spin's template of mystery is however rooted in the emergence of cricket's modernity when bowlers in the nineteenth century defied and resisted convention to enable the game's

Illustration 9.1 Bishan Singh Bedi

progress from under-arm to over-arm/round-arm bowling. This critical moment fashioned a self-awareness among bowlers of seeing themselves and their practices as somewhat different from the past, of making a break with earlier forms or conventions, developing a sense of their art and especially of spin as an art that is imaginative, full of

Illustration 9.2 Subhash Gupte

possibilities and self-consciously creative and innovative.[3] A leg spin great from the 1920s, Arthur Mailey, offers a telling observation which links together the imprint of modernity with the originality and the display of individualism by the spinners:

...the great spin bowlers of cricket were personalities and men of character—not always pleasant but invariably interesting. They may have lacked the charm and friendliness of their faster confederates; they may have been more temperamental and less self-disciplined; but there seemed to be an absence of orthodoxy about them and they were able to meander through life as individuals, not as civil servants.[4]

This process is more intensely dramatised in spin's colonial and post-colonial cultures—the preference for unorthodoxy, the display of extreme individualism and inventiveness, even the appearance of some freakish and very temporary skills. It is fascinating to note here, as Rajan's book points out, that in the period following the legalisation of over-arm bowling in 1864, bowlers, Australian bowlers such as F. R. Spofforth, Hugh Trumble, and Monty Noble happily blended medium pace and spin to produce subtleties of turn and swerve: their practice finding its fullest expression in the nearly unclassifiable bowling of the Englishman Sydney Barnes in the first decade of the twentieth century.[5] Some years later in the 1930s, it was the Indian, Palwankar Baloo, a member of the Chamar caste, who inaugurated the sub-continent's list of spin improvisers, and blended left-arm spin—that included a cleverly disguised armer—with left-arm medium pace.[6]

In this tradition of self-conscious innovation and its registers and resonances within colonial and post-colonial cultures, Sonny Ramadhin's unusual, aberrant skills—the deceptive deliveries, the concealment, the texture of his bowling nearly unclassifiable—make a rewarding case study. 'Of Indian origin', Sonny, as his school mates at the Mission school he attended called him (the name on his birth certificate just said 'boy') came to be part of the West Indies team in 1950 when he acquired the name K. T. Ramadhin. To quote Sonny: "The kids at school had called me Sonny and so I adopted that. But when I got to England they insisted that nobody could go through life without initials. The next time I picked up the paper I'd become K. T. Ramadhin. I never did find out what my new English names were supposed to be."[7] Wearing a cap like W. G. Grace and shirt sleeves buttoned at the wrist, Sonny Ramadhin bowled a bewildering mix of off-break and leg-break with a flick of his fingers and a barely perceptible movement of the wrist. An off-break bowler, Sonny spun the ball the other way—hint of the 'Doosra' perhaps long before Saqlain Mushtaq bowled it—or pushed it straighter on. There is an echo of Grimmett here in his quality of concealment, the slight build and even in his self-absorption. John Arlott suggested a parallel with Sydney Barnes in the way both spinners deployed the first finger and the middle finger to push the off-break and the leg-break, the many shades and variations that produced that made their bowling difficult to define.[8]

Illustration 9.3 Sonny Ramadhin

How does one explain Ramadhin's mystifying skills? Was it an effect of the complex interaction of bodily difference, negotiation and tension with technique that is inadequately mastered? Marcel Mauss in his 1935 essay, 'Techniques of the Body' notes that techniques of body movement with their 'biological echoes and effects' constitute a 'corporeal and technical habitus' that is acquired and is social in nature.[9] Sporting techniques and practices function as grounds of training and discipline embodying social, collective practices and relations of power. Developing Mauss's notion of 'techniques of the body' and 'habitus', Pierre Bourdieu examines sporting activity and pursuits as choices, 'predispositions', practices that acquire a set of social and historical meanings. Sporting activities according to Bourdieu constitute a set of embodied practices that cannot be interpreted as autonomous choice: the 'function and meaning' of each sport will depend upon the context within 'which agents consciously or unconsciously choose their sports'.[10] So in order to be able to understand the meaning of a sporting practice it becomes important to examine in what context the sport is played and learnt. Bourdieu's terms help us to understand how cricket, particularly in colonial and post-colonial societies, becomes the ground for negotiations and struggles that have shaped distinctive body cultures. These include the many pleasurable varieties and ambiguities that spin's diverse cultures have thrown up. C. L. R. James's descriptions of Gary Sobers's bowling and of other West Indian cricketers can be understood against this landscape of complex social and historical meanings manifested by cricket. James describes Gary Sobers 'hurling himself into his fast bowling' as 'a living embodiment of centuries of a tortured history'.[11] In his collection of autobiographical essays, *Beyond A Boundary*, Matthew Bondman's batting and Arthur Jones's cut-shot become types of physical action that plot a public memory.[12] The history of complex feelings, feelings of anger in particular, that sporting practices in a colonial context attempt to remember and articulate, according to C. L. R. James, produces a complex tension between the playing body and events outside the game. This tension marks negotiations and practices that may even be hostile to the rules of sport.[13] The idea of a productive bodily tension played out in different social and pedagogical contexts, the way in which a game is chosen and learnt could be of some assistance in helping us understand alterations and negotiations in technique through which new forms like the Doosra and the Carom ball were forged, rediscovered and legitimated.[14]

Sonny Ramadhin's skills were rooted in a sense in the unacknowledged and isolated life of an immigrant playing a game that he had taught himself (he sharpened his skills by spinning limes), while he was never considered good enough to be part of its institutions. Sonny's bowling had all the bewildering variations that came from the uncertainties and contingencies of such an identity and sometimes its lucky encounters. It was one such lucky encounter when he was twenty years old and working as a storekeeper that got him onto a boat to tour England as a member of the West Indies team alongside the three Ws. Sonny formed a partnership with the West Indian Alf Valentine, a classic left-arm orthodox bowler, tall and strongly built, and together they were responsible for the first series victory against England. The Afro-Indian pair became a popular theme in celebrations of that victory in England, and inspired a calypso:

At Lord's where I saw it,
Yardley tried his best,
Goddard won the test,
They gave the crowd plenty fun,
The Second Test and West Indies won,
With those two little pals of mine,
Ramadhin and Valentine.[15]

Ramadhin and Valentine's inventories of spin anticipated the more politicised body cultures that were to follow, led by Sobers and company.[16]

A Life Too Short: Loss and Melancholia

Throughout his career Ramadhin led a very solitary life. Trevor Bailey who played with him thought this was the consequence of the pain of assimilation into the West Indies team. Perhaps it was a sense of difference bound up with his self-absorption in the demands of his own singular skills that sharpened his sense of isolation and made him vulnerable to fits of depression.[17] For an art that has to be so rigorously thought-out—delicate wrist movements exactly calibrated—spin's catalogue of imaginative possibilities accommodates an inevitable provisionality: the sense of an exacting, unreliable skill counterpointed by feelings of loss and emptiness. Amol Rajan suggests that spinners as a group tend to show a tendency toward obsessive and neurotic behaviour.[18] Peter Roebuck who commented on why the rate of suicide was so high in cricket (higher than in any other sport according to some findings) suggests that cricket, in many ways, an individual and lonely sport (despite being a team game) has always attracted 'sensitive men of aesthetic temperament, the very men who are, in the end, least well served by it.'[19]

The Australian, Jack Iverson (a contemporary of Sonny Ramadhin) was the archetypal mystery spinner, who spun the ball using the unusual grip of holding the ball between the thumb and the middle finger, releasing the ball with a flick of the bent middle finger (it demanded immensely strong fingers). The grip, the unconventional release (later also perfected by the Australian, John Gleeson in the 1970s and continued by the current Sri Lankan slow bowler Ajantha Mendis) made it impossible for the batsmen to tell his variations apart.[20] Iverson was not much of a bowler at school but during the war years he learnt to spin, spinning a ping-pong ball as a nervous tic. A magic spell, and a moment of great personal triumph during the 1950–51 test series against England (he took 21 wickets) followed, but then Iverson lost interest and abandoned Test cricket. In a thoughtful review of Gideon Haigh's incisive and affecting biography of Jack Iverson, Robert Winder seeks an explanation for Iverson's mental battles in the very nature of play. 'Games', Winder writes, 'are hard taskmasters—plumb their trivial mysteries too deeply, and they can drive you mad.'[21] Iverson knew that but found it difficult to embrace the ephemeral nature of the game: the triumph that instantly became memory, a magic spell that quickly dissolved into emotional oblivion. Iverson laughed at the game, thought it made men do silly things, but the irony masked an inner despair. Richie Benaud and Keith Miller, both Iverson's contemporaries, thought that if Iverson had joined the Australian team for the Ashes tour of 1952–53 they would have won and not lost the series 1–0. Jack Iverson had refused because he thought he had lost his form. Driven to the edge of depressive melancholia he felt a deep sense of inadequacy and thought that no one remembered a cricketer like him. Ultimately it became a difficult burden to carry, and some years after his career was over Iverson put a gun to his chest, shot and killed himself. The fear of invisibility haunts many sportspersons because they know that the perfection of their skills is bound to a time and a place, they know how quickly their actions dissolve into memory and their feeling of joy and fulfilment of a goal transforms into loss and emptiness. Cardus writes movingly that a 'cricketer's art is thrown out on the summer air; it enchants us for a while, and then it is gone.'[22]

Illustration 9.4 Jack Iverson

The sporting body that engages in an attempt to overcome human limits, physical and psychological, gains meaning from the notion of a lived body as the basis and ground of existential experience. In his 'Construction of a definition', Bernard Suits suggests that the 'play-world' (using Huizinga's term) sustains itself because it is inseparable from a set of 'constitutive rules' that make such a world available. This requires us to find purpose and meaning in bodily performances tied to the acceptance ('lusory attitude') of difficult and even arbitrary rules. The classic definition that Suits provides of playing a game is the 'voluntary attempt to overcome unnecessary obstacles'.[23] Elaborating further on Suits's thesis, Thomas Hurka suggests that the negotiation of difficult skills, precisely and even precariously executed, together with the acceptance of physical risk or danger, are intrinsic to entry into the 'play-world'.[24] The playing body is driven by a particular, individual necessity to extend and overcome human limits that cannot be explained in terms of everyday existence and morality.[25] In his 'Nature and significance of play as a cultural phenomenon', Johan Huizinga writes that play is constitutive of a 'temporary' world that 'contains its own course and meaning' and stands 'outside the range of good and bad'. Yet the 'ethical value' lies in the 'tension', the ordeal: the inevitability of rules and the uncertainty of bodily performance bound to those rules. The 'play-world', Huizinga suggests has an element of 'secludedness', the game is 'played out within certain limits of time and place'. The elements of 'uncertainty' and 'chanciness' stand out and according to Huizinga are intrinsic to the 'test' that imparts 'ethical value' to play. Will the player be able to make something 'come off' or make it 'go'?[26] The player, Thomas Hurka notes, should be able to 'grasp an extended content, including all the pieces on the board or all the players on the ice or court, in a single act of consciousness'.[27] The continual adjustment of body to technique, the limited nature of time and space, mean that the central content of the sporting experience is never fixed and unchanging but always subject to newer battles and newer kinds of tension. Melancholia always seems to thrust itself on the sporting life. In what may be considered as one of the most remarkable biographies to come out in recent times, Ronald Reng's biography, *A Life Too Short*, of his friend Robert Enke (the German footballer who died tragically in 2009) is an evocative and affecting portrait of the footballer as a melancholic man playing the agonisingly shifting role of the goalkeeper.

The world of the goalkeeper, Reng suggests, is particularly pitiless: a heroic save fades away behind a goal let in, and failure is an ever-present possibility. When Robert Enke was a teenager, he was already a star footballer, and was portrayed by German magazines as the one likely to become the footballer of his generation, certainly Germany's future goalkeeper. In an interview that Enke gave at that time to a magazine after a very successful performance in the German National youth team, he puzzlingly said that he did not often think about the world but he had the 'feeling the Apocalypse is coming soon.'[28] What Enke verbalised here was the shadow of loss and emptiness that slowly took root in his heart, and that perhaps lurks at the heart of all sporting experience: one failure and Enke thought it could be all over for him, the 'pure joy' of a spectacular save that he experienced on the field but that felt 'pointless' soon after, the moment instantly slipping away into memory, into an inescapable void. On a bus journey to a match during his stint with Barcelona, Robert felt that whatever happened he 'could only lose.'[29] The key mood of our relationship to the world, Heidegger writes, is anxiety, and fear is a particular aspect of that relationship. The world confronts us with the threat and the fear of losing—through the actions we may or may not perform—what one already possesses.[30] When anxiety began to take hold of Enke, he had to battle the feeling that he would become 'invisible' to others in some way, and paradoxically, at the same time, he had to battle the desire not to play.[31] Goalkeeping became a metaphor that Enke lived out and that explained Enke's struggle and fight to hold off this world of anxiety and fears.

When Enke went into therapy, he was diagnosed with a 'deep melancholy of a kind many people experienced after bereavement, after being fired from a job, or after being bullied.'[32] In his classic essay, 'Mourning and Melancholia', Freud suggests that melancholia is not just a 'reaction to the loss of a loved object', but it 'is a loss of a more ideal kind'. In many cases the melancholic may not know what he has lost, something undefined or even possibly imagined. This suggests according to Freud that 'melancholia is related in some way to object-loss which is withdrawn from consciousness in contradistinction to mourning in which there is nothing about the loss that is unconscious.'[33] We may turn here to Haruki Murakami's *What I Talk About When I Talk About Running* in order to be able to understand Enke's battles, the larger truths that confront and define a sportsperson. At the end of running an immensely difficult ultra marathon in Japan, Murakami felt as if he had lost interest in running: he felt he had lost something, like the loss one feels when the initial crazy feeling of falling in love disappears. He felt that something had left him.[34] The end of a race, Murakami writes, does not promise meaning but rather its opposite, the absence of meaning. He writes that he continues his pursuit of running, pushing his body, 'lugging' it around like an 'old suitcase most likely headed toward another anti-climax' and moving toward a 'taciturn unadorned maturity, an evolving dead end.'[35] But Murakami is not a professional footballer like Robert Enke. Running made him into a writer, an activity that offered freedom and solitude. Football never gave Robert Enke any sense of freedom but instead intensified in him a sense of tragic lack. It absorbed him in a way that made his life unbearable to him: feelings of dejection and inadequacy consumed him and made him incapable of playing football. Freud writes that 'in mourning the world becomes poor and empty' but in melancholia it is the ego which feels 'empty' and 'impoverished'. Enke was polite, sensitive and generous to a fault but he put himself through severe self-criticism, guilt and on occasion a delusion of punishment. Freud suggests that the self-reproach and guilt of a melancholic man is an effect of the withdrawal into the ego (via identification with the lost object) of feelings of anger and hatred felt against the external world. Thus 'object-loss' is transformed and experienced as an 'ego-loss': a 'shadow' falls, overwhelming the ego and grounding suicidal impulses.[36]

Robert Enke's biographer Ronald Reng writes that Enke was a 'goalkeeper's goalkeeper', one who was revered by his fellow footballers but who never attained mass popularity.[37] Enke had a classical, restrained style, no unnecessary spectacular moves or dramatics, and he was alone in this regard among his contemporaries, many of them preferring a more flamboyant style. In the month of May, 2008, Robert Enke was selected along with Jens Lehmann as the goalkeeper of the German team for the European championship. During the World

Cup qualifiers in the same year when he was the number one German goalkeeper Robert developed a wrist injury and had to opt out. The press was quick to announce the more flamboyant and crowd-pleasing René Adler as the new number one goalkeeper. Enke felt he was treated unfairly: the sense of unfairness, Freud writes attaches itself easily to the melancholic's sense of inadequacy.[38] The demons swarmed in. This time Enke could not hold them back and on 10 November 2009 he stepped in front of a passing train. Enke was thirty-one years old.

The heart of a sportsperson (especially in the case of a deeply sensitive footballer like Robert Enke) is in some sense unknowable. Murakami writes in his memoir that only runners know what other runners go through. 'There are, Murakami notes, things that only runners understand and share'.[39] Robert Enke wrote a series of poems that he referred to as 'dwarf' poems. He loved the image of the dwarf because he thought he was a dwarf: the irony, the darker symbolism is apparent. Here are a few lines:

Your heart is something you can't define
It's easier to find a mountain to climb
Now climbing a mountain's a hard thing to do
When that tiny dwarf down at the bottom is you.[40]

The Lure and the Despair

The pursuit of sport, if we follow Bernard Suits's definition, comes from the impulse or the drive to measure oneself against an obstacle. In his moving memoir *The Lure Of Long Distances*, long-distance runner Robin Harvie describes the nature of this pursuit, in this case long-distance running, as the denial of the longing to 'return'. It means submitting to the pull of a world revealed only in motion: its end 'out there' and unknown at the outer limits of human experience.[41] Running, writes Harvie is a kind of 'suffering' that offers the possibility of 'experiencing the expansive nature of human sentience, the felt-fact of aliveness'.[42] In *Modernity and Subjectivity: Body, Soul, Spirit*, Harvie Ferguson suggests that this freedom and abandonment co-exists with willed repetition of pain to the body that in its extremity manifests a death drive (Thanatos).[43] Toby Miller in *Sportsex* suggests that the spectacle (in the context of professional sport) does not generate freedom but rather instantiates new forms of enslavement tied to practices of commodification and capitalist marketing. The spectacle also generates conflicts that get played out in far more insidious ways in women's sport. Miller picks up the example of women gymnasts: the expressive demands of their sport are tied up with 'body shapes and practices' that are 'occasioned by norms of femininity', subjecting them to body disorders and illnesses.[44]

The runner seeks an intense vision but it is lived out at the limits of human capacity; it is what can only be experienced on the 'edge of our own extinction'.[45] There is a fundamental otherness to the pain of the long-distance runner that cannot be understood and explained through language. Robin Harvie writes that to 'listen to the ultra distance runners' after they return 'requires an acknowledgment that there is a radical subjectivity to their suffering, which language alone cannot communicate'.[46]

Self-imposed as it may be, the playing body's desire and determination to discover its skills in a temporary and limited world grounds an existential striving, anchoring it in a process of self-creation and self-destruction. The playing body lives out a world poised between striving and non-striving, regimentation and destruction, contingency and loss.

Many of the themes discussed above, the obsession, the punishing self-regimen, the precariousness, the melancholy, structure an existential conundrum that the tennis player Andre Agassi movingly describes in his autobiography *Open*. The playing body, Agassi suggests is subject to a negotiation between the force of the spectacle and the erosion, even the destruction of the body, between the desire to overcome the body and the drive to repossess it. I end with a few lines from Agassi's autobiography:

> The finish line at the end of a career is no different from the finish line at the end of a match. The objective is to get within reach of that finish line, because then it gives off a magnetic force. When you're close, you can feel that force pulling you and you can use that force to get across. But just before you come within range, or just after, you feel another force, equally strong, pushing you away. It's inexplicable, mystical, these twin forces, these contradictory energies, but they both exist. I know because I've spent much of my life seeking the

one, fighting the other, and sometimes I've been stuck, suspended, bounced like a tennis ball between the two.

Please let this be over
I don't want it to be over[47]

Notes

1. Neville Cardus, *Cardus on Cricket*, repr. ed. (Delhi: Rupa&Co, 2008), pp. 136–38.
2. Amol Rajan, *Twirlymen: The Unlikely History of Cricket's Greatest Spin Bowlers* (London: Yellow Jersey Press, 2011), p. 23.
3. Amol Rajan's *Twirlymen* provides a fascinating account of the early history of spin that coincides with and underpins cricket's modernity.
4. See Amol Rajan, *Twirlymen: The Unlikely History of Cricket's Greatest Spin Bowlers* (London: Yellow Jersey Press, 2011), p. 69.
5. Ibid., p. 99.
6. Ramachandra Guha, *A Corner of a Foreign Field: The Indian History of a British Sport* (London: Picador, 2002), p. 93.
7. See Vaneisa Baksh, 'Sonny Ramadhin', *ESPN cricinfo*, http://www.espncricinfo/westindies/content/player/52804.html (accessed on July 3, 2012).
8. John Arlott, 'Ramadhin and Valentine-little friends of mine', *ESPN cricinfo*, January 1990, http://www.espncricinfo.com/ci/content/story/140863.html (accessed July 3, 2012).
9. Marcel Mauss, 'Techniques of the Body', in *Techniques, Technology and Civilisation*, ed. Nathan Schlanger (New York: Berghahn/Durkheim Press, 2006), pp. 77–93.
10. The discussion here on Pierre Bourdieu's engagement with sporting practices is based on Alan Tomlinson, 'Pierre Bourdieu and the Sociological Study of Sport: Habitus, Capital and Field', in *Sport and Modern Social Theorists*, ed. Richard Giulianotti (New York: Palgrave Macmillan, 2004), pp. 162–66.
11. C. L. R. James, 'Garfield Sobers', in *Cricket: The Great All-Rounders*, ed. John Arlott (London: Pelham Books, 1969), p. 169.
12. C. L. R. James, *Beyond A Boundary* (London: Yellow Jersey Press, 2005), pp. 4–8.
13. For an insightful account on the relationship between 'play' and 'resistance' in the context of West Indian culture, see Richard D. E. Burton, 'Cricket, Carnival and Street Culture in the Caribbean', in *Sport, Racism and Ethnicity*, ed. Grant Jarvie (London: The Falmer Press, 1991, Taylor & Francis e-book, 2005, chap. 1). Burton examines the relationship between 'play' and 'resistance' through a complex account of the interrelationship between

cricket, carnival and the street. Burton makes an interesting reference here to the argument made by the Jamaican writer Orlando Patterson that the West Indian attitude to cricket is 'a deeply ambivalent one in which love and hate co-exist, but in which, contrary to appearances, it is actually the hate element that predominates'.

14. The Doosra is an object of many competing claims. Credited to Saqlain Mushtaq, the Australian Jack Potter is said to have bowled it in the 1964 Ashes series against England. Amol Rajan, in his book *Twirlymen,* debunks the myth that any of these new deliveries could be attributed to any single player given that they were always deployed before or had become dormant only to be restored or rediscovered through familiar processes of creative reinvention. For further discussion on the question of mystery bowling—see Gideon Haigh, 'International men of mystery', *ESPN cricinfo,* April 28, 2008, http://www.espncricinfo.com/magazine/content/story/347392.html (accessed July 3, 2012). In his piece, Haigh argues that 'mystery bowling is classically an individual pursuit, the result of lone experiment and lateral thought'. The Australian Jack Iverson leads this group of unusual spinners and like him his contemporary Sonny Ramadhin, the Australian John Gleeson, and India's Bhagwat Chandrasekhar were all self-taught. It is instructive to note here that the question of mystery and imaginative improvisation associated with spin calls into question the experience of disability and deformity. Spin as a practice is not only compatible with deformity but the presence and experience of disability has been the reason for much originality in spin's body cultures. Chandra and Muralitharan are best examples of startling skills enabled by their bodily disabilities. It has been suggested that Sydney Barnes too had a deformity in his wrist that enabled him to send out such unusual deliveries.
15. After the win at Lord's on June 29, 1950 the *Times* reported (post-match report) that the West Indians ran into the field armed with 'guitar-like instruments'. Among them was Lord Kitchener who composed this now well-known calypso. For an account of this match, see Martin Williamson, 'Those two little pals of mine', *ESPN cricinfo,* June 24, 2006, http://www.espncricinfo.com/magazine/content/story/251196.html (accessed July 3, 2012).
16. It is important to note here that Sobers though perceived as the embodiment of West Indian political culture always preferred to delink his engagement with sport from West Indian political life unlike for example Viv Richards.
17. Trevor Bailey, 'Those two little tormentors of mine', *ESPN cricinfo,* August 21, 2008, http://www.espncricinfo.com/magazine/content/content/story/365667.html (accessed July 3, 2012).
18. Amol Rajan, *Twirlymen: The Unlikely History of Cricket's Greatest Spin Bowlers* (London: Yellow Jersey Press, 2011), pp. 53–6.

19. See Suresh Menon, 'The Loneliness of the long-distance cricketer', *ESPN cricinfo*, February 24, 2008, http://www.espn.cricinfo.com/magazine/content/story/337858.html (accessed July 3, 2012).
20. Ajantha Mendis perfected the carom ball releasing it by flicking the ball between the thumb and the bent middle finger in the same fashion as Jack Iverson and John Gleeson (the famous Iverson-Gleeson grip).
21. Robert Winder, 'A Dying game. Why would a cricketer commit suicide?', *NewStatesman*, 19 June, 2000, http://www.newstatesman.com/node/137938 (accessed July 3, 2012).
22. Neville Cardus, *Cardus on Cricket*, repr. ed. (Delhi: Rupa & Co, 2008), p. 66.
23. Bernard Suits, 'Construction of a definition', in *The Ethics of Sports: A Reader*, ed. Mike McNamee (London: Routledge, 2010), pp. 26–8.
24. Thomas Hurka, 'Games and the good—I', in *The Ethics of Sports: A Reader*, ed. Mike McNamee (London: Routledge, 2010), pp. 54–7.
25. It is in this context that J. S. Russell argues that 'play in general', especially dangerous and risky sports, implies a 'suspension of the ordinary' and we cannot evaluate it by using 'considerations found in everyday morality'—see J. S. Russell, 'The value of dangerous sport', in *The Ethics of Sports: A Reader*, ed. Mike McNamee (London: Routledge, 2010), p. 453.
26. Johan Huizinga, 'Nature and significance of play as a cultural phenomenon', in *The Ethics of Sports: A Reader*, ed. Mike McNamee (London: Routledge, 2010), pp. 31–32.
27. Thomas Hurka 'Games and the Good—I', in *The Ethics of* Sports: *A Reader*, ed. Mike McNamee (London: Routledge, 2010), p. 56.
28. Ronald Reng, *A Life Too Short: The Tragedy of Robert Enke*, trans. Shaun Whiteside (London: Yellow Jersey Press, 2011), p. 19.
29. Ibid., pp. 137–161.
30. The discussion here is based on Paul Gilbert and Kathleen Lennon, *The World, the Flesh and the Subject: Continental Themes in Philosophy of Mind and Body* (Edinburgh: Edinburgh University Press, 2005), p. 102.
31. Ronald Reng, *A Life Too Short: The Tragedy of Robert Enke*, trans. Shaun Whiteside (London: Yellow Jersey Press, 2011), p. 36.
32. Ibid., p. 154.
33. Sigmund Freud, 'Mourning and Melancholia', in *Essential Papers on Object Loss*, ed. Rita V. Frankiel (New York: New York University Press, 1994), p. 40.
34. Haruki Murakami, *What I Talk About When I Talk About Running: A Memoir*, trans. Philip Gabriel (London: Vintage, 2009), p. 117.
35. Ibid., p. 151.
36. Sigmund Freud, 'Mourning and Melancholia', in *Essential Papers on Object Loss*, ed. Rita V. Frankiel (New York: New York University Press, 1994), pp. 43–6.

37. Ronald Reng, *A Life Too Short: The Tragedy of Robert Enke*, trans. Shaun Whiteside (London: Yellow Jersey Press, 2011), p. 301.
38. Sigmund Freud, 'Mourning and Melancholia', in *Essential Papers on Object Loss*, ed. Rita V. Frankiel (New York: New York University Press, 1994), p. 43.
39. Haruki Murakami, *What I Talk About When I Talk About Running: A Memoir*, trans. Philip Gabriel (London: Vintage, 2009), p. 75.
40. Ronald Reng, *A Life Too Short: The Tragedy of Robert Enke*, trans. Shaun Whiteside (London: Yellow Jersey Press, 2011), p. 207.
41. Robin Harvie, *The Lure of Long Distances: Why We Run* (New York: PublicAffairs, 2011), p. 29.
42. Ibid., p. 63.
43. For further discussion on this aspect see Harvie Ferguson, *Modernity and Subjectivity: Body, Soul, Spirit* (Charlottesville & London: University Press of Virginia, 2000), p. 74.
44. Toby Miller, *Sportsex* (Philadelphia: Temple University Press, 2001), pp. 4–26. Chris Shilling too argues that the expressive body is subject to a rationalized sporting world making it vulnerable to many forces such as the constant demands of performance and the use of drugs. For further discussion on this aspect see Chris Shilling, *The Body in Culture, Technology and Society* (London: Sage Publications, 2005), pp. 101–06.
45. Robin Harvie, *The Lure Of Long Distances: Why We Run* (New York: PublicAffairs, 2011), p. 64.
46. Ibid., pp. 66–7.
47. Andre Agassi, *Open: An Autobiography* (London: HarperCollins, 2009), pp. 7–9.

10

Refugee City: Football and Other Divides of the Self in Post-Partition Kolkata

Debjani Sengupta

This essay looks at a particular moment in the history of football in Kolkata, during the heyday of the league matches between two city clubs, Mohun Bagan and East Bengal, to show how the game, introduced by the British in the late nineteenth century, became a site for the expression of local conflicts between regional and class adversaries. This in turn generated films and literature based on the language of sport in post-Partition Kolkata.

Football in Colonial Calcutta

The undivided province of Bengal had been the centre of Indian football since the British established the IFA in its capital Calcutta in 1893. Football, like cricket, was an important aspect of the colonial project and it was actively introduced in the missionary run schools and colleges of the city that helped to create a band of young Indians who would be loyal and lively aides of empire. The game was encouraged among British and Indian soldiers by their officers to promote fitness and discipline, and further, this resurgence of physical education and sporting activities under the British was an active intervention by the colonialists to shape the 'effete' Bengali.[1] Western sports became popular among the Bengali elite from 1880s onwards and many Bengali intellectuals and educationists like Raj Narayan Basu (1826–99) and Gurusaday Datta (1882–1941) wrote about the Bengali self-image that needed to emulate the masculinity and vigour of the English. Datta's Bratachari, a Scouts like movement amongst the youth of Bengal in the nineteen thirties, sought to question and remedy the stereotype of the feminised Bengali that the British propagated.[2] Early writers, including the novelist Bankim Chandra Chattopadhyay (1838–94) and the religious leader Vivekananda (1863–1902), sought to revive and regenerate the Bengali people by awakening them through sporting and other physical activities. British inspiration and support were often forthcoming and the introduction of cricket and football was met with enthusiasm amongst the Bengali upper class bhadralok. As Partha Chatterjee notes, 'The 'games ethic', in other words, was appropriated by the Bengali middle class and turned into an instrument for matching up to the power of the British,' and the humiliation and emasculation in politics and economy were to be reversed on the sports field.[3]

Football, early in its history, came to be embedded in the paradoxes of nationalism and colonialism both as imitation and resistance and was a fraught terrain where questions of class and race were intimately bound up with the Indian resistance to 'ideologies of empire'.[4] Football gained popularity as nationalist feelings began to develop and harden and the game was seen by many Bengalis as an opportunity to beat the masters in a sport they had introduced to the colonised.[5] Mohun Bagan's famous victory over a British team in the IFA Shield in 1911 was a case in point. That unexpected triumph was given a range of political and national undertones by the local press and venerated for decades to come. In the Calcutta of the nineteen thirties and forties, even football could not remain untouched by the playing out of institutional and popular communalisms. From being a contestation of colonial power, the status of football changed to reflect the growing communal tension between the Hindu majority and Muslim minority in Bengal.[6] This transition from 'community to communal' had several shifts and points of convergence with other issues of economic and political change too, especially with the increasing divisive politics that the British advocated through separate electorates. Social and religious identities were invested in the Mohammedan Sporting Club's successes (supported by many Muslims of the city and seen as a marker of Muslim resurgence) throughout the nineteen thirties and, even when the British left India, football continued to express the fissures inherent in Bengali society especially during the post-Partition years when thousands of Hindus migrants crowded the city and gave another dimension to the communal conflicts that had earlier pervaded the game. The contours of the game changed with a sharpening of the rivalry between the two Calcutta clubs, Mohun Bagan and East Bengal, that had been growing since the latter was established in 1920 and run by East Bengalis to 'ameliorate their sporting grievances born out of continuous discrimination waged against them by Calcutta's Bengali clubs'.[7] At the turn of the century, football had spread from the metropolitan centres to other districts of North and East Bengal. East Bengal was home to a great number of notable players who often came to Calcutta to play in the city clubs. Gostho Paul, the legendary Mohun Bagan defender came from Faridpur district in East Bengal while eight out of the eleven players of the victorious Mohun Bagan team in 1911 came originally from the eastern part as well. On the eve of the Partition of India in 1947, simmering social tensions off the pitch influenced and found expression in the hostility and mob violence that surrounded important matches supported by rival groups. East Bengal's League triumph of 1946 witnessed rampant hooliganism with supporters ransacking the Mohun Bagan tent after the match.[8] This bitter and fanatical rivalry between the supporters of the two clubs reached new heights after Partition, especially during the years 1949 and 1953, when the East Bengal club, led by its 'Five Pandavas' playing in the forward line, achieved spectacular successes at all national level tournaments, winning the IFA Shield thrice.[9] A virulent form of sub-regionalism replaced nationalism as a fundamental principle of football in nineteen fifties Calcutta.[10]

The First City, the First Railway Platform

In the nineteen fifties, Calcutta also mutated from being the first city to becoming a refugee city. The journey of the East Bengali Hindu refugee, culturally and psychologically, was a one-way journey. The refugees came to stay. According to later Calcutta Municipal Development Authority (CMDA) statistics, in 1961 the refugee migrants to the city comprised 18% of the total population of a city of 29.27 lakhs and the conservative estimate was that 'since 1947, a total of about 7,00,000 refugees were counted to have entered the city'.[11] The public space of Sealdah station, where the waves of refugees arrived from East Bengal, became for many the first space where they could rest their weary heads. The influx of refugees in huge numbers, crowding the city pavements and the railway platforms, created an unprecedented social and economic problem for the state, already under the trauma of the 1943 famine and the devastating fallout of the Second World War. A reporter from *Amrita Bazar Patrika* described the suffering and degradation of those thousands of people who made the railway platforms their homes:

On Thursday I spent a few hours amongst the refugees in Sealdah station. The refugees have come by train to Sealdah. As long as they are not sent elsewhere, they will continue to live here. As soon as they arrive they will stand in a queue to be inoculated against cholera and other diseases. Then, along with all family members, they will have to stand in front of the office of the relief and rehabilitation department where they will be given a certificate stating they are eligible for shelter in relief camps. When all this is over, only then will they spread whatever bedding they have on the South platform and wait for transportation to the camps. Someone has divided up a portion of the platform by a rope. Until they get a place in the relief camps, the refugees consider this roped area as their homes. Can you imagine how, within this barely manageable space, five to six thousand people were packed, spending their days with their sons, daughters and wives! The drinking water for so many people came from three taps; women have two lavatories while the men have twelve.... How were these unfortunate people spending their days on the platform? Imagine young girls bathing in front of hundred commuters in open spaces, people sleeping under the sky a few feet away from overflowing lavatories, cooking their meals in roadside ovens made with three bricks and lit by the refuse collected from streets.[12]

Prafullakumar Chakraborty in his book *Prantik Manob* (The Marginal Men) wrote about those early days: 'The refugees in Sealdah station had come away leaving behind all to live here with self-respect. They could never guess what death in life awaited them in West Bengal. They got their first poisonous taste at the Sealdah station... What did this merciless city give them? The stone and brick city stared at them with deep contempt. I doubt if the thousands of commuters who came to Kolkata everyday ever glanced at these ragged dirty human faces... Who were they? Were they really human? The cloak of civilisation has fallen from the dirty, pale, shameless bodies and the minds of these refugees'.[13] How long did this condition last? What happened to those who came to West Bengal in the early years after the Partition before the government rehabilitation processes sluggishly commenced in the 1950s? It is well documented that the new government of West Bengal did its utmost to discourage migration and its lack of sympathy towards the refugees was one of the many charges brought against the Bidhan Chandra Roy-led Congress government. Throughout the years immediately after the Partition, newspapers were full of pictures and accounts of the overcrowded unsanitary conditions of the refugee transit and permanent camps with unforgivable delays in dispersal of relief materials.

Over a period of time, the migrants began to rehabilitate themselves by forcibly occupying abandoned, marshy lands and built squatter colonies in and around the city and its suburbs. In the years after 1950, their numbers began to swell with fresh incidents of communal tensions in East Pakistan. Deserters from the refugee camps outside West Bengal joined their ranks and by 1955, squatter colonies were mushrooming in and around Kolkata at a tremendous pace. Besides railway tracks, in marshy lands, in abandoned World War II army barracks, the refugees came and settled down, driven by a strong desire to get a foothold in the city. The colonies consisted of shacks and shanties and were grossly lacking in civic services, even though they were always named after great nationalists leaders like Netaji Subhash Chandra Bose or Mahatma Gandhi or Deshbandhu Chittaranjan Das. The refugees extended the city's limits and filled its slums. Commenting on this, sociologist Benoy Ghosh wrote in 1967, 'The New Suburbia has expanded in the last twenty-five or thirty years. The old boundaries of the city suburbs have expanded to accommodate wave after wave of population—abandoned land, fertile land, rice field, marshy lands, ponds, lakes, jungle and gardens all took in the rising tidal waves of population'.[14] Contemporary literature, films and plays seemed to grasp these new changes in the city much more sensitively than city planners so that 'the theme of an overall moral crisis generated by a violent uprooting and the compulsions of survival appeared often in contemporary literature'.[15]

The Green Passport

In 1967, the poet Tarapada Roy writes of his first arrival as a refugee in the city, a city that is evoked in the poem, 'That Green Passport', full of the alienation of a country bumpkin bewildered by the glittering metropolis. For the East Bengali exile, Kolkata, in the poem, remains forever a mystery, but one where, not accidentally, the hope and aspiration of the refugee can only be expressed through a haunting football image, of a penalty kick in which the football soaring through space is not just a winning goal but achieving the 'moon'. The poem indirectly voices the way in which the game, played especially by a club that carried the name of the lost homeland, became a source of hope and avowal of the refugee's identity:

That Green Passport

Do you remember, Kolkata
That green passport, my dark green shirt;
Arriving, drenched, at Sealdah Main
That day on the train from the border
I saw a shoeshine boy for the first time in my life.

It was a thrill, my dream city,
My first tram-car, my earliest first-class,
First class Kolkata,
Where pet clouds hover over every roof.
Within every window
A mystery of darkness and light.
My green shirt, my ragged shoes,
Fear in every step.
Madmen with beggars, beggars with drunks,
Processions, rainbow hued, stretching
Right up to the horizon,
The crowded teashops, the futile mob on the road.
On windy afternoons dry leaves scatter,
In the sunlight, tram tracks glisten
Pale as ivory,
Reaching nowhere.
Sometimes I feel,
I am no longer within your limits,
Nowhere can I find that city of mine

Where, between two lamp-posts, in a long penalty kick
Someone sends the football moon to space
While shadowy figures in the gallery yell,' Goal, goal.'

These twenty years,
I have found nothing in common with you, Kolkata.
My torn dreams, my ragged pieces of poetry
In dirty paper bags the tramps
Have collected them all.
Those dream-words
Have been sold like rubbish.
Not a single mystery window opened anywhere
Nowhere could I reach the clouds on the roofs.
Only the colour of my shirt,
My shoe size changed,
Needlessly.[16]

'Ghoti-Bangal' and Other Divides of the Self

Partition, then, provides the context for an invisible divide that goes deep into the psyche of the city of Kolkata even today. Yet the divide itself predates the historical event of the Partition of India in 1947, and may be traced to a set of earlier social and linguistic distinctions between *ghoti* and *bangal,* between people from the west and east Bengal. In undivided Bengal, before Partition, Calcutta had offered education and jobs for the middle classes from east Bengal. Educational institutions like the Hindu College, Ripon College, Presidency College, Scottish Church College were filled with students from the East while the merchant and trading houses, the government departments, had many workers who came from east Bengal. Every year they travelled back home, crossing the Padma, waking up the sleepy villages with tales of the many-coloured city. In return they carried back to the city their language, the nostalgia for their land, the smell of their rivers Buriganga, Dhaleshwari, Padma, Meghna, the tug and pull of memories. Living in cramped *mess-bari* or shared lodgings, they dreamt of making it big in the city.[17] Even though they lived and worked in Calcutta, it was never home; in their minds there always existed a division of culture, of landscapes, of food and flora and fauna. Calcutta, claustrophobic in its interiors, such as the lodging-houses, the rented rooms, the restaurants, the cinema halls, was a place of isolation. Placed against this were what the community had left behind: the green vistas of riverine East Bengal, the village *puja mandap*, the laughter and the togetherness of family and friends.

After the Partition, when it was increasingly clear to the East Bengalis that they would never return, that distant taste of a lost landscape fuelled the passion and the strength to negotiate the city, to make it home and to re-create in imaginative ways their abandoned villages. The reason east Bengalis felt alien in the city was certainly strengthened by the *ghoti-bangal* divide that existed as an invisible but strong line of separation in Calcutta. Dipesh Chakraborty writes of his adolescence in Kolkata: 'We had not heard about academic critiques of essentialism in those days, so *bangals* and *ghotis* proceeded to elaborate and ritualise their differences with the enthusiasm of peoples whom anthropologists sometimes call *warring tribes*. We both spoke Bengali, but with different accents; we loved the *hilsa* fish, while they loved prawns; our songs were set to different tunes; our traditions of courtesy were different; and every act of intermarriage was noticed and commented upon.'[18] The *ghotis* lived in the older part of Kolkata, the north, while the *bangals*, especially after the Partition, made south Kolkata their home. Although the East Bengali gentleman or *bhadralok* class had made Kolkata its second home, the *ghoti-bangal* divide was palpable and quite open. This divide became even more prominent after the Partition of India in 1947, with the influx of thousands into the city. Historian Tapan Raychaudhuri, in his autobiography *Bangalnama*, remembered how he was ridiculed in Ballygunj Boys School as a *bangal* from the country who couldn't speak English.[19] The figure of the *bangal* had always been a butt of jokes as early as the *Chaitanyacharitamrita* (1612) where we find witticisms about the inhabitants of East Bengal. In the Kolkata of the nineteen-fifties and -sixties, the rivalry went up several notches of the barometer on the days of League or Shield soccer matches. East Bengalis supported their club of that name (founded on 1 August 1920) while *ghotis* supported Mohun Bagan (founded on 15 August 1889). Even if one did not follow football, one knew which team had won by the market price of fish that day. East Bengal's icon was the *hilsa* while the Mohun Bagan supporters relished prawns. I remember many feasts of *hilsa* from my childhood that my East Bengal-supporter father organised when his club won crucial matches. Even as a child, I had little need of sociology to understand the blatantly parochial attitudes of the respective football club fans that simultaneously bound and divided my refugee city.

Football: A Stratagem of Social Safety

Given the hostility and resentment against the *bangals*, the question that remains is, why did the city of Kolkata, when hundreds and thousands of refugees invaded it, accept the newcomers? Why were there no violent flare-ups in the nature of riots between the older inhabitants and the newcomers? In what ways did the city accommodate and accept this influx of population? In what ways did the newcomers negotiate the city that was largely alien? The answer is probably very simple: through comedy and through football.

Dipesh Chakraborty theorises that the *ghoti* and *bangal* rivalry was an example of 'proximity', where physical contiguity throws up difference: a situation 'in which difference is neither reified nor erased but negotiated'.[20] This notion of proximity is opposite to 'identity' which is a mode of relating to difference in which difference is either concealed or congealed and claims of being identical are foregrounded. I see the *ghoti-bangal* rivalry, especially where football is concerned, as a means by which larger, more public crises were averted and nullified. In the Calcutta of the nineteen-fifties, football had a unique place, which was to a large extent associated with regional identity. Manna Dey's popular song, '*Shob khelar sera Bangalir ei football*' (Bengali's football is the best game of all the games) talks of the game as belonging to all Bengalis, but this homogenising aspect of football was a myth. On the football grounds passions ran high with small and large-scale incidents of violence breaking out repeatedly whenever important matches took place. In 1948, for example, the IFA Shield final between East Bengal and Mohun Bagan had to be abandoned on the first occasion due to spectator violence. Sports writers often lamented that the unseemly behaviour of the fans marred the 'sacred' ground of the football field.[21] It may be conjectured that these acts of shouting and stone throwing in the Maidan offered a relatively safe and non-politicised means of releasing the mutual bitterness and distrust between *bangals* and *ghotis*. Like warring tribes they fought their battles in the rituals of the football fields and not in Kolkata's alleys. The madness over and enthusiasm for football is clearly indicated in the following extract from the sports pages of *Desh*, 21 May 1955: 'Every year, on the Maidan, the arguments, researches, rumours, excitements and enthusiasms eddying around football are countless. The question of whether their favourite team will win is endlessly discussed in the field, outside it and inside homes. Mohun Bagan and East Bengal supporters, mostly young colleagues in workplaces, begin with juicy arguments that often end in laughter...actually it is very apparent that in the five months of the football season, this game creates a huge upheaval in the minds and hearts of Calcutta's citizens that few other games can match.'[22] In the city's history the anguish of dispossession has only on rare occasions been translated into open aggression. Identity politics may thus seem to have been less important than the human interactions between the two groups.

The truth of this is also borne out by the films of that era. The *ghoti-bangal* divide and its associations with football is captured very evocatively in a film *Ora Thakey Odhare* (They Live On that Side, 1954, directed by Sukumar Dasgupta) based on a story by Premendra Mitra and featuring famous actors like Chhobi Biswas, Molina Debi, Uttam Kumar and Suchitra Sen. The film revolves around two families, one *bangal* and the other *ghoti*. They are neighbours and often resort to bickerings and fights, trading insults about each other's cultural characteristics. On the day of a football match between Mohun Bagan and East Bengal a quarrel erupts. 'Why drag a quarrel of the football field inside the home?' asks a lady of the house, but to no avail. This hostility ensures that a romance between a grown up son and a daughter belonging to each of the two families is nipped in the bud. The film however had a strong message for the times. In the face of adversity, when the head of the *ghoti* family Harimohunbabu loses his job, his *bangal* neighbour comes to his rescue. In the last scene, the families are united and they agree that 'we are two hands, sometimes raised in fists and sometimes brought together in a clap.'

As in the film, the *ghoti-bangal* resentments were sorted out on the football field, in cinema halls, in theatre, and in other cultural fields. The culture industry after the Partition fed on the rich source of oppositions arising from this divide and films often had caricatures of the countrified *bangal,* a butt of well meaning jokes. Acceptance of the *bangals,* the refugees was partly effected through the medium of laughter. In hit films, of the times like *Sharey Chuattar* (Seventy Four and Half), *Bhanu Pelo Lottery* (Bhanu wins a Lottery) and *Bhanu Goyenda and Jahar Assistant* (Bhanu the Detective and Jahar his Assistant), the noted artists Bhanu Banerjee, a *bangal,* and Jahar Roy, a *ghoti,* formed a comic pair and became a box office success. Comedy and football were thus able to diffuse the tensions that in reality were often palpably felt in Kolkata's social fabric.

Parimal Goswami's 1948 short story called *Khelar Mathey* (On the Sports Field) is set on this premise of cultural accommodation that accompanied the refugee influx. The story was first published in the newspaper *Jugantar* and later collected in Goswami's volume of short stories titled *Marke Lengey* (We Shall Fight and Win).[23] It is a satirical take on the *ghoti-bangal* rivalry over football, but what is interesting is the way the writer extends the metaphor of play into the political and social discourses of a time when the city faced an unprecedented refugee crisis. The story, probably inspired by the media reports of mob violence on the IFA League's final match of 1946, begins with a description of the Maidan as a war zone where thousands are engaged in an uproar: fisticuffs and armed attacks are the order of the day. The irate fans calm down only after the arrival of the military police, a common enough occurrence on the Maidan. Footballing demands—related to the scarcity of good players—are extended to the larger issues of rehabilitation when the East Bengal supporters yell: 'We will not tolerate injustice. If we lack players in the team then the rest of the Hindus still in East Bengal will also take refuge in this city.'[24] In the ensuing melée, the players on both sides decide that they will no longer play, since to do so would endanger their lives. The fans are aghast at the decision and the narrator states that 'if the game is stopped then the whole city will turn into a war zone. The nation will collapse under misrule. This was the only way in which we forgot our sorrows and our tribulations. The sports field absorbed all the existential curses of our lives.'[25] The government became equally worried: 'Those who made the city hell with their want and poverty, what is to be done with them?'

The reason that the riots that took place on the sports field should not and cannot be stopped was: 'because the sports field was the safest place for a riot.' In Goswami's ironic narrative, 'the government is sure that the rioting inside the field must be contained within it so that they can sell tickets to people who can come to see a game of riots if they so wished; that would be the first instance of nationalisation of Sports Rioting'![26]

The semiotic transference of play into rioting is effortlessly produced, to gesture at the larger symbolic structures of power and dispossession that marked the *ghoti-bangal* relationship within the city space. Like Dipesh Chakraborty's warring tribes the two sides are forever engaged in bloodthirsty skirmishes on the playing field but Goswami's depiction of the East Bengali and the West Bengali is not based on the logic of 'proximity' alone. By using irony and satire, Goswami's portrayal of a game of football produces an effect of juxtapository transference: the vicious energy and planning of a riot is now projected into an imaginary arena where instead of the players, the spectators will engage in 'playing' out a riot. The story's larger trope of containing the energies of the warring tribes within the sports field is not lost on the reader. Goswami's ironic take on the rioting possibilities of a football game transform the seriousness of the encounter between the migrant and the original inhabitant of the city: through laughter he subverts the aggressive possibilities of a cultural confrontation to an enjoyable 'spectacle' of riot as a game. The story ends with a bacchanalian twist: a Mohun Bagan/East Bengal game erupts in 'warfare' but soon the rioting members realise that the players and the referee are encased in a strong steel cage, watching the spectators as *they* engage in a 'war' outside. The inversion of the players into the spectators and vice versa blurs the line that the spectacle of football imposes on its followers. This transposal points to the ominous ways in which Goswami's irony works: the parochial attitude of the fans is displaced onto the players as they too become tainted with a bloodthirsty desire 'to enjoy' a riot. Given the fact that Calcutta had seen the most sustained days of communal conflagration in August 1946, still fresh in public memory, the playing at riots underlies the fragile communal/sub-regional identities (that could so easily erupt into a blaze) that needed a cautioning buffer that only humour could provide.

Satire and Containment

As with much Bengali humour of his time, Goswami's satire also has a sharper edge. The venting of aggression on the football field, the use of organised sports as a means of containing potentially anarchic social energies, suggests a kind of banalisation of the real issues of dispossession, homelessness, poverty and unemployment. By bringing the government into his imagined scene of crisis, Goswami suggests that the *lumpen* proletariat refugee's obsession with football is deliberately encouraged by a state that cannot offer them other satisfactions: football, thus, becomes 'the opium of the people'.[27] While I have so far been arguing that the East Bengal-Mohun Bagan rivalry served a positive social end in that it reduced and absorbed the tensions and enmities that might otherwise have taken a more violent form, it is also possible to see a more negative side of this mechanism of control. To understand this, we should recall that there was a third major football club that also had a fanatic following, Mohammedan Sporting (founded in 1891).

Partha Chatterjee has argued that football, a mass-based sport which had the potential, especially after the historic victory of Mohun Bagan in 1911, to become a focus of national unity and patriotic sentiment, lost that potential largely because of the identity politics that divided its support base between *ghoti* and *bangal*, Hindu and Muslim.[28] In a sense, his argument is the reverse of mine. While I have suggested that football rivalries helped to contain regional and communal hostilities (it should be noted that while Hindus and Muslims were indeed ranged on opposite sides when Mohun Bagan or East Bengal played Mohammedan Sporting) Chatterjee suggests that the petty factionalism of the Maidan helped to divert and dissipate energies that could have been better utilised for political and nationalist purposes. In both readings, football is a vehicle of social control: viewed positively by some, negatively by others. We may recall that sport has always had this dual purpose: in the nineteenth century British public school it was used to contain the aggression of young boys, while Baron Pierre de Coubertin, founder of the modern Olympics, viewed sport as a means of inculcating friendship and peace between the European nations.

Goswami's double-edged satire in *Khelar Mathey* (The Playing Field) demonstrates how literature can both critique and illuminate the place of sport in society. For post-Partition Bengal, football was indeed a source of collective solace, a means whereby the anxieties and frustrations of everyday life could be worked out in a relatively safe environment. For the refugee migrant new to the city, the game helped to establish a link to his lost community and home, and further enabled him to situate himself in West Bengal's football loving *bhadralok* society. At the same time, it could be seen as a means whereby the suffering and anger of these same people were drawn out and contained in such a way that people were only 'playing at' riots. Given that there was indeed communal tension between Hindus and Muslims, and that riots were not unknown in the city, this 'safety valve' mechanism was not entirely safe. The football field was a violent place. Nevertheless, as Goswami's story shows, the violence of the playing fields in the Maidan was a form of social turbulence that authority might in fact encourage. It was better to riot at football than to riot in the streets. The story of football then becomes one of the many Partition narratives of modern India that show us the close relationship between literature, sports and politics.

Notes

The author acknowledges the help of the editors in honing the argument of this paper. A special thanks to Ashis Nandy whose work has deeply influenced mine.

1. John Rosselli, 'The Self-Image of Effeteness: Physical Education and Nationalism in Nineteenth Century Bengal,' *Past and Present,* no. 86 (1980): 121–2. See also Mrinalini Sinha, *Colonial Masculinity: The 'Manly Englishman' and the 'Effeminate Bengali' in the late 19th Century* (Manchester: Manchester University Press, 1995).
2. John Rosselli,'The Self-Image', pp. 140–1.
3. Partha Chatterjee,'Football and the Politics of Identity in Colonial Calcutta'. Keynote paper at the conference on 'Sport and the Nation', Jadavpur University, Kolkata, 19–20 January 2012. Reference supplied by Supriya Chaudhuri. The paper has been incorporated in Chatterjee's book, *The Black Hole of Empire: History of a Global Practice of Power* (Princeton: Princeton University Press, 2012).

4. Paul Dimeo, 'Football and Politics in Bengal: Colonialism, Nationalism, Communalism', in *Soccer in Asia: Empire, Nation, Diaspora*, eds Paul Dimeo and James Mills (London: Frank Cass, 2001), p. 71.
5. Gary Armstrong and Crispin Bates, 'Selves and Others: Reflection on Sports in South Asia,' *Contemporary South Asia*, 10, no. 2 (2001), 254. See also, *Sports in Asian Society*, eds J. Mangan and Fan Hong (London: Frank Cass, 2003), p. 12.
6. Kausik Bandyopadhyay, *Scoring off the Field: Football Culture in Bengal 1911–1980* (New Delhi: Routledge, 2011), pp. 108–9.
7. Ibid., p. 174.
8. James Mills, 'A Historiography of South Asian Sport,' in *Contemporary South Asia, 212*. Also Bandyopadhyay, *Scoring Off*, p. 175.
9. The five famous players were Vengkatesh, Apparao, Dhanraj, Ahmed Khan and Saleh who brought victory to the club by winning the League matches thrice in 1949, 1950 and 1952 and the IFA Shield in 1949, 1950 and 1951. They were called the Pandavas after the five brothers in the *Mahabharata*.
10. Soumen Mitra, 'Nationalism, Communalism and Sub-Regionalism: A Study of Football in Bengal 1880–1950', Unpublished M.Phil Thesis, Jawaharlal Nehru University, New Delhi, 1988.
11. Maitreyi B. Roy, *Calcutta Slums: Public Policy in Retrospect* (Kolkata: Minerva), p. 16.
12. Quoted in Prafullakumar Chakraborty, *Prantik Manob*, Translated by me (Kolkata: Protikkhon, 1997), pp. 18–9.
13. Chakraborty, *Prantik Manob*, p. 19.
14. Benoy Ghosh, 'Metropolitan Mon', *Metropolitan Mon O Modhyobityo Bidroho* (The Metropolitan Mind and Middle-class Revolution), Translated by me (Calcutta: Orient Longman 1973), p. 67.
15. Moinak Biswas, 'The City and The Real: Chinnamul and the Left Cultural Movement in the 1940s' in *City Flicks: Indian Cinema and the Urban Experience*, ed. Preben Kaarsholm (Calcutta: Orient Longman, 2006), p. 53.
16. Tarapada Roy, 'Sei Shobuj Passport' (That Green Passport) in *The Oxford Anthology of Bengali Literature*, vol. 2 (Delhi: Oxford University Press, 2010), pp. 82–3.
17. See Bibhutibhushan Bandopadhyay's short story 'Sitanather Bari Phera' (Sitanath's Homecoming) in *Galpo Shomogro* (Collected Stories), vol. 2 (Kolkata: Mitra O Ghosh, 2002), p. 291.
18. Dipesh Chakraborty, 'The In-Human and the Ethical in Communal Violence', in *Habitations of Modernity: Essays in the wake of Subaltern Studies* (Delhi: Permanent Black, 2002), p. 139.
19. Tapan Raychaudhuri, *Bangalnama* (Kolkata: Ananda Publishers, 2009), p. 179.
20. Dipesh Chakraborty, 'The In-Human', p. 140.

21. Eklavya, 'Khelar Mathey' (On the Sports Field) in *Desh*, no. 31 (Kolkata: Ananda Bazar Publications), June, 1955, p. 628.
22. Eklavya, 'Khelar Mathey', in *Desh*, no. 29 (Kolkata: Ananda Bazar Publications), May 1955, p. 316.
23. Parimal Goswami, 'Khelar Mathey,' in *Maar ke Lengey* (We shall Fight and Win) (Kolkata: Bibhash Corner, 1950).
24. Goswami, *Khelar*, p. 238.
25. Goswami, *Khelar*, p. 240.
26. Goswami, *Khelar*, p. 242.
27. Karl Marx, *Introduction to A Contribution to the Critique of Hegel's Philosophy of Right*, 1843. Cited from e-text at http://www.marxists.org/archive/marx/works/1843/critique-hpr/intro.htm (accessed on June 2, 2012).
28. Partha Chatterjee, 'Football and the Politics of Identity in Colonial Calcutta'. Keynote paper at conference on 'Sport and the Nation', Jadavpur University, Kolkata, 19–20 January 2012.

11

The *Matter* that Matters—Re-thinking Corporeality in a Computer Game

Aratrika Das

On the one side the physiological and biological data, which present a 'simple' nature (no matter what their complexity may be) because they hold entirely within the field in which they appear...on the other side, the phenomena belonging to the interhuman milieu, which have the characteristic that they can never be taken as simple data or defined in the order of their own nature but must always be understood as double from the fact that they are connected to something else, whatever their "referent" may be.

—Benveniste, *Problems in General Linguistics*

What is real always pushes back... '[R]eality' *is* that which displays intractability and intransigence relative to our will.

—Benedikt, *Cyberspace: First Steps*

This essay is about a child playing games on a computer. The child shows where she is about to go in her computer game. The German soldiers, from whom she is trying to escape, are coming closer. And while she is trying to understand the situation, her hand touches the mouse very quickly and her eyes are looking at the screen. 'Achtung', says the German soldier. The child's game avatar is now standing and the two military tanks are driving on the screen. When the fight starts, she is jumping back and forth and is shooting the German soldiers with the mouse. The activity ends with a 'yes—I made it', and she is about to go to the next 'level'.

This is just one of many examples of this climate of biotechnologies, virtual worlds and digital manipulation where the relationship between the organism and the machine emerges. It is a relationship that contests organic bodily boundaries, the locus of identity and the status of the human. Clear distinctions between what is real and what is virtual, where the body ends and technology begins, what is nature and what is machine, fracture and implode. The story of how I came to undertake this research, then, stems from an ongoing fascination with how the relationship between human and technology has been disrupted. This essay is not a linear critical analysis but an ongoing investigation of conditions of possibility for understanding the embeddedness and entanglement of the 'human' in this climate of biotechnology. First I will map the new form of corporeality that emerges within a seamless articulation of software, hardware, flesh, machine, mind and computers and the critical inquiries this has lead to. Second, I will attempt to negotiate the terms in which one may imagine alternative modalities for locating the materiality of a body playing a computer game.

A Seamless Flow: Body-to-Interface-to-Critical Analysis

My urgent need to inquire into the materiality of the playing body comes from the answers that my questions have occasioned. For example, to the question—where is the body of the child located while playing—the answer is often 'Of course the body is here where she is playing'. The sheer absurdity of my question is further emphasised in the critical works on virtual reality, game studies and theories on 'posthuman'. However, as I remain dissatisfied with this sort of answer that pretends to know the nature of matter and where it resides, I begin my point of departure by mapping the field of investigation that seem to be strangely blind to corporeality, the material body of the child playing the game.

In *Cyberspace: First Steps*, the collection of essays that marked the first serious academic engagement with virtual reality, Michael Benedikt describes virtual space as a world of hyperbolic agency, a post-corporeality that seems to at last answer the desire for utopia, that no-place that defies the conventions of location by its very ubiquity.[1] Vivian Sobchack, a writer on phenomenology, puts it that this desire for an ultimate escape actually 'demands' 'Getting rid of the Meat'.[2] For Sobchack, the cyberspace is the magical space that promises a virtual escape route from the constraints of life. Allucquere Roseanne Stone reads these electronic worlds as a 'succession of prosthetics' that can augment what has been deficient, or lacking in our lives. Stone reads technology as the supplement that repairs a body rendered incomplete before its augmentation. Paraphrasing Donna Haraway, Stone reads cyberspace as a domain of 'total representation', 'purely conceptual', 'pure information' and therefore a 'geography of elsewhere'.[3] Further as Michael Benedikt puts it, VR technology is an Edenic, primordial existence. With nothing between us and our desires, he says, '[w]e would become again as 'children', but this time with the power of the mind of summoning worlds at will and impressing speedily upon others the particulars of our experience'.[4]

This form of academic writing reminds us again and again that there is no body in virtual space, or more precisely, the cyberspace may transcend the Cartesian coordinates. Virtual reality or cyberspace is permanently ephemeral, the space where the perfect body is paradoxically acquired through an annihilation of flesh. It is interesting to note that in most critical works on cyberspace the complex nature of identity is a topic of discussion (for example, the anonymity and impersonation that social networking sites allow), but what constitutes that complex nature of identity is assumed unproblematic.[5] The nature of corporeal substance 'as such' is not the matter of contestation. This refusal to include the question of corporeality explains how the flesh is read as something residual against which the complexity of cyberspace is articulated. The interface, visibly present as a computer screen, is merely read as separating two entities. On one hand is the human body and on the other hand, the virtual space, wherein the subject may upload into the network. Even when critics such as Stone say, '[n]o matter how virtual the subject may become, there is always a body *attached*'[6] (emphasis added), one is reminded of the mind/body division.

My contention is that the problem of corporeality does not derive from a splitting process, but how one understands corporeality in virtual space.[7] The subject who is playing a computer game is either read as being physically put into cyberspace in such a complete and immersed manner that matter or flesh becomes an impediment to the fullest realisation of transcendence. Or, the interface is read as a supplement to the playing subject. That is to say, the virtual existence that acknowledges the physical body, reads the body as a supplement that is always 'attached'. In either case, the corporeality of the playing body remains intact, severed from the mind/consciousness. The implication is that the uploading consciousness has autonomy of form and substance. Donna Haraway's notion of cyborg is alert to this problematic assumption of cyberspace as a composite of separable coordinates. A cyborg, which is short for 'cybernetic organism', comprises not an impermeable organic wholeness, but symbiosis, prosthetic devices, hybrids, chimeras and mosaics.[8] However, though Haraway celebrates the notion of cyborg as a 'monstrous and illegitimate' identity who 'skips the step of original unity', she fails to interrogate what one understands as the 'original unity' or the 'before' against which the cyborg is defined.[9]

Virtual reality becomes in this mode of critical understanding a transcendent technology. The body and materiality itself are left behind and the user becomes one with a virtual technological whole. In focusing on how the effects of new technologies may be evaluated and managed, critical analysis often leaves unexplored the more immediately empirical issue of how a human body actually experiences and interacts with technologies. Bogard, for example, contends that, while recognising the transparency of the virtual system, the 'operator too' disappears, giving way to the disembodied traveller, the astral projectionist, the 'interface, data cowboy' in cyberspace.[10] Stone, to some extent, warns us to avoid the 'Cartesian trick' because, she argues, physicality is as important in cyberspace as it is in everyday environments. 'No refigured virtual body', she warns, 'no matter how beautiful, will slow the death of a cyberpunk with AIDS. Even in the age of the technosocial subject, life is lived through bodies'.[11] My argument in this essay is in line with Stone, the experience of using VR is an embodied experience. However, what begs investigation is the nature of this embodiment.

What is integral—the game/player/screen?

To begin with, it is extremely important to recall the notion of 'play' as an attribute of the human (as Johan Huizinga, following Schiller and Nietzsche, argued in *Homo Ludens*, 1938), and read it against a taxonomic model of 'games'.[12] Though I would sidestep the complexity of play-game here, it is significant to note that without the control of the player, all that remains in a computer game is an algorithm that cannot be executed because of a lack of input. Mark Hansen establishes a connection between the player and the video game image which exceeds the notion of the video game controller (or the system as such) as being a 'mere vehicle for translating the real into a form', but rather being an 'operation of the real itself'.[13] Exactly because the movements on screen are either directly controlled (the avatar by the player) or at least indirectly influenced, the computer screen is not an intermediary, but located more closely to the human agent. The game, in this sense, becomes a medium of immersion wherein the playing subject has an active bodily experience within a spaceless-space. Hansen terms these bodies which experience technology as an extension rather than a limitation: 'bodies in code'. Bodies in code are defined as

> mediators which use the concrete technology of virtual reality *to stage a disconnection of the (fundamentally motile) body schema from the (fundamentally visual) body image*. [...] Such technical mediation of the body schema (of the scope of body-environment coupling) comprises [...] a body in code.[14]

Here embodiment is realised in 'conjunction with technics'.[15] The bodily (motor) activity that the playing subject experiences then fractures any easy definition of corporeality (a question discussed in subsequent sections).

Thus a child playing the video game not only transforms into an image but also occupies two spaces at the same time. The moving image of the video games is an eternal flow of present tense. The video game image makes sense only in relation to a player who perceives it. It cannot be stored in albums and fulfils its original purpose only in relation to the playing body. The video game opens into the present and this extension of the field allows the body to enter the image in the here-and-now. This creates the spaceless-space of the video game image.

Within this spaceless-space of the video game image the child playing the game is often reduced to a set of eyes fixed on a screen. Contrary to this mode of understanding, let us adopt a more nuanced conceptualisation of the player–game relationship—one that erodes the sovereignty of the 'seeing subject' and reconsiders the practice of playing video games as a powerfully performative one with both 'intersubjective' and 'interobjective' dimensions. The first step in this manoeuvre entails broadening the scope of inquiry and expanding the object of analysis in a refusal to reduce the video game player to a mere set of eyeballs. Such a move emphasises what the child is doing when she is playing video games, not merely what or how she is watching.

Let us attend to the 'intersubjective' and 'interobjective' aspects of a computer game. 'Intersubjectivity' is the element that allows the human and the machine components to combine. 'Intersubjectivity' is inherent in the practice of video gaming: the interpersonal relations manifest in the experience of play, the disciplinary systems inscribed on and invoked by the body in its very movement, and the discursive power relations that 'play out' in play. Without the subjective potential of 'intersubjectivity', a computer game would be only software with an algorithm unavailable for 'playing'. The first-person experience that a computer game affords draws its energy from this subjective component.

Now let us realise the provocative *ekstasis* of video gaming's 'interobjective' dimensions: the ways in which bodies are literally given shape and configured in performances of video gaming, the practice's capacity to subvert dominant systems of meaning, and the insistence on new ways of meaning and mattering; the autonomy and power of the video game's material body, its complicity in shaping the game experience and facilitating passion. Further, the gaze of the gamer is already a wholly embodied sense. Merleau-Ponty reminds us:

> My mobile body makes a difference in the visible world, being part of it; that is why I can steer it through the visible. Conversely, it is just as true that vision is attached to movement. We see only what we look at. What would vision be without eye movement?[16]

If anything, the child playing a game brings to the forefront the role of the body in the practice of video gaming, to 'go back to the working, actual body—not the body as a chunk of space or a bundle of functions but that body which is an intertwining of vision and movement'.[17] Play, in this sense is about *being* in play, or as Mihaly Csikszentmihailyi describes this 'flow':

> People become so involved in that they are doing that the activity becomes spontaneous [...] they stop being aware of themselves as separate from the actions they are performing.[18]

To be in play, then, is a sudden way of being, a specific state of mind. With the 'intersubjective' and 'interobjective' elements, 'playing' a computer game becomes a first-person event with its own unique physiological conditions determined by objective structures and algorithms. As a result, the experiential materiality that this game affords is never a *pure* subjective or an objective experience. One is physically grounded with hands and fingers moving in the keyboard and eyeballs in the screen, but extended in a way that makes it difficult to define.

Further, the computer game, the game with its structures, rules and systems, not only has a physical material, as a hand-on CD-ROM or a file on the computer, but in a sense a part of the practice around the game is also delineated. One learns the game while playing the game. This means that one does not have to have competences before one starts the game. One gets them while playing. But does it mean that all practice is materialised in the game? No, the point is that when it comes to materialisation of the practice, the existing play practice, the practice around other games and play products will be integrated or used as an inspiration for the specific play practice as well. This reveals then that the notion of the play, game (both as a practice and as a shared experience) and the playing subject—all enter into a structure that makes the normative understanding of a computer game inadequate.

Sketching Materiality

While an entire project for a new understanding of materiality as encapsulated within virtual space is beyond the scope of this essay, I shall sketch—the operative word being 'sketch!'—what I believe is central to the new modality of locating the material body of the playing child.

My point of departure is the definition by Pimentel and Texeira: 'In general, the term virtual reality refers to an immersive, interactive experience generated by a computer'.[19] While the term 'computer generated' accounts for the virtual character of the game, 'immersive' and 'interactive' explain what makes the computer-assisted game an experience of reality. To apprehend a world as 'real' is to feel surrounded by it, to be able to interact physically with it, and to have the power to modify this environment. The conjunction of immersion and interactivity leads to an effect known as telepresence. In order to feel immersed, the player must be able to move around the virtual space and to apprehend it under various points of view. The computer tracks his movements and generates the sensory data corresponding to his position in a continuously shifting display. Insofar as immersion is 'the blocking out of the physical world',[20] it cannot be experienced if the user remains aware of the physical generator of the data, namely the computer. The 'virtual reality effect' is the denial of the role of signs (bits, pixels, and binary codes) in the production of what the player experiences as unmediated presence. Jaron Lanier, a leading developer of VR systems, echoes: 'With a VR system you don't see the computer anymore—it's gone. All that's there is you'.[21]

Paradoxically, it is at this juncture that the body of the playing child may be located. The game may proceed only on moving the sensors. The virtual world must respond to the player's actions. Games are something that is 'done': an active process, something experiential. One of the earliest and most formative game studies texts, ESPEN Aarseth's *Cybertext,* refers to digital media texts—including digital games—as 'ergodic', a term borrowed from contemporary physics that describes something requiring nontrivial effort to consume.[22] In a typical computer game, the creative processes of playing and 'writing' the game are conflated. One is both playing and writing the story as one moves through the computer world. The player can be inconsistent; he can change his mind, rearrange the story, remake the characters, redesign the set. The creative process is not the playing out of narrative conventions or structures. There can be alternative versions, differing interpretations, purposeful ambiguity. However, his fictional world is always according to some prescribed grid. When the game takes place, each player is making a different interpretation from the same visual region, and it is in the progress of action as a result of those interpretations that their common game is played. What this reveals is then a paradoxical structure of game and play. The player of a computer game must be free—enter voluntarily into the game and leave it voluntarily—but is still constrained by the rules and boundaries of the virtual circle of codes and digits. Borrowing Roger Caillois' notion of play in *Man, Play, and Games*, a computer game could then be said to be as being free *within* the rules of the space.[23]

Consequently then the idea of play as separate from reality and taking place in a prescribed space bounded by rules continues to be salient. As Caillois succinctly puts it:

> [t]he confused and intricate laws of ordinary life are replaced, in this fixed space and for this given time, by precise, arbitrary, unexceptionable rules that must be accepted as such and which govern the correct playing of the game.[24]

A computer game is then a space which represents the refutation of a popular myth: the personification of the computer as an autonomous mind (a myth fostered by artificial intelligence and its attempt to endow machines with creative thinking). Instead what comes up is a complex web of 'body as such', a body in code, a bio-logical body that refuses to serve as a residual 'something' against which virtual cyberspace may be defined and a bodily presence that cannot be differentiated from the interface in terms of 'before' or original.

Sliding Dimensions: Body/Being/Matter/Flesh/Substance

> Beyond the Aristotelian terms, above that categorisation, there is the notion of 'being' which envelops everything. Without being a predicate itself, 'being' is the condition of all predicates. All the varieties of 'being-such', of 'state', all the possible views of 'time', etc., depend on the notion of 'being'.[25]

Recalling Benveniste's comment on separate coordinates of data with which I began this essay, contemporary critical writings assume that there 'is' some untainted, unmediated space of subjective interiority where one can stand aside from, totalise, and critique the codes and roles without at the same time being bound by them, some unquestioned and unquestionable yardstick by which the socially and linguistically constructed codes of ethics may be judged. Here one could cite any number of sources: Lacan's rereading of Freud in light of the realisation that 'the unconscious is structured like a language', that it is 'outside' the subject; Derrida's deconstruction of the 'auto-affection' and self-presence of voice in both Husserl and Saussure; Althusser's dismantling of humanist Marxism; or beyond that, Levi-Strauss's critique of Sartre's neo-Hegelian reliance on the category of consciousness. The presumption of such a space of pure interiority, pure self-presence of the subject, receives its most rigorous and devastating critique, perhaps, in Derrida's reading of Husserl in *Speech and Phenomena,* which would no doubt draw our attention to the demotion of writing and iteration thinly veiled (if at all) in Bauman's privileging of 'moral conscience' over the realm of the ethical. My aim here, however, is not to retrace any of these arguments, but simply to point out that all we get by way of confrontation is an engagement with the surface that ignores the commonsense understanding of the body.

Curiously Benveniste's comment that I quoted at the beginning of this section takes us beyond Benveniste's original brief. 'Being' is the transcategorical condition of any category. As the notion that makes possible the category of 'language', it also opens the possibility of an outside of language. Can this notion of 'being' serve a suggestive opening onto the enlarged scene of materiality that the playing body of the child affords? Can the very tissue of substance, the ground of Being, be read as a mutable intertext that both circumscribes and exceeds the conventional divisions of mind/body, man/machine, etc.? The matter of the child's playing body, then, following Derrida, 'the most elementary processes within the living cell' is also a part of the 'play' (in the sense that I had delineated in the earlier section) and one whose 'system' is never closed.[26] This would mean that the body is unstable—a shifting scene of inscription that both plays and is played upon—a scenario where the subject takes itself as its own object, and where an image could be said to rewrite the image-maker in a movement of production that disrupts the temporal determination of what comes first. The common understanding of materiality as rock-solid is called into question through such an approach.

But even then my initial doubts about the body of a child playing a computer game remain unanswered. The body of the playing child with tissue and anatomy seems to be inaccessible and posits itself as a field through which the bodies-in-code, as explained earlier, may be seamlessly articulated. Is it possible to think through the body of the playing child? Or can only the 'Being' be captured in our disembodied speculations and the body that itches at a mosquito bite be left behind as a closure?

In the landmark text *The Second Self: Computers and the Human Spirit*, Sherry Turkle documents the responses of children, adolescents and adults interacting with new digital communication.[27] For Turkle, the advent of computer culture incites a radical rethinking of who we are and the nature of being human. Central to her analysis is the issue of how individuals forge a sense of self in relation to an emerging computer culture. As she explains:

> Technology catalyzes changes not only in what we do but in how we think. It changes peoples' awareness of themselves, of one another, of their relationship with the world. The new machine that stands behind the flashing digital signal, unlike the clock, the telescope, or the train, is a machine that "thinks". It challenges our notions not only of time and distance, but of mind.[28]

From her perspective, the question is not whether technology is good or bad for people and society, but how it serves as a means by which the self may be articulated. For Turkle, 'the machine can act as a projection of part of the self, a mirror of the mind',[29] or as she goes on to state, 'computers enter into the development of personality, of identity, and even of sexuality'.[30] She isn't suggesting here that the computer is a passive screen or neutral entity onto which the self is projected. Rather, it is how individuals perceive themselves and their relationship to the world that is radically altered through the virtual medium.

I discuss Turkle's work at length as her work has taken into account the question of corporeality and has made a huge impact. An alternative means of theorising identity is posed by the author—one that recognises the context, location and embodied experiences, which impact on the formation of the subject. Turkle advocates a subject that is neither unified nor fixed, but constantly formulated and reconstructed through her/his diverse relationships with computer culture, a self within a culture of simulation, virtuality and the digital.

It is a new mode of existence by which the subject comes into being, as distinctions collapse between nature and artifice, self and computer, virtual and real, animate and inanimate.

The theoretical perspective offered by Turkle encourages us to question the relationships between the real and virtual, nature/machine and human/non-human. Yet in distinguishing between real life and life on the screen, Turkle fundamentally maintains the categorical distinction between the two, albeit complicating the status of each. For Turkle, computer technology affords a means to reflect upon real life, rather than problematise the very status of the real. This proves problematic to a rethinking of the materiality of the playing child as his playing body is read as a separate entity from the machine.

Similarly, in 'Virtual Bodies and Flickering Signifiers', Hayles forges valuable insights toward refiguring the signifier/signified relationship by way of a shift from the presence/absence dialectic to one of pattern/randomness.[31] In a world where the emerging cultural aesthetic of the digital is transforming our very mode of signification, Hayles contends that discursive formations that rely on a presence/absence dialectic are no longer effective in making meaning in a virtual world. Theories of the subject discussed in these terms make little sense in a digital domain characterised by simulation and virtuality because signifieds and signifiers have no direct relationship and meaning is no longer grounded by a fixed origin. Hayles proposes a new theory of signification based on pattern and randomness to replace Cartesian dualisms of presence/absence.[32] Extending on the Lacanian idea of the floating signifier, Hayles suggests that 'information technologies create what I will call *flickering signifiers,* characterised by their tendency toward unexpected metamorphoses, attenuations, and dispersions'.[33] While this concept offers an effective tool to consider how technologies of textual production affect signification, it cannot be sustained at the point where the circulation of signs has no relation to the material world. By replacing presence and absence with pattern and randomness, and establishing a divide between the material (presence/absence) and the virtual (pattern/randomness), Hayles maintains an approach to signification based in a dialectical logic.

In my opinion, in this digital era a radically new means of configuring materiality is required—one that questions the very status of real and virtual, machine and organism, Self and Other. This is because our engagements with the world around us take the form of simulated realities. That is, the categories of embodied existence collide with virtual experience so that the two are no longer separable. Instead of approaching the playing child through a study of 'real life', as Turkle does, or through Hayles' lens of 'material reality', perhaps an interpretation of the materiality within virtual space needs to take into account the representational economy of simulation in which images exist and are circulated, and hence reside beyond the codes of signification and their enactments. Conversely speaking, that representational economy need not read 'biology' as a supplementary ingredient to be included or excluded. The body is more than a mere supplement to the interface.[34]

Extending Perspectives—Virtual Reality to Haptic Visuality

Hansen in *Embodying Technesis: Technology Beyond Writing* and *Framing the Digital Image* offers a conceptual framework on technology that frees it from being embedded in discourse and representation.[35] The position he stakes out draws deeply upon Henri Bergson's defence of the affective, prediscursive body as the active source of meaning. From Hansen's perspective, technologies alter the very basis of our sensory experience and drastically affect what it means to live as *embodied* human agents. The technologies reconfigure the senses at a precognitional or even paracognitional level (not to privilege one level over the other), prior to conscious perception and assimilation to language. What interests me is how Hansen argues for displacing an abstracted sense of vision as the primary sense in favour of the internal bodily senses of touch and self-movement. Vision becomes 'haptic' in Hansen's effort to relocate visual sense-making in the body. He generates a 'haptic spatiality', an internally grounded image of the body prior to and independent of external geometrical space.

This view has a range of interesting consequences with respect to the playing body of this essay. For instance, Virtual Reality in Hansen's view is not the simple product of technical advances in computer graphics. It is not only the ability to process more polygons and run hierarchies of shading algorithms faster that creates the Virtual Reality experience. Rather, that experience is grounded in the biological potential of human beings. Virtual Reality is, Hansen argues, a body-brain achievement. The source of the virtual is thus not technological, but rather a biologically grounded adaptation to newly acquired technological extensions provided by new media.

Laura Marks recently dealt with this 'genre', which 'appeals to a tactile, or haptic visuality'.[36] She distinguishes this type of perception from optical visuality.

> Haptic perception is ... defined as the combination of tactile, kinaesthetic, and proprioceptive functions, the way we experience touch both on the surface of and inside our bodies. In haptic visuality, the eyes themselves function like organs of touch. Haptic visuality ... draws from other forms of sense experience, primarily touch and kinaesthetics. (...) The relationship between viewer and screen in the case of haptic visuality is a relationship of the viewer with another skin or another body, reason why it can become erotic...for one not only touches this screen-skin or screen-body with one's own eye/body, but the touched also reaches back with a caress as if it belongs to or is a 'subject'.[37]

I borrow Hansen's notion of 'haptic spatiality' and Marks' distinctions to reflect upon the peculiar kind of corporeality that a computer game occasions. Rather, by embedding a computer game within debates of mind-body dualism, the conceptual framework of haptic visuality opens alternate modes of gaming experience that involve bodily dimensions of spacing and duration—modes that, in short, capitalise on the flexibility of the body, and indeed, on the cross-modal or synesthetic capacities of bodily affectivity. In this way, it exemplifies the inversion of a normative critical analysis, such that the body becomes the stable point of reference around which the interface might be said to move. In various ways, this mode of understanding channel perception through the computer, not as a technical extension beyond the body-brain, but as an embodied prosthesis, a catalyst for bodily self-transformation. In so doing, this foregrounds the body as an agent of a sensorimotor connection with the interface. The body, in short, becomes integral rather than a mediator between the playing subject and the interface.

Speculations

I have deliberately titled the last section 'Speculations' and not 'Conclusion' as I am yet to discover the terms that allow me to account for that playing child who has consistently remained with me as a synonym for the palpable matter of body that evades critical inquiry. In the previous sections I have tried to engage with this problem amidst growing unease that once provoked my interest. My increasing impatience with the morphology of such critical arguments in some ways is born from my sympathies with them. The problem is this: how does one argue with the theoretical positions when one's own intellectual location is filtered through such analysis? It is not a straightforwardly simple relocation of notions of causality and production of (counter) claims. It is a process of individuation that is necessarily contingent and yet attempts to individuate itself within species-being, and identifies itself as possessing sufficient stability to ground the destabilisation of grounds, however unclear they may be. The inevitable result is only speculation and not a conclusion.

More graphic than before, soliciting a more visceral experiential response, a computer game alters the very ways in which one imagines the human subject. Unlike a stable integrated human body, this game offers the prospect of a corporeality that is fragmented and permeable. The body is in a kind of frictionless flow. The purpose of this essay was to delineate that the subjective and the objective elements of a computer game have to be considered in a mode of complementarity to comprehend this 'body-in-code'. The experiential and creative elements of the game confirm that without the 'intersubjective' part, the game would be reduced to a set of algorithms. Yet one of the essential elements of 'playing' a computer game is that the player becomes unidentifiable from the game—an 'interobjective' experience. The result is thus a 'telepresence', an embodied awareness through which the player 'appears' to transcend the bodily boundaries. Playing a computer game evokes the hope that cyberspace technology may render the tangible world of biology null and void. Yet what one actually witnesses is a haptic spatiality and an extended experience of corporeality that make distinctions and thereby definitions difficult.

As this essay has tried to explore, matter for critical theorists may not be a blank or passive surface, but it is still a surface, and one that demands to be interpreted or written upon, by something other than itself. Although matter possesses the capacity to call upon thought, it is apparently incapable of calling upon itself to interpret itself. The substance of matter, the concrete and tangible thing called body, is excluded from critical enquiry. What I have tried to conjure here is in some way how flesh is deeply implicated within the 'system'. The flesh and substance of fingers and eyes of the playing child cannot be exteriorised from the domain of technics—none of these are autonomously enclosed upon themselves. Rather they are all emergent *within* a field of differentiations that has no exteriority in any final sense. The conjunction of mind *and* body that is assumed to happen at *one* surface *between* entities, might be a myriad partitioning. The body—flesh, bone, tissue, fingers, eyes, brain—may itself be a field of infinite interfacings. My principal concern is neither the history of ideas nor epistemology, but the pragmatics of coping in everyday life with such questions that are perpetually dismissed. My contention is that the enclosure of the category of materiality will not generate fertile critical enquiries. But, by putting the sustained refusal within critical enquiry to acknowledge this flesh/substance/matter/body into question and exploring the category of corporeality on the atomic level of its constitution, matter may become substantially re-marked.

Notes

1. Michael Benedikt, *Cyberspace: First Steps* (Cambridge: MIT Press, 1992).
2. Vivian Sobchack, 'New Age Mutant Ninja Hackers: Reading Mondo 2000', in *Flame Wars: The Discourse of Cyberculture*, ed. M. Dery (Durham, NC: Duke University Press, 1993), p. 577.
3. Donna Haraway, 'A Cyborg Manifesto: Science, Technology, and Socialist-Feminism in the Late Twentieth Century', *Simians, Cyborgs, and Women: The Reinvention of Nature* (New York: Routledge,1992), p. 109.
4. Michael Benedikt, *Cyberspace: First Steps* (Cambridge: MIT Press, 1992) p. 13. For a detailed discussion on the various theoretical readings of cyberspace, see Vicki Kirby, *Telling Flesh—The Substance of the Corporeal* (New York and London: Routledge, 1997) and Geoffrey Batchen, 'Spectres'. *Afterimage* 23, 3: 1995, 6–7.

5. Various critics have questioned the nature of identity that is encapsulated within cyberspace. Bailey, for example, writes extensively on the ways in which race is embedded in cyberspace. In his article 'Virtual Skin: Articulating Race in Cyberspace' he suggests that race matters in virtual experiences: 'The discourse of race is, by history and by design, rooted in the body. Cyber-subjectivity promises the fantasy of disembodied communication, but it remains firmly connected to bodies through the imaginative act required to project into cyberspace. See Cameron Bailey, 'Virtual Skin: Articulating Race in Cyberspace', in *Immersed in Technology: Art and Virtual Environments*, ed. Mary Anne Moser (Cambridge, MA: MIT Press, 1996), p. 42. Zoe Sophia, on the other hand, locates VR technology as a military desire and reads the human-computer interaction as a contemporary expression of masculine anxiety about the maternal body: 'Masculine envy of, and identification with, maternal fertility fuels the sublimation of infantile epistemophilia into cultural quests to discover or create new bodies of knowledge, land, resources, or technique as brainchildren for the mother's body'. See Zoe Sophia, 'Virtual Corporeality: A Feminist View'. *Australian Feminist Studies* 15: 1992, 14. In Sophie's reading, the inability to cut from the mother's body, refigured here as a machine, marks masculinity. The feminine associations with 'mother boards, 'consoles', 'user friendliness'—are seen as the ways in which the computer is fetishized as the body of a woman. What is significant to note is that in each of these readings, the debate is about the ethical and political valuation of the subject who achieves an electronic life in cyberspace. The nature of corporeal substance, the material nature of the body that is being represented in cyberspace is assumed self-evident and uncomplicated.
6. Allucquere Roseanne Stone, 'Will the Real Body Please Stand Up?', in *Cyberspace: First Steps*, ed. Michael Benedikt (Cambridge: MIT Press, 1992), p. 111.
7. I have borrowed Elizabeth Grosz's reading of a Mobius strip as a guiding framework for this paper. As Grosz puts it, 'a Mobius strip, the inverted three-dimensional figure eight ... has the advantage of showing the inflection of mind into body and body into mind, the ways in which, through a kind of twisting or inversion, one side becomes another'. This model provides a way of rethinking the relations between inside and outside, the psychical interior and corporeal exterior of a subject. The attempt here shall be not to show the reducibility of one onto another, but the passage or the uncontrollable tension flowing through the inside into the outside and the outside into the inside. Elizabeth Grosz, *Volatile Bodies—Toward a Corporeal Feminism* (Bloomington and Indianapolis: Indiana University Press, 1994), p. xii.
8. Haraway puts it as, 'Biological organisms have become biotic systems, communications devices like others. There is no fundamental, ontological

separation in our formal knowledge of machine and organism, of technical and organic. The replicant Rachel in the Ridley Scott film *Blade Runner* stands as the image of a cyborg culture's fear, love and confusion'. See Donna Haraway, 'A Cyborg Manifesto: Science, Technology, and Socialist-Feminism in the Late Twentieth Century'. *Simians, Cyborgs, and Women: The Reinvention of Nature* (New York: Routledge, 1991), pp. 177–8.

9. For Haraway, the cyborg's 'monstrous and illegitimate' identity provides a promise of disrupting political space: 'An origin story in the 'Western', humanist sense depends on the myth of original unity, fullness, bliss and terror, represented by the phallic mother from whom all humans must separate...both Marxism and psychoanalysis...depend on the plot of original unity out of which difference must be produced...The cyborg skips the step of original unity, of identification with nature in the Western sense... Nature and culture are reworked; the one can no longer be the resource for appropriation or incorporation by the other' Ibid., p. 151. This image of an instable, unfixed and volatile contour of the cyborg does provide an access to disruptive politics. However, what this very construction of the cyborg's identity ironically dismisses is the infinite partitioning through which its disruptive force is mediated and generated. In other words, the self-evident nature of cyborg's reality that this definition seems to embrace, implicitly, re-states the Cartesian hierarchisation. By not recognising the matter of corporeal existence, the cyborg seems to dissolve the legibility of conventional politics. Yet, this very dissolution legitimises the need to take matter as the determining premise for identity formation. What this paper seeks to do is to ask how and in what terms can matter in itself, be considered without being caught in a structuralist commitment to identity versus difference, substance versus form, presence versus absence, or reality versus representation.
10. William Bogard, *The Simulation of Surveillance: Hypercontrol in Telematic Societies* (London: Cambridge University Press, 1996), p. 37.
11. Allucquere Roseanne Stone, 'Will the Real Body Please Stand Up?', in *Cyberspace: First Steps*, ed. Michael Benedikt (Cambridge: MIT Press, 1992), p. 113.
12. Cited from Supriya Chaudhuri, 'Bodies at Risk: Gender and Sport', in *Women Contesting Culture: Changing Frames of Gender Politics in India*, eds Kavita Panjabi and Paromita Chakravarti (Kolkata: Stree, 2012), p. 185.
13. Mark Hansen, *Embodying Technesis: Technology Beyond Writing* (Michigan: University of Michigan Press, 2000), p. 200.
14. Ibid., p. 20.
15. Ibid.
16. Merleau-Ponty, *The Primacy of Perception* (Illinois: Northwestern University Press, 1964), p. 162.
17. Ibid.

18. Mihaly Csikszentmihalyi and Susan A. Jackson, *Flow in Sports: The Keys to Optimal Experiences and Performances* (Champaign, Illinois: Human Kinetics Publishers, 1999), p. 4.
19. Ken Pimental and Kevin Texeira, *Virtual Reality: Through the New Looking Glass* (London: Mcgraw-Hill School Education Group, 1992), p. 11.
20. Frank Biocca, 'Immersive Virtual Reality Technology', in *Communication in the Age of Virtual Reality*, eds Frank Biocca and Mark R. Levy (Hillsdale, NJ: Lawrence Erlbaum, 1995), p. 25.
21. Jaron Lanier, *You Are Not a Gadget: A Manifesto* (New York: Alfred A. Knopf, 2010), p. 2.
22. Espen Aarseth, *Cybertext: Perspectives on Ergodic Literature* (New York: JHU Press, 1997).
23. Roger Caillois, *Man, Play, and Games*. Trans. Meyer Barash (USA: The Free Press, 2001).
24. Ibid., p. 7.
25. Emile Benveniste, *Problems in General Linguistics*. Trans. M. E. Meek (Coral Gables, FL: University of Miami Press, 1971), p. 61.
26. Jacques Derrida, *Margins of Philosophy* (Chicago: University of Chicago Press, 1984), p. 9.
27. Sherry Turkle, *The Second Self: Computers and the Human Spirit* (New York: Simon and Schuster, 1984).
28. Ibid., p. 13.
29. Ibid., p. 15.
30. Ibid.
31. Katherine Hayles, 'Virtual Bodies and Flickering Signifiers'. *October* 66: 1993, 69–91.
32. Katherine Hayles, *How We Became Posthuman: Virtual Bodies in Cybernetics, Literature, and Informatics* (Chicago & London: University of Chicago Press, 1999), p. 28.
33. Ibid., p. 30. Hayles writes: 'First, the posthuman view privileges informational pattern over material instantiation, so that embodiment in a biological substrate is seen as an accident of history rather than an inevitability of life. Second, the posthuman view considers consciousness, regarded as the seat of human identity in the Western tradition long before Descartes thought he was a mind thinking, as an epiphenomenon, as an evolutionary upstart trying to claim that it is the whole show when in actuality it is only a minor sideshow. Third, the posthuman view thinks of the body as the original prosthesis we all learn to manipulate, so that extending or replacing the body with other prostheses becomes a continuation of a process that began before we were born. Fourth, and most important, by these and other means, the posthuman view configures human being so that it can be seamlessly articulated with intelligent machines. In the posthuman, there are no essential differences or absolute demarcations between bodily existence and

computer simulation, cybernetic mechanism and biological organism, robot teleology and human goals'. Ibid., pp. 2–3.

34. Theorists, such as Turkle and Hayles, who express misgivings about the exclusion of 'biology' from the 'embodied presence', seem to have an almost consensual agreement that a limit must be determined with regard to the notion of materiality and anatomy in cyberspace. 'Biology' in these accounts is not open to the problematic of recognition. It is the 'given' of body that must not be confused with the complexities of identity politics. The inevitable result is that the productive force of these excellent readings is confined to the notion of 'inscription' upon the body's surface when in virtual world. Anatomy is interpreted as the body's external shape. My own argument is not in opposition to these readings, as I am entirely indebted to their intelligent provocations. I see this essay as a further elaboration of this trajectory, an attempt to read it to the letter. In other words, though I agree with the conceptual frameworks provided by these theorists, I want to insist that such frameworks are possible through and through corporeal.
35. Mark Hansen, *Embodying Technesis: Technology Beyond Writing* (Michigan: University of Michigan Press, 2000).
36. Laura Marks, 'Video Haptics and Erotics'. *Screen* 39(4): 1998, 332.
37. Ibid., pp. 333–41.

Part IV

Sport and Cinema

12

Shoonya (The Zero Zone, 2007)

Arindam Mitra

The difficulty in talking about my film *Shoonya* [The Zero Zone] is that it was never released in India. It was one of the early selections at the Rotterdam International Film Festival (2007) and at the Pusan International Film Festival the same year. It even played at the Museum of Modern Art, New York and got Kay Kay Menon the best actor prize at Osian's Film Festival; but it was never viewed in India by an Indian audience. Most of readers of this essay, therefore, will never have watched the film at all. I will say more about that later. Let me begin with a synopsis of the film to set a context for this discussion.

The film's central character, Mahendra, is the captain of the Indian cricket team. He is hauled up on match-fixing charges. His first reaction is to go to the CBI and confess his crime. He meets the investigator and does exactly that. He is asked to come back to sign his statement a few days later. He thinks that he has buried his demons and has sacrificed himself to the purity of his sport (or art, if I may call it that), but the world around him will not let this happen. His wife will not allow the glittering life she co-owns with the country's biggest sporting star crumble around her. His teammates and friends will not let this dangerous confession destroy their careers. The betting syndicate threatens to kill him if he signs the statement. Mahendra is assailed relentlessly from every direction to withdraw his statement. He feels weaker by the hour and feels the ground shift beneath him. In the end, he must confront himself and his own weaknesses to resolve the situation. The decision he takes is to withdraw his statement, thus maintaining a deadly *status quo*.

When I made the film, I had access to the CBI papers on the match-fixing controversies that rocked cricket and shocked the nation in the late nineteen-nineties. I built up the narrative by adhering fairly closely to the facts, or alleged facts, to be more precise. But unlike *Black Friday* (directed by Anurag Kashyap) that I produced a couple of years earlier, this was not a film about a central event or set of incidents. I did not want to make a documentary on match-fixing. I wanted to put the character of Mahendra in a situation that was both imagined and real, examining him closely to see what became of him. In some respects I wrote *Shoonya* as a Greek tragedy. Or perhaps *Shoonya* for me is my interpretation of T. S. Eliot's *Murder in the Cathedral*. Mahendra is my Becket. His wife, friend and the syndicate are the tempters. And the final tempter is Mahendra himself.

I even structured the film exactly like a Greek tragedy. The film begins abruptly at the middle of the story where Mahendra, with his friend, meets the lawyer to retract his statement given to the CBI. I tried to underline the tragic inevitability in that scheme of things. As viewers, we subsequently go back to the beginning of the narrative and the story unfolds according to the time-line of the incidents. The cricket fans play the role of the chorus. They demonstrate a blind faith in their captain in the beginning, but as the film progresses, they lose every atom of that faith. As the film ends, we see a shattered Mahendra wearing all his cricketing gear, sitting by himself, while the fans burn his effigy outside.

It was in *Shoonya* that sports, literature and cinema collided for me. I grew up in the Kolkata of the early nineteen-eighties where sports was a way of life. We used to swim, play soccer, cricket and badminton. I was a serious swimmer and represented the state. Later, I started rowing and represented the country. Like my team-mates, I knew the euphoria of winning and the wretchedness of losing. We knew every bone that creaked and every muscle that ached when we went for the final push. We would climb on the rooftop to fix a booster antenna to catch Bangladesh TV transmission, so that we could watch Brazil play. Socrates and Zico were household names, as were John McEnroe and Björn Borg. I remember the whole family being glued to the radio when Sunny Gavaskar was playing his epic knock of 221 at the Oval against England in 1979. The fates of Mohun Bagan and

East Bengal were matters of life and death. In that kind of world, Moti Nandy's fiction and the struggles of his heroes seemed only natural. His breakaway success, the novel *Striker*, a story about a young, impoverished soccer player, thrilled us all. We read it and re-read it, living every moment of the striker's struggle and replaying every move that led to the glorious final goal. This was followed by *Koni*—the story of a swimmer, later to be made into a film. And all this while the Bengali daily newspaper, *Ananda Bazar Patrika*, was reporting sport almost like philosophy. Some years later, after a dull Brazilian World Cup win, ABP carried a headline that said—'Nation pays tribute to Ayrton Senna'. Senna, the Brazilian Formula One champion, had died in a fatal crash a few months before this, and it was as if Brazil was still in mourning.

I must have carried this passion for sport along with me when I left Kolkata and settled in Mumbai. So when I looked at the match-fixing documents that my journalist friends gave me, I looked at this crisis as something that cut deep, as a pain in the gut, as an intensely personal matter. My journalist friends were disappointed. They were expecting another *Black Friday*, not the grim, personal tale of a disgraced sportsman.

I had watched Emir Kusturica's documentary on Maradona in Spanish (a language that I don't understand), without sub-titles. But I was drawn in compulsively from the very first shot. Kusturica, himself a shining light of modern cinema and the lead guitarist in a rock band, reaches Maradona's home town. He is allowed no access but he remains in the town. After many days of waiting at Maradona's doorstep, Kusturica finally gains access. They become close friends and start talking to each other. Maradona says that he is not ashamed of his 'hand of God' goal against England. He would have broken every rule to beat England that evening, since the victory was his protest against Britain's war in the Falkland Islands. Kusturica's documentary is for me is a true example of the meeting of sport and cinema. The film is sport. It is life. It is the picture of a whole nation's anguish.

In *Shoonya*, I added a third layer to Mahendra's narrative and the cricket fans' chorus, by inserting glimpses from Mahendra's childhood interactions with his father. The film attempts to show how a pure, open space was created around the child, a space where acceptance and endeavour were discussed. I felt that this would be the space that had built Mahendra, the cricketer. He would have carried this space with him when he stepped out to bat for the first time in a Test match. It is this space that would have resonated in the first boundary that he hit. And then it would be this space that would be usurped by the commercial madness of modern cricket.

Children do not play anymore. Sport, even with spectacular TV coverage, has become far more distant from the ordinary viewer, and India's recent (2011) cricket World Cup win had none of the adrenaline rush of the one in 1983. But sport continues to offer excellent plot lines for cinema. Producers are excited by the notion of creating genres behind which they can hide. Boxing films constitute such a genre, and are popular in India even though the sport of boxing has few genuine followers. The greatest single film to emerge from this genre is probably *Raging Bull*. Whether a sports story can be turned into cinematic material depends on the writer, the director, the music director, and all the other assistants. Yet, at the same time, sport is often just a formula. Mainstream cinema uses the formula and invests heavily in it to turn the subject into a spectacle. Few independent films (with exceptions like Jafar Panahi's *Off-side*) use sport as a subject. This brand of cinema does not have the budget or funding to create a spectacle. And if one were to get into the human side of sports, the yellow tape marking the distinction between the viewer, the crime, and the detective, might have generated larger audiences for the 'cut'. *Shoonya* fails to be a cricket film. And this is probably why it never got to the screens in India.

I had to put the film together on the edit table, yet it still seemed to me that I didn't have an opening sequence. I then shot one simple scene, a dead body going into the electric crematorium. It is Mahendra's father. And it is the end of the pure space for the captain. As he hurtles down the tunnel of corruption, this is an image that the captain dismisses. In the end, however, that image of nothingness is all that awaits him: literally, hero to zero, *shoonya*.

Playing Fair, Playing for Money: A Note on the Film *Shoonya*

Poonam Trivedi

'Fair play' has become a contested concept in sports today, noted more in the infringement than in the observance. Corruption in sport surfaces frequently, and institutional scams, doping, betting and match-fixing seem to have become the order of the day. The invasion by capital of sports, its corporatisation as it is termed, is seen as the source of these ills; the very investment and money which has contributed to the exponential expansion of the cache of sports—viewership and fandom—is seen as threatening to undermine the very basis of the existence of games and fair play. In India the most devastating incident has been the match-fixing scandal which broke out in 2000 after the ODI series between India and South Africa in which well-known players of both teams were indicted for accepting large sums of money from bookies for throwing away matches. The whole nation watched in horror and disbelief the unfolding of events which brought shame and dishonour to the most beloved game of all, cricket. In South Africa the shock was more severe: 'people were absolutely speechless. It is as though the entire country came to a standstill' recounts cricket writer Luke Alfred.[1] It is therefore appropriate that cinema which is a cultural barometer of the country should come out with a film, *Shoonya* (The Zero Zone), directed by Arindam Mitra, 2007, which encapsulated the trauma of this first instance of match-fixing in Indian cricket. The film was, however, denied public release through a legal injunction—a testimony of its truth value perhaps. A private screening was however permitted as part of the sports seminar out of which this book has emerged. The essay will examine this cinematic intervention, its unusual investigation into match-fixing, through a flashback narrative, into the heart and mind of a star cricketer. Press coverage, while informative, can rarely reveal the inner stories, the whys and wherefores, of a fall from grace. More crucially, the film problematises the ideal of fair play when the player is pressurised from all sides not to confess the truth. Hence the essay interrogates the entities of fair and foul play, especially with regard to sub-continental cricket, to provide a larger contextualisation to the accompanying archival piece by the director, Arindam Mitra, on the making of *Shoonya*.

Sport and Mammon

Money, capital of different kinds, has always been part of organised sport. The athletes of the original games in Olympia in ancient Greece, it is now known, were supported and sponsored by wealthy patrons and civic authorities. The ideal of amateurism, of playing but not for prize money, was an ideal created by the landed and leisured gentry who could spare the time and capital to developing sporting skills. And though professionalisation and mediatisation has changed the structure of sport into an arena of entertainment to a large extent, it has bought benefits of better fees, facilities and stadia for players and fans. Advertising revenues have glamorised sportspersons into celebrities. 'It is', as Adrian Walsh and Richard Giulianotti assert, 'naïve' to be repulsed by 'Sport as Business'.[2] Rules too have been changing to suit the times: the acceptance of the professional sportsperson in the Olympics has resulted in better and bigger events and records. The conflicting ambiguities of 'competing' versus 'winning' as ideals are illustrated very well, again, in a film, *Chariots of Fire* (1981), where the athlete Harold Abraham's openly demonstrated determination to win is contrasted unfavourably with the more playful manner of his Cambridge cohorts. Technology has further complicated the rules of fair play: line review, third umpire, DRS etc, while ostensibly compensating for human error are not infallible measures in themselves. Morality and ethics play out differently in sport: for many it constitutes a separate world with a bracketed morality which does not always apply in the mundane world. For others, like George Orwell, 'serious sport has nothing to do with fair play. It is bound up with hatred, jealousy, boastfulness, disregard of all rules and sadistic pleasure in witnessing violence.'[3] Thus while it is undeniable that money has become a major factor in sports and is subjecting it to market forces, the notion of fair play is perhaps no longer as clear cut in many minds as it used to be.

Different sports have a differing equation with capital. Cricket, the gentleman's game, is particularly caught up and fractured in its ethos: as Mike Marqusee has observed, 'cricket with its pre-industrial baggage,... despite recent embrace of the market, what might be called its political economies, continues to function in a parallel universe not quite conforming to the norms that govern other commercial ventures.'[4] Ashis Nandy, in a similar vein, calls cricket an essentially 'ethical game'. Its uniqueness he sees in its greater share of 'luck and probability'. Therefore the 'ethics of cricket', according to him 'depends primarily on the players': self regulation is crucial—players are required to start walking if they know they are out even before the umpire's decision. Today, however, he concedes, with the hardening of rules and the introduction of technology, the 'moral universe is different'. A 'player does not feel ethically compelled not to cheat. Everything is being dictated by rules and they judge the game. And on top of it, the cricketing boards are full of politicians and businessmen.'[5] We can now begin to unravel the sense of betrayal of 2000.

Sport and Cinema

Shoonya is not a typical sports film. It is not a celebratory bio-pic like *Bhaag Milkha Bhaag* or even a realistic one like *Pan Singh Tomar* or a nationalist or postcolonial sports film like *Chak De! India* or *Lagaan*, nor even a cricket crazy film like *Ferrari ki Sawaari* or *Kai Po Che*. It is not about match-fixing *per se*, but instead is a somber look at the fall of a great player, from 'hero to zero'.[6] It is also prophetic, in that it shows up for the first time, what was not so well known then, how players are lured by betting syndicate bosses, how they are tempted bit by bit with gifts and freebies until they are infected with the gambling virus. Rasik Bhai, a fat, bluff, teeth-picking fixer in dark glasses, played with consummate ease by Satish Kaushik, who calls himself Mahendra's 'bada pankha' [big fan] befriends and pursues him, plying him with expensive watches and cars, refusing to take a no. Moreover, the film exposes what is being revealed as fact today, the systemic rot which is infecting not just cricket, but also many other spheres of public life, of an entire underground system of illegal betting run by a mafia in which the players seem to be the smallest components. Lord Condon, head of the ICC anti-corruption unit, has estimated that up to $ 1billion can be gambled away on a one-day international of a World Cup series; and that 'in some countries, it is now more lucrative to engage in sports corruption than drug dealing or robbery'.[7] As the latest controversy of Indian Premier League VI played in 2013 is proving, corruption in cricket is not an individual aberration of a single player but of a cartel of bookies in which the very management and club owners are betting on their own teams in as illegitimate a manner as insider trading. And while a vociferous debate has been triggered off about how to save the game—from scrapping the Cricket Board, governmental takeover, legalising betting to jettisoning the IPL format—the changing complexion of fair play is not being fully addressed. Several of those charged with match-fixing in the 2000 case have been exonerated because of a lack of a specific law for this crime.[8] The current valency of the film is being reasserted.

Shoonya is not a documentary on the tribulations of cricket, competing with television footage and highlights. It is not an expository but introspective film, which, taking a cue from literary narratives, traces a soul-searching journey into the inner being of a superstar cricketer, Mahendra Naik, who is beset with temptations. And it plunges one into the heart of the conundrum of 'playing fair' when the player admits to taking money for throwing away matches and giving insider information, but is forced to retract the truth by his wife and his closest friend, who find no place for Harishchandra-like absolute 'truths' which will also drag them into ignominy. He also receives threatening phone calls from syndicate bosses. For him there is no recourse, no shred of heroism left, not even of the seeming martyr to the cause of truth. Not only is he sucked into the vortex of corruption but even his dilemma and his inner urge to come clean, to finally sacrifice himself to the cause of cricket is ridiculed as sentimental sympathy seeking and inexpedient. Kay Kay Menon gives a controlled and felt performance, which won for him the best actor award at the Osian Film festival, to show how the player's sense of self is so torn apart that he does not know what is right or wrong, or how to play fair, any more.

Most of the film is a dramatic visualisation of this vacillation, a moral 'pitch and toss'[9] which becomes a confounding of certainties. A Mephistophelian urbane old man, conjured by Mahendra's inner trauma, and played persuasively by Naseerudin Shah, repeatedly dogs him with discomfiting questions: '*Tum shoonya ke baare mein soochte ho?* [Do you think about zero]... as a cricketer are you not afraid of *shoonya* (also a duck in cricketing terminology)?' He berates him: 'You have sold our honour, the country's honour. ...Do you think that if you tell the truth you won't go to jail? ... It is not so easy to free yourself.' Initially Mahendra avoids these questions and brushes him off, but the old man argues not only on behalf of the family, but also on behalf of the game of cricket. 'Cricket is not in the constitution of Hindustan but it certainly is in the constitution of the public... as soon as this news spreads all of India will be on the streets ... your effigies will be burnt, the stadium will be wrecked, pitches will be dug up overnight, the cricket club will be reduced to ashes and like the Buddha of Bamiyan, Dalmiya (the then BCCI president) will also be obliterated,' he warns. Ambiguities proliferate when this seeming father figure tries to persuade Mahendra not to follow his instincts to own up but to choose a more realistic and pragmatic path. Towards the end both are seen together, dangling their feet in a pool, gauging their depths and sharpening the ethical issues: 'Do you think that by telling the truth you will achieve your repentance?... aren't you being a bit selfish? ... If you try to escape from the hell of your own creation you will drag your supporters with you. Either you burn or you let the others burn.'

Mahendra is finally confronted with a doppelganger, a saturnine image of himself in the washroom mirror, who tauntingly demands the *hisab* of his life, the 'debit/credit', and forces him to face up to himself. The ensuing debate tears to shreds his emotional subterfuges: starting from 'I didn't want all this... only wanted to play cricket' to 'cricket has ruined me, ... it lifted me up so close to the sun that my clothes got burnt ... I have been denuded'. But this 'other' self, who calls himself a *shaitan ki aulad* ['devil's creation'] does not stop until he has goaded him with some harsh truths, '*Mercedes mein phasa hua, middle-class ki aulad* [trapped in a Mercedes you son of the middle-class]'. For the first time Mahendra loses his composure, and hits out at him in the mirror hurting his fist into the bargain. Following this scene, he rushes to a lawyer and takes back his confession to the CBI, but not before his mind flashes hallucinations of dark waters closing over him, and drowning him.

Throughout the film, Mahendra's one refrain is 'life ban'. He already feels punished and victimised because he had nothing else in his life except cricket, and, as he says, 'without cricket his life is a *shoonya*'; he recalls with pride how once he made 147 not out despite being hit by a bouncer in the match. The film juxtaposes the space of actual sport with its inevitable corruption; the heroism of skill and dedication as an inviolable space is ironically contrasted with the growing lionisation and a god-like status which immunises the player against morality and makes him feel he can get away with corruption. Pursuit by bookies is one thing but succumbing to mammon another. As Hansie Cronje, captain of the South African (1994–2000) team, who shocked his country and the world of cricket when he was convicted of amassing 82,000 GBP by match-fixing, admitted at a press conference that 'it was the Devil who led him down the path of corruption ... that he became obsessed with money'[10] And that it was 'easy money, ... money for jam.'[11] In the film after the CBI officer has made the last bid to persuade Mahendra to tell the truth, by pleading on behalf of the game: '*Agar ho sake tho cricket ko bachaiye* [if you can, save cricket]', the hallucinatory figure of the old man reappears to congratulate him on suppressing the truth and saving the game: '*logo ka ab khel par se viswas kabhi nahi uthega* [now the people's trust in the game will never be breached]' he assures him. The irony of the muddying moralities is further complicated by the fact that Mahendra's actual father, *Baba*, a failed musician, seen in flashbacks, had brought him up with stoic guidance: '*jis cheez ki sabse zyada zarurat hoti hai woh kabhi kabhi nahi milti* [the thing you want most sometimes eludes you]'.

If we compare *Shoonya* with *Jannat* (Heaven, 2008, directed by Kunal Deshmukh) a film on a bookie's love story in the backdrop of match-fixing, which proved fairly successful grossing thirty-five crores in five weeks, the treatment of the ethical issues in the two films is fore-grounded. *Jannat* with its Bollywoodian absolutes does not debate, but instead polarises: Arjun Dixit, its hero, is a compulsive gambler who lies with impunity. He is also an angry young man who must win at all costs to achieve his heaven on earth. Hence, while the moral implications are spelt out, as in *Shoonya,* by his father, that 'the path of crime looks wonderful from a distance', they are never complicated, relativised or blurred either for the protagonist or for the audience as in *Shoonya.* There is no dilemma about playing fair, no introspection about the fall into temptation and its consequences. And though the bookie hero in *Jannnat* is caught and shot dead in the end, it is a gratuitous and sentimental end in which he moves to pick up a diamond ring—the token of his love—which has fallen out of his pocket, a move which is misread by the police. *Shoonya,* on the other hand, chooses a more starkly realistic, albeit full of pathos, ending: Mahendra is seen sitting alone in a corner of his house fully dressed in his cricketing gear while right outside fans are burning his effigy, jeering and hooting him. As the Mephistophelian figure exhorted him, '*shoonya mein baith kar socho*' [sit in nothingness and think]. While the tainted player finally has nothing left with his fans breaking down his gate, his only sense of a stable self remains in clutching to his playing persona, the 'pure space' of sport. Far from condoning the suppression of evidence, the film underlines the view that one can never escape the consequences of an unethical act.

'Why can't Bollywood keep its sports films real?' questions film critic Shubhra Gupta, 'Why do we need to dress them up to make them palatable?...Why are we so afraid of seeing the truth on screen?'[12] The sports film is doubly challenged: while it cannot compete with actual sport footage in terms of action, it is inevitably under pressure to effect some compromises in the interests of the box office. *Shoonya* made few compromises and that's why it has yet to acquire a following, or, in fact, even a commercial release. It eschewed the song and dance titillation in favour of a soul-searching problematisation of the ideas of fair and foul, the pure, but now tainted, space of sport.

Sport and Ethics

Mammon or commodification is not the only problem in sport today. Equally pernicious and difficult to root out is doping, where the innate desire to excel pushes sportspeople into indulging in drugs which ultimately do more harm than good to the sporting body. Other unsavoury practices like sledging, ball tampering, underarm bowling, or no balls keep cropping up every now and then. At this moment when Indian cricket is again caught in the throes of a spot-fixing and betting controversy involving reputed players, and history seems to be repeating itself, the notion of playing fair needs to be examined not just by players but by administrators too, especially in terms of their responsibility to the game and its fans. It is the public, i.e. the fans, whose investment of time and money keeps professionalised sport rolling and whose support should not be taken for granted. The film has an acute portrait of the role of the fans in the idolization and then, being left bereft, in the disgrace of Mahendra. The case of the considerable diminution of support for rugby in Australia after the struggle for control of the game between two rival pay television channels (Packer vs Murdoch) and the institution of a rival tournament, the Super League, in the 1990s is well documented and may happen elsewhere too.[13]

In the Preface to a new edition (2007) of his provocative book, *The Tao of Cricket* (2000), Ashis Nandy seriously questions whether matches can actually be fixed in cricket given the high unpredictability of the game: 'Someone has to convince me that by buying off a few players or by depending upon a few tips about ground conditions from players, one can control results in cricket.'[14] He refers to the infamous test between England and South Africa, played at Centurion Park (January 2000) captained by Cronje, in which he admitted to taking money to declare on the last day and make a game out of it but which ultimately resulted in a victory for England, as an example of the working of 'fate' versus 'fixing' in cricket. Fate, or the element of chance, he argues, is more instrumental in cricket than other games like football or hockey in which environmental factors are roughly the same for both teams: 'Fate is the first identifier of cricket...In true cricket, one incidentally wins against one's opponent; one mostly wins against one's fate. That is why a drawn match can be such an enriching, exciting result in traditional cricket'.[15] He also points to the conventions and paradoxes of the game which are 'unique in providing ample scope for unjust play as well as having strong taboos against such play', and that it is this very condition of 'elasticities and inelasticities', that is 'the unique structure of the ethics of cricket' which forms 'the basic bond between cricket and Indian culture'.[16] 'One of the cultural attractions of cricket in India is the moral universe that it invokes and sustains', he pronounces[17] and then consolidates his argument by linking the other great passion of the Indian populace, films, with cricket, noting their 'common concern' with the contradictions of fate.[18] One does not need to be fully persuaded by Nandy's views to assert that he would approve of *Shoonya* where these very contradictions, the twists and turns, and the confusions between fate, truth and fairness are enacted in the life of an individual Indian cricketer.

Despite professionalisation, and the questioning of amateurism notwithstanding, the notion of sports for sports' sake remains an ideal not just for setting right the rules and ethics of fair play, but also of an acknowledgement of the intrinsic skills, techniques and the beauty and pleasure of playing a good shot, getting a stroke right, and of the pure, and possibly incorruptible, space of playing 'fair'.

Notes

1. Luke Alfred, *BBC 1* 'Panorama' 20 June 2001, transcript, accessed 30 Sept. 2013.
2. Adrian Walsh and Richard Giulianotti, *Ethics, Money and Sport: This Sporting Mammon* (New York: Routledge 2007), p. 4.
3. George Orwell, 'The Sporting Spirit', in *The Penguin Essays of George Orwell* (Harmondsworth: Penguin, 1994), pp. 321–23.
4. Mike Marqusee, *Anyone but England: Cricket and the National Malaise* (London: Verso, 1994), p. 119.
5. Ashis Nandy, Interview by Ajoy Ashirwad Mahaprashasta, 'It has become a real business,' *Frontline*, 28 June 2013.
6. Arindam Mitra, 'Connections' .... I am thankful to Arindam Mitra for permitting a viewing of this film.
7. 'The Shadow over Cricket', *BBC News*, 4 June 2007, accessed 30 Sept. 2013.

8. Dhananjay Mahapatra, 'Lack of a law saved Azhar, Jadeja', *The Times of India*, May 26, 2013.
9. L. C. Knights' comment on the blurring of moral verities in Shakespeare's *Macbeth*, *Explorations: Essays in Criticism Mainly on the Literature of the Seventeenth Century* (London: Chatto & Windus, 1958), p. 18.
10. Walsh and Giulianotti, op. cit. p. 41.
11. As reported by David Lomax in *BBC 1*, 'Panorama' 20 June 2001, transcript, accessed 30 Sept. 2013.
12. Shubhra Gupta, 'How to be a Sport', in 'Eye', *The Sunday Express*, 1–7 September, 2013, p. 20.
13. See Walsh and Giulianotti, op. cit., p. 107.
14. Ashis Nandy, Preface to the OUP Edition, *A Very Popular Exile*, Oxford India Paperbacks (New Delhi: Oxford University Press, 2011), p. xiii.
15. Ashis Nandy, 'The Tao of Cricket', in *A Very Popular Exile*, ibid., p. 21.
16. Nandy, ibid., pp. 30–1.
17. Nandy, ibid., p. 37. He elaborates his argument by some provocative comparisons: 'The apparent slowness of cricket ... would tax the patience of most peoples except the *Gita*-devouring ahistorical Indians, who continue to see it as pleasurable and as an epitome of desireless, *karmic* life; the savage, frolicsome West Indians, allegedly innocent of the idea of the productive use of time; and England's antiquated Victorian gentry, still trying to see cricket as both pleasurable and as a Calvinist moral lesson', p. 21.
18. Nandy, ibid., p. 44.

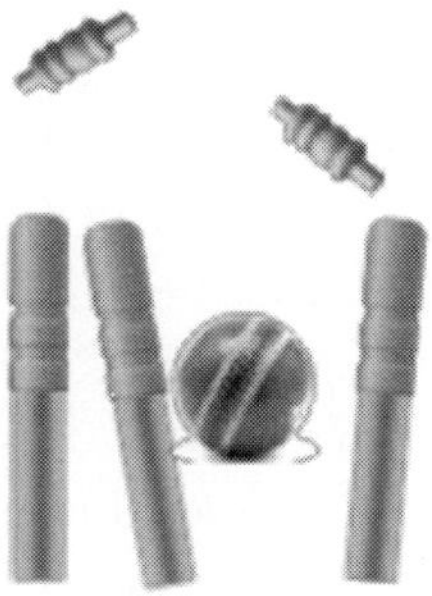

13

The Underdog Bowling to the Cultural Field in Kukunoor's *Iqbal*

Anas Tabraiz

Nagesh Kukunoor's *Iqbal,* produced by Subhash Ghai's Mukta Searchlight films in 2005, was released at a momentous period in the history of the growth of the Indian nation. Even though the viewers' response to the film was at best average, it did raise certain important questions about the reach of the concept of the Indian nation, the proliferation of the national identity and narratives of integration amongst its people. After Independence, the national media, cinema and sports played a crucial role in reaching out to the masses to make them participate in the national imaginary and to fashion an image for the new India. The diversity of cultures, regions and religions and the initial technical inadequacy of the media made it a challenge for the Indian state to capture the imagination of people in far flung and remote areas of the Indian territory. National telecast on television, came as late as 1982, with Doordarshan. The patchy representation, in national organisations and teams, of people from several states, regions and communities reflected the irregularities in the sway of the national imaginary in India. It is only since the last few years that a boom in the field of information technology and mass communication has brought about a sea change in the possibilities of the world of representation and images. The recent rise in the popularity and availability of television sets, internet and mobile phones has made it easier for the state to convey its discourses to the masses. The entry into the new century has witnessed a torrent of reality and game shows like 'Indian Idol' and 'Kaun Banega Crorepati' on television that exercise and stimulate the imagination of a much larger audience. If we were to talk of the changes in the Indian national cricket team, in the context of Kukunoor's *Iqbal*, usual names from expected pockets have given way to new blood from across the country. The new policy of tapping enterprise in every sector is reflected in the surfacing of new cricketing talent in the last few years. According to the sports historian Boria Majumdar, 'Sanjay Bangar, Harbhajan Singh, Zaheer Khan, Virender Sehwag and Mohammed Kaif are men from the middle class and relatively modest backgrounds, who have become national icons in the years 1998–2003.'[1] Majumdar acknowledges this new inclusive trend in the Indian team:

> The presence of men from humble backgrounds in a team is significant, because Indian cricket, till recently, continued to be dominated by the economically privileged, affluent sections of the society. In India caste and class status has, in most cases, tended to overlap, and the economically privileged stratum has been for decades, and remains, predominantly upper class.[2]

He further points out that the team's popularity after the victory in the 1983 World Cup in England 'opened up among the middle class and the underprivileged sections of Indian society the possibility of cricket being a viable career option.'[3] The prospect of joining the Indian team allowed the 'lower caste, economically underprivileged men to come to the fore and don national colours.'[4] Yet, while the appearance of new faces from small towns and suburbs is a welcome phenomenon there is still a huge rural population that cannot look up to the city for its provisions and needs. In portraying the rise to fame of a deaf-mute boy, from the very germ of desire to its fruition, *Iqbal* reiterates the need for a deeper penetration of the national narratives. It is in this context that I have read the film as an indirect call to all those who do not have the means to voice their concerns on the screen of Indian popular culture. The choice of cricket as a theme to discuss the changing face, scope and potential of the Indian national imaginary in the early years of the twenty-first century secures a safe place for *Iqbal* in the history of Indian cinema. It is a film that uses cricket and its mass appeal to make meaningful statements about the reach of the narratives of nationalism across the Indian nation. The film achieves a kind of metaphorical transcendence, drawing its audience so powerfully into its story that, at times, it would be difficult to convince viewers that, beneath the story of the deaf-mute hero's rise to fame, there are deeper socio-economic and political issues involved. Kukunoor's film makes effective use of theories of linguistics and psychoanalysis to analyse the participation of some sections of the Indian masses, especially the minorities, in national policies, examining how this facilitates India's participation in the global economy. In doing this, the film also fulfills the function of subtle propaganda by urging the marginalised sections of the Indian masses to enter the national imaginary; to utilise its common resources to earn a place for India in the global community. Read in this context, the story of Iqbal seeks to inspire the new generation of Indians to dream; to imagine a world of better opportunities, and to use national resources towards the realisation of their dreams. It also addresses that part of the rural Indian population that has hitherto been indifferent to the dreams and desires that drive modern, urban India. Iqbal's life is presented as a model for his minority community and for rural India in general. He becomes exemplary for his ability to imagine a community with a hallowed circle of the national elite (represented by the national cricket team), in spite of being born in an oppressively unpromising reality. The film participates in the discourse that urges the deprived, castaway sections of the Indian masses not to forego their stake in the national identity, because of its lack of inclusiveness, and to imagine unconventional ways to deserve membership in that community, however exclusive it may appear. It, therefore, seeks to eventually pull them into an economy of desire and make them participants in a power-game that they otherwise would hardly ever play on their own.

Disability, Imagination and Desire

The path of the transformation of the deaf-mute Iqbal into a circumspect, competent bowler is structurally homologous to the description of a 'little man's' acquisition of language in the Lacanian theory of the Mirror Stage. The child in the mirror stage follows a trajectory of growth that emancipates him from a position of congenital physical powerlessness. The imaginative identification with the mirror image makes the intransigent body subservient to the logic of the mirror and the self-image in it. This is how Lacan traces the growth of natural man, out of a state of essential powerlessness and subjection, into what he terms the 'Symbolic' order. Like the congenitally 'disabled' little man in Lacan, Iqbal, the central character of the film, is born deaf-mute. The film shows us how the protagonist overcomes a material, physical shortcoming, by exercising his will to attain 'subjectivity'. He imaginatively participates in an alternative semantic field, where he might overcome physical disabilities and reclaim his capacity to assert and articulate himself. It is not only for Iqbal that the film traces the passage from an essentially voiceless existence to acquiring voice and language; Iqbal's desire and his pursuit of it are meant to be an inspiration for his region and the community that he belongs to. The film, therefore, addresses not only individuals but also the communities marginalised out of the national image, to rise out of their immediate reality and to participate in the national imaginary for national and individual interests. At a subtler level, the film tries to urge the unassimilated sections of the Indian population, the minorities, remote tribes and rural communities, to forge an identification, however false, with the mirror image of the unified nation. The benefits that accrue from such participation in the national, or at a deeper level, the global, imaginary are implied in the deaf-mute hero's emancipation to a version of 'speech' on the cricket field.

Iqbal was released in 2005, at a time when the minority question was being rethought by the nation. The Gujarat riots in 2002 had raised the question of the sense of belonging and the stake that the minority community had in the 'secular' state. The Sachar Committee was appointed by the Prime Minister on 9 March 2005 and its report was submitted in the last week of November 2006. The Sachar Report conclusively proved that the bulk of Indian Muslims suffer from grave deprivation in social, economic and educational opportunities because of lack of access to education, health care and other public services, and to employment. The level of deprivation has increased to such an extent that in certain sectors Muslims are lagging even behind Dalits. That this deprivation affects Muslims more than any other Socio-Religious Category (SRC) has also been the conclusion of many previous studies like those of C. Ramamanohar Reddy, Imran Ali and Yogendra Sikand, Zoya Hasan and Ritu Menon. The fact that the government felt the need to appoint yet another committee to look into the affairs of the community reflects the growing need in the state to incorporate this second largest community of India into the nation. In the specific case of Indian minorities, scholars have pointed out 'conceptual and political contestations between 'citizens' and 'people' on the one hand and between the dynamics of hegemonic majoritarianism and the consequences of minority marginalisation on the other.'[5]

Iqbal's father is a typical member of the Muslims in India in seeking to be independent of the state machinery for earning his livelihood. He refuses to be led by images and believes in physical labour. Unlike the other minorities, Muslims have always been a special case in the Indian context. The prioritisation of religious law and community interests over the interests of the nation has always kept them in the realm of suspicion. It is in national interest that the suspicious image of the Indian Muslim has been continually denied by films like *Chak De! India* and *Sarfarosh*. *Chak De! India* portrays Kabir Khan (played by Shah Rukh Khan) as the coach of the Indian National Women's Hockey team, who is suspected of privileging community over country for having failed to convert a penalty into a goal, in an all important world cup final against Pakistan. It is only by training the national women's hockey team and leading them to victory that Kabir Khan proves his allegiance to the nation and silences his critics. Similarly, *Sarfarosh* has a brief episode where the ACP (Aamir Khan) is suspicious of a subordinate Muslim police officer's alliance with anti-national elements. The suspicion turns out to be unfounded and leads to regret and remorse on the part of the patriotic ACP. Notwithstanding the representation in cinema, the triumph of religious law and community bonding over the pull of the national imaginary has made the Muslims merely dispassionate participants in the narratives of the nation or of globalisation. In order to participate and gain from the national imaginary it is imperative that the community set aside its religious priorities to participate in a syncretistic, secular society. Participation in the syncretistic community of the nation would be comparable to the Lacanian child's complete identification with his image in the mirror. The problem that the film presents, especially with the character of Iqbal's father, is that of a lack of recognition of the benefits of participation in the national imaginary. The refusal to acknowledge and desire the benefits of participation in the nation, affects not only the minorities but also a huge population inhabiting relatively remote areas of the Indian territory. The inability of the various media to reach these remote parts is responsible for the lukewarm appeal of the nationalistic discourses in these areas. The tiny television set on which the whole village watches the national team play, in the opening scene of *Iqbal,* is a reminder of the limited access that mass media have to the remote interiors to bring the nation together. To increase its mass appeal the discourse of nationalism needs to make the mirror image generally accessible to the masses in order for its promise to be recognised. Iqbal's father, therefore, has an argument with his son's trainer, that works equally well for nationalism as for cricket, over the sagacity of gambling with one's life in a game that bestows its jackpots on the elect few.

The fact that the film consciously uses the Lacanian schema for its theoretical background implies that it seeks to present the protagonist's 'disability' in terms of the failure to identify with the mirror image. In the context of the Lacanian theories of language and psychology, Iqbal's disability with language is structurally comparable to his community's inability to participate in the imaginary community of the nation. The growth into the secular, syncretistic society is similar to the imaginary phase of the Lacanian mirror stage, as diverse subjects 'misrecognise' themselves in the image of a unified nation. According to Anika Lemaire, 'The subject is in effect represented in symbolism by a stand in; a signifier which may be the personal pronoun 'I', the forename which devolves upon the subject.'[6] Every subject of the nation participates in the national imaginary for the liberal space that the nation promises to provide for individual development. Everyone, therefore, is driven by self-interest but keeps this self-interest hidden while performatively participating in the national community. Any objective reality that the subject encounters has to be structurally mediated and transformed to suit the self-interest and the structure that furthers that self-interest. The symbolic space that thus emerges is a circular formation in which the structure provides opportunities to the individual to grow, and the individual grows to perpetuate the structure. The closed structure implies that rather than encountering objective reality and being affected by it, the subject begins to affect objective reality. Rather than facing the world outside, the subject turns away from it towards an interior space of ready made signifiers. The harmony that the subject achieves by such a turning back from external impulses has been called a 'palintropic harmony' by Heraclitus in ancient Greek texts.[7] This palintropic, or back-turning harmony has the structure similar to cupid's bow, where the string gives tension to the stick and the stick maintains the tautness of the string.

The narrative of the nation is the order of signifiers that the self has to 'subject' itself to, in order to attain 'subjectivity'. Emile Benveniste describes the purely linguistic basis of the notion of subjectivity as follows: "The subjectivity we are discussing here is the capacity of the speaker to posit himself as 'subject'. It is defined not by the feeling which everyone experiences of being himself...but as the psychic unity that transcends the totality of the actual experiences it assembles, and that makes the permanence of the consciousness."[8] The call for participation in the national community is, therefore, a call towards subjection to a system of 'pure signifiers' that shall not have any direct referential relation to the objective world. The 'pure signifiers' will structure a discursive field that shall absorb the shocks of pure objective reality and shall alchemically transform it to the point of making it palatable. Through the ensuing discussion I would like to discuss Nagesh Kukunoor's use of the cricketing field (and the Indian nation) as a metaphor for the linguistic field of 'pure signifiers'. The protagonist Iqbal's development into a cricketer, in the above context, would imply his acquisition and learning of the language of 'pure signifiers' and moving into the Lacanian Symbolic (as also the movement of his community into the nation). I would also like to argue that Iqbal's recognition of cricket as a liberating order of the signifier and his consequent triumph over his reality is also a call to his community to participate in the national imaginary for similar benefits.

The most interesting achievement of the eponymous hero lies in his ability to close his eyes and imagine that he is playing for the country, even as he practices bowling on a humble patch of grass. He shows quixotic acumen in transforming the buffaloes that he looks after into a cheering audience at the cricket stadium. The young Indian seeks inspiration from images and does not let the distance, between his goal and his reality, deter him in any way. We come to know a little later that he has made for himself a small hut on whose walls he sticks images of Indian cricketers of international fame. This hut serves to project Iqbal's mind; the inner space to which he often goes to restore his belief in his aspirations. The hut represents the initial flicker of subjective space, and consequently voice, in the otherwise deaf-mute existence of the hero. It is to be noted that the deaf boy 'hears' an imaginary cheering crowd in a stadium only in this secret interior space.

Illustration 13.1 Sequence of Iqbal dreaming *Courtesy*: Mukta Arts

It is the desire to bridge the gap, between the power of the self-image and the powerlessness in real life, that gives an air of urgency to Iqbal's quest. He is divided between this cerebral image of himself and the demands of the mundane world around him. His father allows him just another year to live in his illusory world and dream big before Iqbal is eventually old enough to take his place and share his responsibilities. Iqbal is torn between tapping a liberating imagination, that he inherits from his mother, and the unimaginative subjection to the role of the farmer that his father is waiting to pass on to him.

The self-image that drives Iqbal is sustained, verified and reflected back to him by his mother and his sister. These two members of his family support his belief in his aspirations. It is his sister who performs the important role of a go-between between Iqbal and the rest of the world. In an early part of the movie, we find Iqbal hidden behind buffaloes, trying to read the lips of the head trainer (Guruji) who is giving bowling lessons within a fenced-in field of the Kolapad Academy of Cricket.

Illustration 13.2 Sequence Iqbal fenced in *Courtesy*: Mukta Arts

The scene is well structured in adequately presenting the spatial opposition between the territory bound-in by the fence and the point where Iqbal stands. Iqbal with his 'handicap' is indistinguishable from the cattle that he looks after; the only thing that makes him different is his desire to join the men inside the fence. His sister comes too late from school to join him there. The scene communicates the desire in Iqbal to move ahead by working hard to realise his dream. Kolapad academy is the entry point to the circle of power that Iqbal wishes to master. It is from here that he learns the basics of significantly using the language of cricket that shall lead him to master the discursive field to negotiate with his social, political and economic reality.

It is Iqbal's sister, Khadija, who introduces her brother, and his superior bowling talent, to Guruji. She has so much faith in her brother's capabilities that Guruji agrees to give Iqbal a chance to stage his talent. Khadija is thematically important to the story as she plays the role of a mediator between Iqbal's world and the world of power within the fence. Without her, Iqbal could not have been instructed and trained at all. The fact that Khadija is mostly dressed in a school uniform stresses the need for education in the Muslim community; her role as the mediator emphasises the necessity of education as means to initiate a dialogue with the world of power. At this point, Iqbal is too self-conscious to be able to bowl in front of the other players in the academy. The fact that his sister has to ask him to imagine that the people who were watching him were buffaloes, reveals that the inability was because of the gap between Iqbal's humble reality and his larger-than-life self-image. The problem is eventually solved only by Iqbal's individual belief in a yet unproved sense of superiority over the others around him. The resolution comes about with a complete faith in the subjective reality of the self-image and by making the world around him subservient to that reality. Iqbal becomes a Lacanian subject in giving precedence to his imagination in the face of a smothering reality. Iqbal's first spell, inside the sacred space of the academy, is his first speech-act. Now, he has to find recognition in the eyes of the master. I would like to quote Shoshana Felman in order to clarify my point: 'the psychoanalytic recognition is radically tied up with language, with the subject's analytic speech-act, and as such, its value is less cognitive than performative: it is, itself, essentially a speech-act, whose symbolic action modifies the subject's history, rather than cerebrally observing or recording it, at last correctly.'[9] Iqbal could only have made his entry into this realm of language by a primary act of imagination where he internalises and transforms external reality and tips the scales on his side. He goes on to bowl accurately as soon as this gap between imagination and reality is eliminated. His superior speed and accuracy give enough reason to Guruji to groom him as a prodigy.

Subjective and Objective Reality

Now that Iqbal has entered the Academy, he realises that physical energy, speed and accuracy are not the only attributes that count to attain the mastery over the discursive field, represented by the field of cricket. Guruji tells him that things are very different when one bowls to an opponent rather than just bowling at the wickets on an empty pitch. The conversation between the teacher and his pupil compares the cricket field to the field of language, where various 'players' contend with the others for superiority, backed by their respective self-images. It becomes important not only to learn the straightforward but also the cunning ways of combat. The versions of swing, change of pace and other modes of deception become the staple for a bowler to survive on the field without being mastered. He learns from Guruji that he will have to use his 'pace' as a weapon. Khadija fails to catch up with Guruji's words and signals 'face' instead of 'pace' to Iqbal. The mistake has been scrupulously slipped in to alert and inform the viewers of the presence of a theoretical subtext. The intentional play on using one's face as a weapon alludes to the performative aspect of language, Lacan defines a signifier as 'that which represents a subject for another signifier', in opposition to the sign, which 'represents something for someone.'[10] With training from Guruji, Iqbal is on his way to learning the ways to realise his self-image when a minor incident sends him out of the academy and back into the space fit for cattle.

A rich boy, the erstwhile hero of the academy, becomes jealous of Iqbal's rising popularity and has an altercation with him, off the field. Iqbal, who has by now become too confident of his self-image, answers back by bowling a bodyline ball to this boy, injuring him severely. The injury is serious enough to cost Iqbal his place in the academy. The influential father of the rich boy is, incidentally, also one of the major patrons of the academy. He asks Guruji to either expel Iqbal or to lose funding. The incident is placed in the film to emphasise the yet unbridged gap between Iqbal's reality and his image of himself. It tells us that the subjective image cannot be brought into reality until a reality has been prepared for that image. The self has to negotiate between subjective and objective reality until the time that the reality has been brought to approximate to the subjective image. This incident also teaches Iqbal that there is a structural interconnection between different discursive fields. The mastery of one field does not imply the mastery of the whole structure, and in that one field too, he is not a master yet. Property or money has to be accumulated, apart from and through one's intra-discursive talent, in order to be able to hold power outside one's discursive field. The lesson, however, is learnt too late. Iqbal's self-image is as badly damaged as the face of his rich opponent on the field when he is requested by Guruji to leave the academy immediately. The amount of energy that Iqbal had already spent in earning his entry into the academy makes him powerless to counter this blow of reality. His self-image begins to dwindle as a result of his being too careless in striking a balance between the world of imagination and that of reality. The narrative sequence tells us that it was too early for Iqbal to have let the interior world of imagination come out into an open conflict with the bitter reality of the outer world. Furthermore, the false mirror image given by the Imaginary realm does not have power in the face of reality. In order to give power to the mirror image the self has to move from the dualistic Imaginary order to the ternary realm of the 'Symbolic'.

The return of the little hut, where Iqbal had collected the images of his heroes, reinforces its metaphorical value. Iqbal has to come back to the little hut; he shuts himself in, closes his eyes and tries to repair and resurrect his dying image of himself. This time he finds it hard to hear the voice of the cheering crowds. The brief tryst with power, far from initiating him into the circle of power seems to have left him even more powerless than before. The deaf-mute boy suffers; his handicap redoubles as an overdose of reality scuppers even his ability to imagine.

Illustration 13.3 Sequence Iqbal in anguish *Courtesy*: Mukta Arts

The tragedy seems to have reached its end but only for a tiny string that the writer of the story had left dangling in the early part of the film. Iqbal, before going to the academy, would often rouse a village drunkard by sprinkling water on him, before going back home after finishing his regular practice. He comes upon a little photograph of this same drunkard, while he is burning all the images in his little hut in rage and agitation, after his ouster from the academy. This little photograph becomes a ray of hope that re-illumines the bleak world of Iqbal after his brief encounter with power, at the academy. He picks up the photo and pledges to rebuild his broken fortune with the help of this new teacher, Mohit.

The new teacher, we soon come to know, is too disenchanted, with the constant encounter between imagination and reality, to come back to the field. Whereas Guruji, the teacher at Kolapad academy, represents the extreme of living in reality by cunningly operating from behind the image, the new drunken master represents the other extreme—that of living in a world of intoxication by totally giving up the race for power in the real world. The two masters represent the Apollonian and the Dionysian versions of the human will. The Apollonian represents the constant subjection of objective reality to mental forms as opposed to the Dionysian victory over reality by being intoxicated with the self-image. Iqbal has had a taste of one extreme, he shall learn now from the other. The fact, that our hero has access to both the above mentioned extremes, leads him to the final attainment of a golden mix of the two.

It is a task, for Iqbal and his sister, to get the old master out of his drunken stupor and to inspire him enough to get back at the real world. The youthful enthusiasm and physical prowess of Iqbal can now be combined with the experience and expertise of this new master to set Iqbal back on his road to power. The drunken man realises that Iqbal could become a means for him to hit back at the real world and begin his struggle again from where he had left it. The master's return to the symbolic realm is suitably conveyed through Mohit's agitated outburst where he talks of settling the unfinished business with his (symbolic) father.

Possessing the Symbolic

It is important now, that Iqbal learn from his own mistakes and those of his new master. For this he has to understand the seminal difference between the inner world of the subject and the outer world of reality. The unimpeded beauty of the world of imagination has to be salvaged every moment from the onslaughts of an ugly reality. Iqbal has to learn that objective reality has to be toned down, transformed and adapted to suit the designation of the self-image in the discursive field. He ought to have learnt by now that the uncensored entry and overdose of reality could be seriously detrimental to the world of interiority centered upon, and structured around, one's self-image. The bitter truths of the real world have to be held at bay so that the important business of imagination might be carried on unperturbed. The need for the ternary order of the symbolic that will be made of 'pure signifiers' to mediate between the interior image and the external reality of the subject makes way for Iqbal's entry into the 'Symbolic'.

Fredric Jameson points out that 'the acquisition of the Symbolic is rather a precondition for the full mastery of the imaginary as well.'[11] After having learnt the basics of bowling and having practised the Lacanian Imaginary, Iqbal now has to learn to master the Symbolic. Recalling the triangular schema of Oedipus complex, he is now in the position of a son whose relationship with his mother (objective reality) has to be qualified by the law of the symbolic father (the law of the cricket arena). In other words, Iqbal has to learn to exercise his will to snap his relationship with objective reality in order to optimise his performance in the cricket field. Rather than constantly struggling against a debilitating reality, Iqbal has to sculpt his own reality with the help of symbolic tools and pure signifiers. Once he becomes a subject of the symbolic, he has to learn to 'represent' the mundane reality of the world around him to his advantage. He has to fashion an image of himself and his environment that does not bear any referential relation to his real position in the world outside the cricketing field. Iqbal learns to bowl to a set field. The fenced in field in the earlier scenes develops into a controlled discursive field, an enclosure where every outcome of an action is anticipated and countered in advance. This is done with such mastery that the narrative of interiority, structured with pure (hollow) signifiers, may become impenetrable and could be sustained without any detriment from objective reality.

The cricketing field does not reflect any truth about the objective world, the meaning of every action is defined purely by the law or the rules of the game. In as far as bowling, batting or fielding does not directly make any difference to the real natural or human condition outside the field, it represents the realm of pure signification from which the mother is completely absent. The ball, bat, pitch and the field have come to replace the conventional field of human effort. It becomes clear through a structural comparison with the Oedipal triangle that the real mother has been replaced by the symbolic mother. The film compares learning to bowl to a set field to the Freudian *Game of the Occult*, where the child learns to deal with the mother's absence by playing Fort/Da with the spindle that stands in for the absent mother. This phase of learning is directed at gaining control over and being able to 'effect' a willed reality. By learning to master the spindle in the Fort/Da game, the child becomes free of the painful reality of an absent mother and can maintain his state of pleasure by exercising his will. By imaginatively practicing to replace the absent mother with the spindle, the child attains autonomy and becomes independent of the mother and replaces her with another object. The Oedipal child has to impose a beginning, middle and an end on an otherwise unyielding and amorphous reality. The child's proficiency at maintaining his pleasure is comparable to Iqbal's learning to control the outcome of each one of his deliveries and making the batsmen play the shots that the bowler desires. Mohit interestingly quibbles with Khadija as he points towards his head and says *'yeh dil ka khel hai'* ('this is game of heart'), and points towards his heart and says *'jo dimagh se khela jaata hai'* ('which is played by the mind'). What the master clearly implies is that once in the symbolic sphere one has to learn to do the work of the mind with his heart. The heart and the mind have to be locked into a relationship where the mind provides images for what the heart desires. The relationship hinted at, between the heart and the mind, the seat of desire and imagination, respectively, is explained by this quotation from Edmond Ortiques:

> Imagination and desire are the realities of a finite being which can emerge from the contradiction between self and other only by the genesis of a third term, a mediatory 'concept' which by determining each term, orders them into reversible and progressive relations which can be developed in language. The whole problem of symbolization lies here, in this passage from a dual opposition to a ternary relation, a passage from desire to the concept.[12]

Through the sustained metaphor of the cricketing field, the film makes a subtle comment on the essential problem of marginalised communities. Iqbal's passionate desire to enter the field of cricket begins to symmetrically overlap a projected community desire to enter the arena of mass/popular culture. The film beckons the marginalised communities, especially the Muslims, to mould a new destiny for themselves by joining an order of images.

The new master therefore teaches Iqbal to control his opponent's (the batsman's) choice of shots rather than constantly straining to anticipate what the opponent's next action might be. He should learn to bowl in such a way that the opponent has no choice but to hit the ball where the bowler wants him to. It is only when one becomes powerful enough to control the response of his opponent, to such an extent that the choice that the opponent exercises seems to be optimum and free, that the field becomes immune to traumatising reality. The self-image, and the Symbolic, has to be believed in to the extent of having complete faith in it. It is with such faith that the actions of the Other and the Self might emanate from the same source. This practice with reality in the imaginary phase helps the subject in its eventual flight into the Symbolic. This is the effect that the control over the opponent's mind by simulating free choice seeks to achieve. The productive complementary interaction between the heart and mind is the key to attaining a 'palintropic harmony' and a relative autonomy from the objective world. This episode gives us a formula for reducing objective reality to an image of desirability before it is encountered by the subject's interiority.

The mastery over objective reality is refined in the final stages of Iqbal's training where he finds the secret formula for the 'Chakravyuh' at his master's place. The Chakravyuh is a peculiar formation in the field which is a grade above the art of controlling the choice of shots for the opponent. Not only should the choice of shots be controlled but also the possible outcomes of these shots. This feat can only be achieved when the field, and the opportunities and avenues that the field holds, changes with every ball according to the desire of the bowler. It is with this final lesson that Iqbal's education of the structure of language becomes complete. He becomes fit to move out into the world of reality with his cherished, although hidden self-image. He can also use his newly acquired art to counter a debilitating reality and to bring about eventual parity between the virtual and the real. The virtual, mental self-image becomes a driving force that will help Iqbal to manage his reality until that reality begins to approximate this image.

According to the logic of the film, it is Iqbal's complete faith in his self-image, and the structure that helps build that self-image, that leads to his salvation from the world of poverty and helplessness that his father inhabits. Iqbal faces his final test in the symbolic field when Guruji tries to use Iqbal's financial crisis to prevent his selection in the National team. Guruji offers Iqbal a substantial sum of money to rescue his father's farm and pay off his debts, on the condition that he would let his protégé, Kamal, be selected by the selection board. Iqbal is too hard pressed at this point to refuse the offer. He keeps Guruji's cheque only to tear it up after having made his arrangements. The logic of the film requires that he does not commit the earlier mistake again. He does not let this blow of objective reality shatter the imaginary world that he had by now made for himself. He finally does use his 'face' as a weapon and goes on to sell his image to media sponsors to get the amount, that he needs to help his father, from the market. The last scene recalls Iqbal's hut as he asks Mohit for five minutes to retreat within himself. In the vacant dressing room he closes his eyes once again to imagine himself playing for the Indian team. The end shows Iqbal as a prospective member of the Indian team. He is a common man who has believed in an image that he had projected for himself and has had the physical and the mental ability to achieve it.

To conclude this essay, I would like to point out that the course that the action of the film suggests is an exact inversion (may one also say, perversion) of the normal course that non-desiring subjects usually take. Whereas the human mind is designed to encounter objective reality, to abstract from it and to reach rational conclusions based on these abstractions, the film lays down a method in which abstractions must precede objective reality. It also implies that the human will and its desire for power should be a part of a combative field where self-centered versions of truth should constantly be working to transform objective reality. According to the logic that the film presents, a relative harmony with reality can only be achieved by turning back from it. The mind, rather than being in a state of flux and becoming, doubles back upon itself. The film urges its audience to distribute its energies between the inner and the outer world. It urges them to carry on their dreary quest for daily bread while also constantly trying their luck in the field of desire.

Even after sixty-five long years of Indian Independence and innumerable conflicts on issues arising from it, the majority of the Indian population refuses to be enchanted by national narratives of development. The sheer immensity and remoteness of this corpus of the world population has kept it inaccessible for the narratives of modernity to affect and transform it. In spite of the constant efforts of the global community to find acknowledgment and emulation, India remains incorrigibly immune to the western imaginary. In this essay, I emphasise the importance of *Iqbal* as a film that uses the two versions of India to structure an argument in favour of more and more public participation in the nation and the liberal global arena. While arguing in favour of the latter, the film associates modernity and globalisation with power and shows them as holding a promise of greater existential and economic autonomy and freedom. In the final analysis, the film is part of the discourses that figuratively underscore the need to incorporate more and more subjects into the field of language. The film suggests that in order to be a part of the nation as an imagined community, the Indians who lie outside the ambit of desire will have to be transformed into desiring subjects. It is only by entering the realm of the Lacanian Symbolic, if only as castrated subjects, that they can attain their dreams. This can only be done by negotiating with reality at the level of signifiers. It is only by negotiating with power that the relatively powerless can think of mastering their reality.

Iqbal is a forerunner in the series of films like *Taare Zameen Par* that project the 'other' in terms of a disability, in terms of language. Their major aim is to make this threatening 'other' outside the narrative of the nation to join the race, to find a place in the culture that represents the masses. It becomes imperative, in this context, to oust the deaf-mute underdogs out of their indifference, to make them learn to bowl to an ostensibly promising cultural field.

Notes

1. Boria Majumdar quoted in Mihir Bose, *The Magic of Indian Cricket: Cricket and Society in India* (London and New York: Routledge, 2006), p. 80.
2. Ibid.
3. Ibid.
4. Ibid.
5. The discussion on the Sachar Committee report and on the condition of Muslims in India can be read in detail in Maidul Islam's paper, 'Imagining Indian Muslims: Looking Through the Lens of Bollywood Cinema', in the *Indian Journal of Human Development*, vol.1, no. 2 (July-December 2007), 403–22.
6. Anika Lemaire, cit. J. A. Miller, 'La Suture', *Cahiers pour l'Analyse*, no. 1, 68.
7. Heraclitus' concept of Palintropos Harmonie has been discussed in quite another context in 'Erôs and Education: Plato's Transformative Epistemology' by John Russon, *Laval théologique et philosophique*, vol. 56, no. 1 (2000), 113–25. I intend to recall the image of the string and the bow and the power that their back turning generates to compare it to the subject's turning away from the external world to live in an autonomous internal world of images and imaginary power.
8. Emile Benveniste, *Problems in General Linguistics*, Trans. Mary Elizabeth Meek (Coral Gables: University of Miami Press, 1971), p. 224.
9. Shoshana Felman, 'Beyond Oedipus: The Specimen Story of Psychoanalysis', *MLN*, 98 (1983), pp. 1026–7.

10. Jacques Lacan, *The Seminar. Book XI. The Four Fundamental Concepts of Psychoanalysis,* trans. Alan Sheridan (London: Hogarth Press and the Institute of Psycho-Analysis, 1977), pp. 206–7.
11. Fredric Jameson, 'Imaginary and the Symbolic in Lacan: Marxism, Psychoanalytic Criticism and the Problem of the Subject', *Yale French Studies*, 55/56 (1977), 360.
12. Fredric Jameson, pp. 388–95.

14

The Gender Games: A Study of *Chak De! India* and *Meerabai Not Out*

Mithuraaj Dhusiya

Sport has supplied some of Hindi cinema's most memorable moments. Who can forget the comical episode in *Gol Maal*[1] (Confusion) when Utpal Dutt spots Amol Palekar at a hockey match, leading to a hilarious set of incidents? Or the car-race scene in *Baazigar*[2] (Gambler) where Shah Rukh Khan deliberately loses the race, only to speak the now unforgettable line '*Haar ke jeetne wale ko Baazigar kehte hain*' (the one who loses to win is called a gambler) that today epitomises the anti-hero as characteristic persona of the Hindi films of the 1990s? The depiction of sport in Hindi cinema has a very unique cinematic history. Anyone who has seen the Hindi films of the 1960s must have memories of, at least one badly played badminton or tennis match, usually between old men fighting to stay fit and vouching for the benefits of modernity. Sometimes, sports were an intrinsic part of the choreography of songs, as in *Humjoli*[3] (Playfellow), often facilitating the hero's wooing of his beloved as in *Chhoti Si Baat*[4] (A Trifling Thing). One of the earliest films to have brought sports into filmic narrative in a major way was Prakash Jha's *Hip Hip Hurray.*[5] It was closely followed by films like *Boxer*[6] and *All Rounder*[7] where the plot gains impetus from the *bildungsroman*-like development of the sporting career of the protagonist, who is usually male. The 1990s saw the production of soft romantic musicals like *Chamatkar*[8] (Miracle) and *Jo Jeeta Wahi Sikandar*[9] (He who wins is King) where love stories blossom amidst amateur sporting contests. *Lagaan: Once Upon a Time in India*[10] (Land tax: Once Upon a Time in India) gave a new dimension to Hindi sports cinema with its exploration of cricketing experiences in colonial India, while *Ta Ra Rum Pum*[11] and *Dhan Dhana Dhan Goal*[12] (Get set goal) deal with the crossover experiences of non-resident Indians in the latter half of the 2000s. A different genus can be spotted if one considers together *Chak De! India*[13] (Come on! India) and a lesser-known (and low-budget) film, *Meerabai Not Out*:[14] these do not centre on the sports*man*. While *Chak De* focusses on the sportswoman, *Meerabai* focalises primarily around the female fan. This article explores how *Chak De* and *Meerabai* in their own way fashion new feminine subjectivities which in spite of interrogating certain normative patriarchal assumptions associated with the largely male-dominated games of hockey and cricket continue to be very much imbricated within the various ideologies and discourses of patriarchy. This study will examine the role played by the media in spotlighting the needs and aspirations of male sportspersons and fans to the point of side-stepping articulations of different feminine subjectivities.

Female physicality is on display in Indian cinema only in a few restricted, often much stylised contexts that emphasise decorum, docility and submission, often to either a visible male body or to an invisibilised patriarchal ethic. *Chak De* and *Meerabai Not Out* offer a point of entry into another aesthetic for the female body. *Chak De* shows a variety of female body types, some 'heavy', some 'dark,' and some 'North-Eastern'; *Meerabai Not Out* does not 'demonstrate' a new physical type for its protagonist, but produces an account of the female protagonist as passionate about something other than the male love-object of the story. These two films, this article argues, produce models of sporting/un-sporting women, to make a play on the idea of sport itself. These films show women sporting desires and bodies not commonly seen in Hindi cinema, and their defiance of patriarchal vocabularies is seen as un-sporting behaviour by patriarchal guardians within these films, leading to their disciplining in various ways, followed by eventual containment within discourses of 'team work,' either that of the national hockey team or that of the extended virilocal patriarchal family. Such narratives of gendering are of course not unfamiliar either in life or in cinema; what *Chak De* and *Meerabai* do different is that they use the vocabulary of sport to contain and stabilise subversive feminine wills. Sport then, must be treated as a gendering discourse, not merely a gendered discourse for the purposes of this essay.

The Unruly Sportswoman

Chak De is an account of Kabir Khan's (played by Shah Rukh Khan) own Tebbit Test.[15] As the Muslim captain of the Indian men's hockey team, who misses a crucial penalty stroke in a match that costs India the World Cup, Kabir Khan is the central focus of the narrative. A photographer—perhaps mischievously—photographs Khan shaking hands with the victor nation—Pakistan's—captain, the first 'piece' of evidence in Khan being accused of disloyalty to the national endeavour. Seven years down the line, the discredited Khan must accept the ignominious office of coach for the national women's team; the ignominy of this role is, however, completely lost on Khan who loves hockey more than he loves any masculinist pride in the sport. The rest of the sporting establishment, however, as the chief selector puts it, has no hopes of the '*bhartiya nari jo lota belan chalati hai*' ('the Indian woman who plies the rolling pin'). The rest of the story features, of course, this team being carefully shaped up into a world-conquering side under their new male coach, Khan. The sixteen members of this team, however, still find themselves outnumbered by the one man coach/superstar machine of Kabir/Shah Rukh Khan. Since they are all novices to acting, their performance often leads to the actor stealing the show, as can be expected. However, the focus of this article will be on the film's own masculinist scopic economy, achieved by conflating the gendered narrative of the assembly of a team from a motley crew of Indian nationals from all kinds of far-flung corners of India with the narrative of Khan's own recuperation from the shock of the accusation of'disloyalty' to the Indian nation because of his religion. The film does raise certain issues like the lack of administrative initiative on the part of the powers that be and the lack of sponsorship and media attention for the development of women's hockey. However there are still strong undercurrents of patriarchal domination in terms of the structures of narrative representation the film employs.

Chak De focuses on 'hero' Kabir Khan's rehabilitation at the heart of the national imaginary. Much work on mainstream Hindi cinema has uncovered its hidden agenda of constructing and nurturing the hypothetical category of the national imaginary. Interestingly though, Hindi films were initially dismissed as an art form unworthy of national importance; as Ravi Vasudevan[16] states: 'The unstable and murky world of film finance and the characterisation of the commercial film aesthetic as inauthentic and hybrid gave it low priority on the agenda for the nation's art'. However, Hindi films over the years have showcased potential for engagement with various nationalist discourses as Jyotika Virdi[17] explains: 'The nation is constructed in Hindi cinema through a complex apparatus of metaphors, discourses, and modes of address. It is imagined through a stock set of tropes, symbols, characters, and narratives that are meant to first air, and then resolve, contemporary anxieties and difficulties'. Unfortunately, the creation of this filmic articulation is not without its share of problems, as by investing in rather narrow definitions of what it means to be an 'Indian' and therefore of 'Indianness', Hindi films have valorised an artificial nationalist discourse created to consolidate a coherent national self, often identifying with the male, upper-caste, North Indian heroic self as the ideal national subject.[18] In the process, these films neglect the pluralities of the Indian experience: they often neglect an adequate documentation of regional aspirations leading to the allegation that much of 'Hindi cinema' is parochial in character with undue pretensions to universality. *Chak De* too reveals a similar ideology at work albeit in the guise of team spirit. Here there is no absence of regional identities as such, but the narrative serves to homogenise these heterogeneous identities in a fashion that serves to marginalise them even in the moment of representation. Each of the sixteen women hockey players comes from a different region of India but these regions are identified through a variety of stereotypes. Thus the girl from Punjab, Balbir Kaur (Tanya Abrol) is shown to be a very loud-mouthed, passionate and temperamental individual while Soimoi Kerketta (Nisha Nair) is depicted as an impoverished and illiterate adivasi girl hailing from a village in the jungles of Jharkhand. Sometimes the joke is on us: we are complicit, the film admits, in making '*mehmaan*' (guests), of North-Easterners and '*junglees*' (savages) of Jharkandis. At the same time, it allows descriptions like 'chowmein' or '*saanp khaane waale junglee*' (snake-eating savage) to pass unremarked or unrelieved by humour with the result that these expressions—which the narrative shows as being produced in passion and anger rather than as endearment—linger unchallenged in all the casteism, racism and parochialism they exhibit. Further, these difficulties are shown to be intractable components of the national imaginary. For instance, in a World Cup match against the Australian team, India is reduced to ten players because of the temperamental Balbir, while Soimoi's inability to understand the English-speaking umpire's directions leads to the award of a penalty corner against India. Since the film plays out in utopian terms, the 'anger' is corrected and Balbir never shows anger any more, but Soimoi's genuine lack of a *lingua franca* never reappears to disturb the narrative of easy bonding and seamless teamwork. One wonders what kind of accelerated language-learning course the poor tribal girl took, sight unseen!

These stereotypical representations straightjacket feminine subjectivities into a normative perceptivity of the regions they represent. The narrative further mars the development of regional feminine subjectivities when Kabir Khan coerces the girls to exorcise themselves of their native identities. A critical establishing narrative shows the team's introduction; various team-members define themselves as 'Balbir Kaur, Punjab', etc., and find themselves sent off the field by the coach till one member says 'Vidya Sharma, India'. Vidya's (Vidya Malvade) 'correct answer' provides the platform for the coach to correctly align the team and for the team-spirit narrative to reinforce itself. The shots and camerawork that compose this segment of the film are worth study: in the opening two-shot, the male coach gets one half of the frame; the sixteen girls together get the other half, a pattern that is most aggressively and frequently reiterated in the film's publicity materials. The line-up of the sixteen is filmed with an over-the shoulder shot that renders them as an agglomeration, with only some of their faces being visible. The same shot, however, is also a medium close-up of the coach, enabling his emotions to be registered plentifully by the audience. In other words, for the spectator, the scopic mechanisms here put the girls on inspection, with all of us joining with the coach in producing the 'correct answer' for the national-imaginary narrative, wherein individual women don't count, but paramount importance must be given to the sporting glory that might be won through patriotic national membership. At the same time, half the screen isn't given over to Khan for nothing, for the film's overall narrative is preoccupied with depicting Khan's anxiety as a Muslim minority representative trying frantically to become part of the national imaginary.

The film, I argue, places female homosociality in a marginal location in comparison to the space given to this repositioning of Khan. The structure of dissidence in these sporting women that the narrative produces or allows is through 'arrogant' characters like Bindiya Naik (Shilpa Shukla) whose dissidence is established as essentially unconstructive. Where the film could have shown debate and discussion between coach and players, the film instead wants the authority of the coach to be accepted by the audience as well as unchallenged by the captain and the team, thus emphatically saying that one of the privileges of maleness is also confirmed authority. Bindiya is reined in by the coach with the edict, '*is team mein ek hi goonda ho sakta hai*' ('there can be only one ruffian on this team'), confirming that the ruffian will be, not her. Even as this authority, one feels, borders on arrogance, the scopic mechanisms of the film engage our sympathy on behalf of the male coach by legitimizing him as a misunderstood 'genius'—Bindiya describes him as *Tughlak*[19]—and therefore, best qualified to lead even if he shows scant respect for other people's intelligence or insights. For example, when he wants a senior and supposedly seasoned player like Bindiya to exchange her usual centre-forward position for a midfielder's, Khan merely sends a new and inexperienced player to the field as her replacement without himself communicating with Bindiya in any way. One can argue that her anger at this is legitimate, but the narrative does not critique Khan for this avoidance of the labour of communicating. Rather it portrays Bindiya as the arrogant person whose presence is not conducive to team spirit. Anderson[20] critiques the overarching power of sports coaches whose actions mostly go unevaluated by their peers or seniors and compares them to military officers in terms of the unchallenged power they wield over their wards. Sportspersons, he notes, are trained to be docile as 'questioning or contesting authority has serious consequences. Should we fail to adhere to a coach's request we can lose playing time, or be socially ostracised and mocked in front of our friends/teammates. Failing to conform gets one stigmatised as not being a team player'. In fact, the narrative fashions Bindiya as a querulous overreacher but the final nail in the coffin of our empathy for her is when she is shown trying to seduce Khan in the changing room. For all her sass, Bindiya reveals herself to be not above using sex to get ahead, making her a typically wily woman rather than a 'leader' worth following. Thus the film produces a stereotypically patriarchal narrative of rebellious sexualities as essentially troublesome feminine subjectivities that need to be corrected and reformed, with the male coach concurrently performing both the paternal and the teacherly functions.

When they are not displaying intransigence on field, the women team-members are shown squabbling over various petty things like dorm beds where, again, they are shown to be unwilling to experiment with positions not their own, refusing bunks that take them away from friends this time. That all these episodes are part of a project of defying maleness is evident, as is the futility of this defiance, in the match this women's team must play, if they want funding, with the men's hockey team. Meant to be a critique of the hockey establishment's apathetic attitude towards the women's hockey team, the film, however, through this narrative ploy shows us in no uncertain terms that men are truly stronger and better, and that it is 'big' and high-minded of them to appreciate and support women at all even as all the earlier episodes show women consistently acting in a petty manner with their large-hearted (male) coach. The men's team appreciates the defeated women's game saying '*changa khela kudiyon ne*' (the girls played well), and this statement by the generous victor serves as emblematic in the film of the generosity with which masculinity ploughs on with weak women, for better or for worse.

That the film is an out-and-out Shah Rukh Khan film is nowhere better evident than from its posters.[21] The one reproduced alongside is typical, with the colossal image of Shah Rukh Khan occupying the centre of the poster with a hockey stick in his hand, towering over his women's team members arrayed in horizontal formation behind with their individual faces hardly visible, their lack of autonomy thus signalled almost unwittingly. Rachel Dwyer and Divia Patel (2002)[22] posit that historically film advertising and publicity materials have

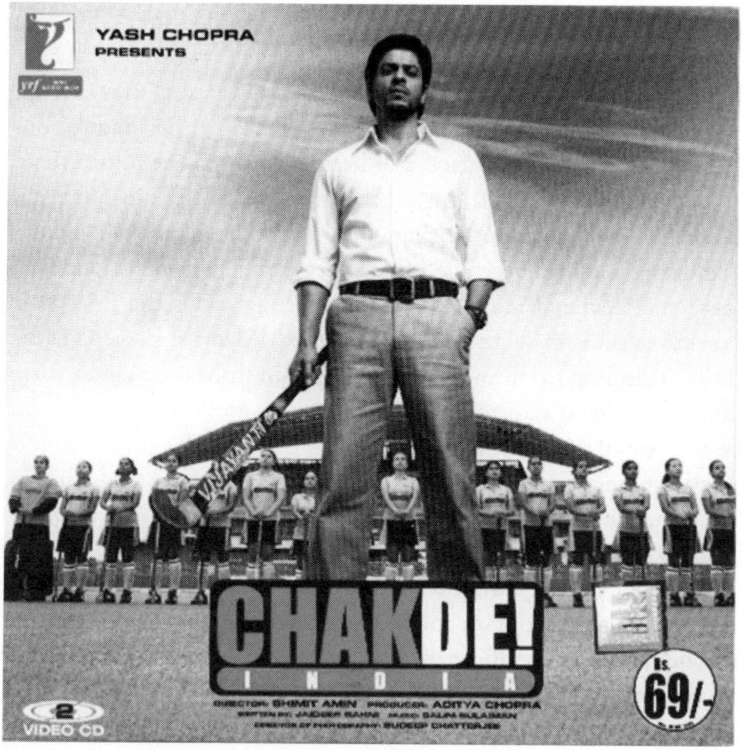

Illustration 14.1 *Chak De! India* poster

had a direct bearing on the content of most Hindi films. This is certainly borne out in *Chak De*'s case, with Shah Rukh Khan's star-power and Kabir Khan's power as coach clearly dominating both the individual women actors and players and the team they collectively populate. Shah Rukh's manner of holding the hockey stick suggests that it is he who runs the show, he who wields the baton, while an atomised species of female hockey player just about barely fills the background.

The Unruly Female Fan

Meerabai Not Out, in stark contradistinction to *Chak De,* individuates the female character—the female sporting fan here—quite clearly, narrating the story of one middle-class woman, the thirty-plus Meera Anant Achrekar (Mandira Bedi),[23] a passionate follower of the game of cricket with an encyclopaedic head for cricket statistics. Meera is also a particularly warm admirer of Anil Kumble: her dedication to him limns virtually every aspect of her life through the film, although she does not get to meet him till the very end of the film. In regular life, she is a very popular mathematics teacher in a school named the 'Vishwaprem Vidyalaya'. She is also very popular in her own locality where she teaches the neighbourhood teenage boys the finer points of cricket, and their team is nicknamed 'Meera's Eleven'. Meera's family, including her brother Mahesh (Mahesh Manjrekar), a former Ranji player who had to give up his cricket ambitions to look after the welfare of his family, are worried for her as she has no interest in getting married. That is, until she meets Dr Arjun Awasthi (Eijaz Khan) and they fall in love. The film then shows how Meera's passion for cricket almost ruins her romance. Through Meera, this film showcases a female fan's life, quite often understated in dominant on-screen male discourses about sports. Meera's passion for the game gives her an inner life of her own, for example, that allows her to create a space within which to sustain herself in all the inadequacies of a life spent amidst overbearing parents and siblings. After meeting her beau, Meera's struggle to balance the roles of a suitable lover and a dutiful daughter-in-law with a private passion for cricket is very poignantly and sympathetically articulated. However, even within this effort to meaningfully delineate how passion endows subjectivity with at least some agency, the film's narrative at key moments once again locates this subjectivity within conventional and normative femininities as defined by a stereotypical masculinist scopic economy.

The promotional marketing strategies of the film centre as much around Mandira Bedi's real life as the female sports commentator clad in 'noodle strap' tube tops in the company of much more fully clad male commentators as they do around Anil Kumble's presence in the film, but both tracks are misleading. As Patchy Nair observes: 'What one sees in movie posters and billboards is not necessarily what one will see in the film itself... For instance, Mandira Bedi does not wear the Indian cricket jersey or noodle-strap sari blouses that we've seen in the posters. Instead we see her in a *churidhar, kurti* and cotton *dupattas*[24] throughout the film. And no, there's no bedroom scene with Anil Kumble in the film'. The filmmakers in a bid to ensure the success of the film chose to cash in on the enduring popularity of televised international cricket in India to invoke curiosity among a select group of filmgoers who were also passionate followers of Indian cricket. This target audience would be what Ghosh describes as a new category of television viewers in the post Doordarshan[25] era, the 'consumer citizen subject', primarily because 'in India, cricket broadcast on entertainment television creates a kind of transtextual experience where textual meaning is overcharged and distracted by apparently disconnected discourses which encircle the text'. Thus, the process of watching cricket in these last one and a half decades has been a 'transtextual experience', almost a package deal with several expert commentary shows both before and after the match. The real life persona of Mandira Bedi as a sports commentator is essentially part of such an experience. However the contrast between the more homely and conservative Meera Achrekar in the film and the outgoing and radical—for conservative Indian sporting audiences—Mandira Bedi in the film's promos serves to highlight the patriarchy-mediated representation of gender by the same media itself. Where deployments of gendered discourses, of criticism and appreciation can be self-reflexively studied, it is more convenient for mass commoditisation to see these discourses as paratextual rather than central to the narrative, as the film will soon proceed to do. Govindan and Dutta point out that media representations of women are 'governed by a paradox: actresses are expected to represent globalised images of a liberated female sexuality, but are still circumscribed by shifting yet narrow definitions of 'Indian' femininity'.[26] *Meerabai Not Out* is caught within such a paradox, deliberately so on the part of the filmmakers as is amply clear when in a self-reflexive moment in the film, the film mocks at Mandira Bedi's real-life noodle-strap persona when Meera, in a rejoinder to boys on the street who remark on her similarity to Mandira Bedi, cements the distinction between herself and Mandira Bedi by saying, '*Main Poore Kapde Pehenti Hoon*' ('I am always fully clothed').

Another key moment in which the masculinist discourse of the film emerges is on the occasion of her engagement to Arjun. It turns

Illustration 14.2 *Meerabai Not Out* poster

out that her day of engagement is also the day when India is playing a cricket match at the Wankhede stadium in Bombay. She confides to Arjun that she would love to watch the match in the stadium as she never misses any that are played in her city, promising that she would come back in time for her engagement as it is a one-day match and would finish by evening. Arjun is none too happy, but she goes anyway. Unfortunately, India loses and mob violence ensures that Meera is late returning home for her own engagement ceremony, after most of the guests have left, tired of futilely waiting for her. Arjun's father, Dr Awasthi (Anupam Kher), is duly enraged and very ironically begs pardon for ever asking for Meera's hand for his son. This sequence is worth examining for the way in which the mise-en-scène establishes the gender divide. The father's lecture conforms to the masculinist stereotyping of women—women, he says, are of two kinds, those who make do with the small but profound joys found within the familial set-up of a happy marriage and those who are born for great things. He ironically offers to free the latter kind of the confinement of living within domesticity saying he will do his bit by refusing to let Meera ruin her greatness for his son, and storms out after this impassioned tirade.

Laura Mulvey[27] says that there are three basic looks associated with cinema: 'that of the camera as it records the pro-filmic event, that of the audience as it watches the final product, and that of the characters at each other within the screen illusion'. She further argues that the 'conventions of narrative film deny the first two and subordinate them to the third' which is then manipulated to provide voyeuristic-scopophilic pleasure to the male audience. However, one can go beyond Mulvey to read the third look as embodying a more direct line of male violence towards women as the analysis of this mise-en-scène will show. Sexual politics allows the narrative to force the two genders present on screen into two symmetrical camps: the scene begins with a long shot where Meera's family of four are all to one side, with the father-son pair on the other side. Arjun's father starts moving towards the women while Meera's elder brother migrates in the course of Dr Awasthi's speech to join the father-son pair to the left of the screen, placing the three men to one side of the frame and three women to the other, with two medium close-ups capturing the gendered segregation. While Meera's brother does not scold her, the cinematic apparatus places him in between son and father, incorporating his agreement, as it were, to their respectively spoken and unspoken grievances against his sister. As the camera slowly pans right, it reveals the women looking at the men now assembled in a straight line, led by the old patriarch. Thus, three generations of men now 'assault' the women with patriarchal discourse. While Mahesh is a little uncomfortable, he is nevertheless, in cinematic language, quite in line with the explicit patriarchal censure of his sister, which as an affectionate though dour brother, he never finds himself able to make in more peaceful times.

Meerabai Not Out depicts a collage of situations which betray the lack of agential roles for the female protagonist. Representations of Meera as actively making decisions are confined entirely to the non-adult world of her teenaged cricket-playing friends, the local boys. In the more serious affairs of the adult world, the film shows her on most occasions to be a very passive recipient of other people's actions. For example, on one occasion, her brother and her lover play out a one-over cricket contest on the condition that the winner will have a final say on the matter of Meera's marriage to Arjun: if Mahesh wins, Arjun forfeits even the right to step into Meera's locality thereafter, while Arjun's winning would entitle him to marry her that very minute. This improvised tournament is almost a modern day rendition of the *swayamvara*,[28] with the caveat of course that such a bridegroom-choice never did offer the bride much agency in any case. Of course, in the case of this film, everything is resolved amicably as the film's genre is comedy and not gruesome drama (as in a similar memorable instance in the *Mahabharata* where Amba's *swayamvara* goes badly wrong, as a result of Bhishma's steadfastly patriarchal attitude). Meerabai's case leaves the viewer with some disturbing questions about the limited authority afforded to women in the social world. In another instance, Meera's father-in-law-to-be asks for her help using the phone-a-friend option available to him to answer a particularly tricky question in a cricket quiz based on the *Kaun Banega Crorepati*[29] model. Meera, of course, answers everything correctly and Dr Awasthi wins the grand prize, but the question one must ask is, why is Dr Awasthi on the show and not Meera? The reason for this narrative choice is that the film is very realistic in its depiction of the larger canvas of patriarchal domination of the female: the subjection of the feminine means that women serve the vested interests of patriarchy even as they are complicit in the censure of the autonomy of their own gender. One of the few opportunities for Meera to play an active social role in the film comes when she is standing in a queue with several of her neighbourhood cricket team members to buy tickets for the cricket match India is soon to play. A tout selling tickets on the black market predictably comes along and Meera just as predictably is didactic in her objections to such dubious practices. When Meera calls out to a policeman standing at some distance for support, she is made aware of the nexus between the policeman and the tout. A tussle ensues and the tout hurls at her the jibe of 'mother India'[30] upon which the group of boys who accompany her beat him up. Throughout the fight, Meera is shown telling her boys to refrain and when the man is badly injured she insists that he be taken to hospital, commandeering a random car on the road—driven, predictably of course, by the male love interest, whom she meets for the first time here.

Sumitra Chakravarty[31] in discussing the film *Mother India* and the implications of its mythical title persuasively argues that the cult of the mother figure so strongly assimilated in the Indian psyche is very much a patriarchal enterprise to objectify women as providers of maternal experience and responsibility in society. This film, replete with so many images of a crestfallen, burdened and crucified 'mother India', offers a point of reference, albeit humorously at this point, for *Meerabai Not Out* to signal the assumption and incorporation of Meera herself into these deeply rooted patriarchal ideologies, with the same fate awaiting Meera if she were to try to claim an autonomous agential role in society.

The film's production of Meera's later repentance and careful self-assimilation into the demands of the father-in-law make up the rest of the narrative: Meera does become mother India in carrying the burden, but without the glory! Meerabai, in a sense, then, is given out. Her innings as Meerabai must cease for her to be someone's wife: she concedes that 'the cricket chapter is now over' and she is shown happily alive ever after. Majumdar and Bandyopadhyay emphasise in the context of India's superb performance in the 2003 Cricket World Cup that 'cricket in twenty-first century India provides a space where all differences are overcome. The assertion of Indian identity, expression of cultural nationalism or feeling of emotional commonality—these are no longer confined to the stadium or post-match activities.'[32] Yet in the context of gender politics, even the game of cricket as an iconic expression of twenty-first century India is unable to facilitate the eradication of gender inequality.

Barring an odd article here or there, Indian film scholarship has not paid much critical attention to sports in Indian cinema. Such an attitude seems to be a world-wide phenomenon: King and Leonard[33] speaking in the context of Hollywood cinema, point out that sports films are not considered valuable enough to merit critical evaluation. A possible reason, as Poulton and Roderick[34] suggest, is the difficulty in identifying and classifying films within the genre of sports films. Further, as Cashmore[35] shows, there can be quite a few variations within this genre, such as 'dramatic/biographical', 'comedy/fantasy' and 'documentary' sports films. Theorising about genre-formation in Indian cinema is beyond the scope of this article. This article studied two Hindi films, produced in the last half of the past decade, that explore the world of sports in Indian society. I have tried to show how sports films are pregnant with possible analyses of the gender-equations in contemporary Indian society. What then is the lesson to take home? The unruly female fan must submit to the joys of the family even as the unruly female player must submit to the canny 'genius' of her male coach. While both films vouch overtly for the entry of women into a set of spaces we don't expect women to inhabit, be it the hard spaces of non-feminine sporting prowess like in *Chak De*, or a woman fan dancing on the street with glorious abandon and unconcern for decorum in *Meerabai Not Out*, the utopian endings of both films are unmistakable in their reiteration of where these women must finally belong. Obey and you shall be rewarded: the female hockey stars win their Cup, the female fan has the great happiness of being her father-in-law's trusted 'phone-a-friend' option on a game show where tellingly, he is the winning player.

Notes

1. *Gol Maal*, directed by Hrishikesh Mukherjee (1979; India: Bollywood Entertainment), DVD. One of the most popular films coming out of the stable of Hrishikesh Mukherjee-Amol Palekar-Utpal Dutt team. The film has only one episode of sports depiction in the form of a hockey match played between India and Pakistan in India. But this scene is pivotal in the development of the entire plot of this comedy.
2. *Baazigar*, directed by Abbas Mastan (1993; India: Eros Entertainment, 2009), DVD. Famous for its kart-racing scenes, this film helped establish Shah Rukh Khan's popularity in solo lead roles as an anti-hero in the early half of the 1990s.
3. *Humjoli*, directed by Ramanna (1970; India: Eros Entertainment, 2009), DVD. 'Dhal gaya din' (the day comes to an end), one of the first and most popular Hindi film songs depicting the lead cast Jeetendra and Leena Chandavarkar playing a private badminton game in the evening.
4. *Choti Si Baat*, directed by Basu Chatterjee (1975; India: Yash Raj, 2000), DVD. The film has a couple of table-tennis scenes and one part of the song 'yeh din kya aaye' (good days have come) picturised on a table-tennis match gives an opportunity to the hero Amol Palekar to impress his beloved Vidya Sinha.
5. *Hip Hip Hurray*, directed by Prakash Jha (1984; India). This film scripts the story of a school sports teacher who deals with soccer-rivalry between

students. This film, a first of its kind, promotes the viability of a non-academic sports-based career.

6. *Boxer*, directed by Raj N. Sippy (1984; India: Shemaroo), DVD. A film based on the intricacies of the boxing sport in India.
7. *All Rounder*, directed by Mohan Kumar (1984; India). This film deals with the sensitive issue of how instant stardom affects lives of young budding professional cricketers in India.
8. *Chamatkar*, directed by Rajiv Mehra (1992; India: Shemaroo), DVD. A friendly ghost helps a group of good hearted boys defeat their rivals in a pulsating college cricket match in this film.
9. *Jo Jeeta Wahi Sikander*, directed by Mansoor Khan (1992; India). An annual bicycle race between colleges is the staple theme of this film.
10. *Lagaan: Once Upon a Time in India*, directed by Ashutosh Gowarikar (2001; India: Sony Pictures Home Entertainment, 2002), DVD. This film, India's official entry to the 2002 Oscars, shows the exploitation of Indians by the Britishers through the metaphor of cricket.
11. *Ta Ra Rum Pum*, directed by Siddharth Anand (2007; India: Yash Raj Films, 2007), DVD. This film showcases some fascinating car-racing events in America.
12. *Dhan Dhana Dhan Goal*, directed by Vivek Agnihotri (2007; India: UTV Motion Pictures, 2008), DVD. This film explores the discrimination faced by the Asian communities settled in England through the metaphor of football.
13. *Chak De! India*, directed by Shimit Amin (2007; India: Yash Raj Films, 2007/08), VCD. Box-office collections show that this film was the third best grossing film of 2007 in India, with revenues of Rs. 67,69,00,000 from the domestic market and earned total gross of Rs. 105,48,00,000 and was declared blockbuster. This film is loosely based on the life and career of Mir Ranjan Negi, the former goalkeeper of Indian hockey team. He was accused of deliberately throwing one match where Pakistan defeated India by seven goals to one in the 1982 Asian Games. Years later, as a goalkeeping coach, he helped India win men's hockey gold in 1998 Asian Games. He was also the assistant coach for the women's hockey team when it won the gold at the 2004 Hockey Asia Cup.
14. *Meerabai Not Out*, directed by Chandrakant Kulkarni (2008; India: Sony Pictures India, 2009), VCD. Though extensively promoted by the Pritish Nandy Communications, the film unfortunately did not do well and could collect only Rs. 21.08 lakhs gross at the box-office. It is one of the first films in the history of Hindi that deals with the predicament of a female cricket spectator.
15. The Tebbit Test refers to a controversial phrase that emerged in April 1990 when the British Conservative politician Norman Tebbit suggested that those Asian and Carribean immigrants who root for their native countries

rather than Great Britain in sports especially cricket might not be sufficiently loyal to their new country.

16. Ravi Vasudevan, *The Melodramatic Public: Film Form and Spectatorship in Indian Cinema* (Ranikhet: Permanent Black, 2010), p. 4.
17. Jyotika Virdi, *The Cinematic Imagination: Indian Popular Films as Social History* (Ranikhet: Permanent Black, 2003), p. 9.
18. Karen Gabriel, *Melodrama and the Nation: Sexual Economies of Bombay Cinema (1970–2000)* (New Delhi: Women Unlimited, 2010). In this book, the author argues that this national imaginary construction severely limits the autonomy of feminine subjectivities especially in war-based Hindi films. This article intends to take this argument further and explore its relevance to sports films as both war and sports based films largely deal with groups and communities and not solely with individuals.
19. Firuz Shah Tughluq (1309–88) was the third ruler of the Tughluq dynasty of the Delhi Sultanate. During his rule over Delhi Sultanate (1351–88), he was highly unpopular for his persecution of Hindus, particularly Hindu Brahmin priests who refused to be forcibly converted to Islam.
20. Eric Anderson, *Sport, Theory and Social Problems: A Critical Introduction* (New York: Routledge, 2010), p. 49.
21. Source: front cover of the Yash Raj Films Home Entertainment VCD pack of the film.
22. Rachel Dwyer and Divia Patel, *Cinema India: The Visual Culture of Hindi Film* (New Delhi: Oxford University Press, 2002). In their highly influential work, the first of its kind in the history of Indian film scholarship, Rachel Dwyer and Divia Patel explore how visual advertisements, promos, song booklets, and particularly film posters act as valuable sources for critical understandings of the film's content as well as a portrayal of the socio-cultural history of the contemporary times.
23. Mandira Bedi's involvement with Indian cricket as a part of television host team for the World Cups of 2003 and 2007 and Indian Premier League season 2, where she was popular less for her cricketing acumen and more for the glamour quotient, serves to bring extra-textual references to this film.
24. Patchy Nair, 'Meerabai Not Out Entertains in Parts,' rediff MOVIES (blog), rediff.com, December 5, 2008, http://www.rediff.com/movies/2008/dec/05meerabai-not-out-entertainment.htm. *Churidhars, kurtis* and *dupattas* are traditional clothes of South and Central Asia. *Churidhars*, better known as *churidhar pyjamas*, are tightly fitting trousers worn by both men and women. *Kurtis* are loose shirts falling either just above or somewhere near the knees of the wearer and are mostly worn by women. Cotton *dupattas* are long multi-purpose scarfs which are generally worn across both shoulders by women.
25. *Doordarshan* meaning 'far vision' is an Indian public service broadcaster, and the oldest audio-visual telecasting agency of the independent India.

26. Padma P. Govindan and Bisakha Dutta, "'From Villain to Traditional Housewife!": The Politics of Globalization and Women's Sexuality in the "New" Indian Media', in *Global Bollywood*, ed. Anandam P. Kavoori and Aswin Punathambekar (New Delhi: Oxford University Press, 2009), pp. 180–181.
27. Laura Mulvey, 'Visual Pleasure and Narrative Cinema'. *Screen* 16, no. 3 (Autumn 1975), p. 16.
28. *Swayamvara* is an ancient Indian practice of choosing a bride-groom from among a list of suitors by girls.
29. *Kaun Banega Crorepati* is an Indian reality game show hosted mostly by Amitabh Bachchan, and briefly by Shah Rukh Khan, with a prize money of one crore and a jackpot question for five crore rupees.
30. *Mother India*, directed by Mehboob Khan (1957; India: Eros Entertainment, 2006), DVD. It is a tragic story of a poor village woman, played by Nargis, who leads a morally upright life and kills her criminal son in the end for greater moral good.
31. Sumitra Chakravarty, *National Identity in Popular Indian Cinema 1947–1987* (Austin: University of Texas Press, 1993).
32. Boria Majumdar and Kausik Bandyopadhyay, 'Cricket as Everyday Life: World Cup 2003', *Economic and Political Weekly* 39, no. 14/15 (April 3–16, 2004), 1453.
33. Richard C. King and David J. Leonard, ed. *Visual Economies of/ in Motion: Sport and Film* (New York: Peter Lang, 2006).
34. Emma Poulton and Martin Roderick, 'Introducing Sport in Cinema'. *Sport in Society* 11, no. 2/3 (March/May 2008), pp. 107–16.
35. Ellis Cashmore, 'Films,' in *Sports Culture: A-Z Guide*, ed. Ellis Cashmore (London: Routledge, 2000), pp. 132–9.

Bibliography

'The Shadow over Cricket', *BBC News*, 4 June 2007, accessed 30 Sept. 2013.

Aarseth, Espen. *Cybertext: Perspectives on Ergodic Literature*. New York: Johns Hopkins University Press, 1997.

Adorno, Theodor W. *The Culture Industry: Selected Essays on Mass Culture*, ed. J.M. Bernstein. London: Routledge, 2003.

Agassi, Andre. *Open: An Autobiography*. London: HarperCollins, 2009.

Alter, Joseph S. 'The Akhara Earth', *The Indian Express*, 12 October 2010.

Alfred, Luke. *BBC 1* 'Panorama' 20 June 2001. Last accessed 30 Sept.2013.

Anderson, Eric. *Sport, Theory and Social Problems: A Critical Introduction* 1st edn, New York: Routledge, 2010.

Appadurai, Arjun. *Modernity at Large: Cultural Dimensions of Globalization*. Minneapolis: University of Minneapolis Press, 1996.

Arlott, John. 'Ramadhin and Valentine-little friends of mine', *ESPN cricinfo*, January 1990, http://www.espncricinfo.com/ci/content/story/140863.html Last accessed 3 July 2012.

Arumugam, K. 'Dhanraj Pillay, the Face of Indian Hockey', in *Top Hockey Stars* ed. by K. Arumugam. New Delhi: Field Hockey Publications, 2004.

Auchmuty, Rosemary. *A World of Girls*. London: The Women's Press, 1992.

Azim, Saadia. 'Tribal girls see football as a game changer'. *One World South Asia*, 13 July 2013 http://southasia.oneworld.net/features/with-new-spikes-and-footballs-tribal-girls-as-game-changers#.UhjenX95dIY. Last accessed 20 August 2013.

Bailey, Cameron. 'Virtual Skin: Articulating Race in Cyberspace,' in *Immersed in Technology: Art and Virtual Environments*, ed. Mary Anne Moser. Cambridge, Mass.: MIT Press, 1996, 29–49.

Bailey, Trevor. 'Those two little tormentors of mine', *ESPN cricinfo*, 21 August 2008, http://www.espncricinfo.com/magazine/content/content/story/365667.html. Last accessed July 3, 2012.

Bairner, Alan. *Sport, Nationalism, and Globalization: European and North American Perspectives*. Albany: State University of New York Press, 2001.

Baksh, Vaneisa. 'Sonny Ramadhin', *ESPN cricinfo*, http://www.espncricinfo/westindies/content/player/52804.html. Last accessed July 2012.

Bandyopadhyay, Kausik. *Playing for Freedom A Historic Sports Victory*. New Delhi: Standard Publishers, 2008.

———. *Scoring Off the Field: Football Culture in Bengal 1911–1980*. New Delhi: Routledge, 2011.

Basu, Jaydeep. *Stories from Indian Football*, New Delhi: UBSPD, 2003.

Batchen, Geoffrey. 'Spectres'. *Afterimage* 23, 3: 1995, 6–7.

Baudrillard, Jean. *Simulacra and Simulation*. Ann Arbor: University of Michigan Press, 1995.

Benedikt, Michael, ed. *Cyberspace: First Steps*. Cambridge: MIT Press, 1992.

Bentham, Jeremy. *Theory of Legislation*. London: Kegan Paul, 1911.

Benveniste, Emile. *Problems in General Linguistics*, trans. M.E. Meek. Coral Gables, FL: University of Miami Press, 1971

Berman, Marshall. *All That Is Solid Melts Into Air: The Experience of Modernity*. New York: Simon and Schuster, 1982.

Bettelheim, Bruno. *The Uses of Enchantment: The Meaning and Importance of Fairy Tales*. New York: Knopf Doubleday, 2010. (First Published, 1975).

Biocca, Frank. 'Immersive Virtual Reality Technolog'. *Communication in the Age of Virtual Reality*, ed. Frank Biocca and Mark R. Levy. Hillsdale, NJ: Lawrence Erlbaum, 1995, 57–124

Blake, Andrew. *The Irresistible Rise of Harry Potter*. London: Verso, 2002.

Blyton, Enid. *Three Great Malory Towers Stories*. London: Armada, 1990.

_____. *Second Form at St. Clare's*. London: Mammoth, 1991.

Bogard, William. *The Simulation of Surveillance: Hypercontrol in Telematic Societies*. Cambridge: Cambridge University Press, 1996.

Bose, Mihir. *A Maidan View: The Magic of Indian Cricket*. London: George Allen and Unwin Ltd., 1986.

Bourdieu, Pierre. 'How Can One Be A Sportsman?'. In *Sociology in Question*, trans. Richard Nice. London: Sage, 1993: 117–31.

Boyle, Raymond and Richard Haynes. *Power Play: Sport, Media and Popular Culture*. Harlow: Pearson Education, 2000.

Bramble, Dennis and Daniel E Lieberman. 'Endurance Running and the Evolution of Homo'. *Nature* 432,2004: 345–352.

Brazil, Angela. *The Angela Brazil Omnibus Book*. London and Glasgow: Blackie, 1937.

Brent-Dyer, Elinor M. *A Problem for the Chalet School*. London: Armada, 1972.

_____. *Tom Tackles the Chalet School*. London: Armada, 1987.

Brookes, Rod. *Representing Sport*. London: Arnold. 2002.

Browning, Robert. 'Pheidipiddes', *Selections from Robert Browning*, ed. Robert Morss Lovett, Boston: Ginn and Co. 1934.

Bruce, Dorita Fairlie. *Dimsie Goes to School*. Wendover: John Goodchild, 1983.

Burton, Richard D.E. 'Cricket, Carnival and Street Culture in the Caribbean'. In *Sport, Racism and Ethnicity*, ed. Grant Jarvie. London: Falmer Press, 1991, Taylor & Francis, e-book, 2005, 5–19.

Cadogan, Mary, and Patricia Craig. *You're a Brick, Angela! The Girls' Story 1839–1985*. London: Victor Gollancz, 1986.

Caillois, Roger and Elaine P. Halperin (trans.). 'The Structure and Classification of Games', *Diogenes* 3, 12, Thousand Oaks, California: 1955, 64–5. doi: 10.1177/039219215500301204. http://dio.sagepub.com/content/3/12/62.full.pdf+html. Last accessed 25 March 2013.

Caillois, Roger. *Man, Play and Games*. Chicago: University of Illinois Press , 2001.

Calvert, Sandra L. 'Children as Consumers: Advertising and Marketing', *Children and Electronic Media*, from *The Future of Children*, 18, 1, New Jersey: Trustees of the Princeton University, 2008. http://futureofchildren.org/futureofchildren/publications/docs/18_01_FullJournal.pdf. Last accessed 25 March 2013.

Cardus, Neville. *Cardus on Cricket*, repr. edn, Delhi: Rupa & Co, 2008.

Cashmore, Ellis. 'Films'. In *Sports Culture: A-Z Guide*, ed. Ellis Cashmore. London: Routledge, 2000, 132–39.

Chak De! India. Directed by Shimit Amin. 2007, India: Yash Raj Films, 2007/8, VCD.

Chakrabarty. Dipesh. *Habitations of Modernity: Essays in the Wake of Subaltern Studies*. Delhi: Permanent Black, 2002.

_____. 'The Rise and Fall of Indian Sports History'. In *Sport in South Asian Society: Past and Present*, ed. Boria Majumdar and J.A. Mangan. London: Routledge, 2005.

Chakraborty, Prafullakumar. *Prantik Manob* (The Marginal Men). Kolkata: Protikhon, 1997.

Chakravarty, Sumita S. *National Identity in Indian Popular Cinema: 1947–1987*, Austin: University of Texas Press, 1993, 152.

Chatterjee, Partha. 'Football and Collective Identity in Colonial Calcutta', draft paper given at International Leverhulme Network Conference on *Commodities and Culture in the Colonial World, 1851–1914*: 'Commodities and Affect', Jadavpur University, Kolkata, 12 January 2011. Later included in Partha Chatterjee, *The Black Hole of Empire: History of a Global Practice of Power*. Princeton: Princeton University Press, 2012.

Chaudhuri, Ahindra. *Nijere hārāye khunji* [I Search for My Lost Self]. Calcutta: Indian Associated Press, 1962.

Chaudhuri, Supriya. 'Bodies at Risk: Gender and Sport.' In *Women Contesting Culture: Changing Frames of Gender Politics in India*, ed. Paromita Chakravarti and Kavita Panjabi. Kolkata: Stree, 2012: 181–98.

_____. 'Literary Modernism and Subaltern Sport.' In *Moving Worlds: A Journal of Transcultural Writings*. University of Leeds: 12:1 (2012), 29–39.

Clark, Andy. *Supersizing the Mind: Embodiment, Action and Cognitive Extension*. Cambridge, Mass.: MIT Press, 2008.

Coakley, Jay. *Sports in Society: Issues and Controversies*. Boston: McGraw Hill, 2006.

Coe, Sebastian. *The Quotable Runner*, ed. Mark Will-Weber. New York: Breakaway Books, 1995.

Collins, Suzanne. *The Hunger Games*. New York: Scholastic, 2008.

_____. *Catching Fire*. New York: Scholastic, 2009.

_____. *Mockingjay*. New York: Scholastic, 2010.

Cook, Daniel Thomas. *The Commodification of Childhood: The Children's Clothing Industry and the Rise of the Child Consumer*. Durham: Duke University Press, 2004.

Csíkszentmihályi, Mihály and Susan A. Jackson. *Flow in Sports: The Keys to Optimal Experiences and Performances*, Champaign, Illinois: Human Kinetics Publishers, 1999

Datta, Nilanjan. 'Bhabani Banerjee: Delhi Football's Last Action Hero' in the *Souvenir* of the 59th 10C-Senior National football championships, ed. Novy Kapadia. New Delhi: 2004, 7

Dayan, Daniel and Elihu Katz. *Media Events: The Live Broadcasting of History*. London: Harvard University Press, 1992.

Debord, Guy. *The Society of the Spectacle*, trans. Donald Nicholson-Smith. London: Zone Books, 1995.

Derrida, Jacques. *Margins of Philosophy*. Chicago: University of Chicago Press, 1984

_____. *The Derrida Reader: Writing Performances*. Lincoln: University of Nebraska Press, 1998.

Dimeo, Paul. 'Football and Politics in Bengal: Colonialism, Nationalism, Communalism'. In *Soccer in South Asia: Empire, Nation, Diaspora*, ed. Paul Dimeo and James Mills. London: Frank Cass, 2001, pp. 57–74.

Dimeo, Paul and James Mills, eds *Soccer in South Asia: Empire, Nation, Diaspora*. London: Frank Cass, 2001.

Dwyer, Rachel and Divia Patel. *Cinema India: The Visual Culture of Hindi Film*. New Delhi: Oxford University Press, 2002.

Fass, Paula. 'Children and Globalization' *Journal of Social History*, 36, 4, Virginia: George Mason University Press, 2003, 963–77. doi: 10.1353/jsh.2003.0090. http://muse.jhu.edu/journals/

journal_of_social_history/summary/v036/36.4fass.html. Last accessed 25 March 2013.

Featherstone, Simon. *Postcolonial Cultures.* Edinburgh: Edinburgh University Press, 2005.

Fein, Greta G. 'Play and the Acquisition of Symbols'. In *Topics in Early Childhood Education,* ed. Lilian G. Katz. Norwood: New Jersey, Ablex-Clio Publication, 1979. Microform 1978. http://www.eric.ed.gov/ERICWebPortal/contentdelivery/servlet/ERICServlet?accno=ED152431Last accessed 26 June 2012

Feldman, Carol Fleisher. 'Mimesis: Where Play and Narrative Meet', *Cognitive Development,* 20, 4, 'Play and Narrative in the Process of Development: Commonalities, Differences and Interrelations', Amsterdam: Elsevier-Science Direct, 2005, 503–13. http://dx.doi.org/10.1016/j.cogdev.2005.08.006. Last Accessed 26 June 2013.

Felman, Shoshana. 'Beyond Oedipus: The Specimen Story of Psychoanalysis', *MLN,* 98, 1983.

Ferguson, Harvie. *Modernity and Subjectivity: Body, Soul, Spirit.* Charlottesville and London: University Press of Virginia, 2000.

Fielding, Sarah. *The Governess, or Little Female Academy,* ed. Mary Cadogan. London and New York: Pandora, 1987.

Fletcher, Sheila. *Women First: The Female Tradition in English Physical Education 1880–1980.* London and Dover, New Hampshire: Athlone, 1984.

Forest, Antonia. *End of Term.* Harmondsworth: Puffin, 1978.

——. *The Cricket Term.* Harmondsworth: Puffin, 1979.

Freud, Sigmund. 'Mourning and Melancholia'. In *Essential Papers on Object Loss,* ed. Rita V. Frankiel. New York: New York University Press, 1994, 38–51.

Gabriel, Karen. *Melodrama and the Nation: Sexual Economies of Bombay Cinema 1970–2000.* New Delhi: Women Unlimited, 2010.

Ganesan, N. 'Hyderabad Football,' *Sport and Pastime Magazine,* Madras: 9 July 1964, 18–19.

Ghosh, Benoy. *Metropolitan Mon O Modhyobityo Bidroho.* Calcutta: Orient Longman, 1973.

Ghosh, Manas. 'Nationalism, Television and Indian Cricket in Global Mediascape: Where has the Local Gone? In *Locating Cultural*

Change: Theory, Method, Process, ed. Partha Pratim Basu and Ipshita Chanda. New Delhi: Sage, 2011, 73–97.

Gilbert, Paul and Kathleen Lennon. *The World, the Flesh and the Subject: Continental Themes in Philosophy of Mind and Body*. Edinburgh: Edinburgh University Press, 2005.

Giulianotti, Richard. *Football: A Sociology of the Global Game*. Cambridge: Polity, 1999.

_____. *Sport: A Critical Sociology*. Oxford: Polity, 2005.

Gonda, Caroline. 'Being Faithful', *Journal of Lesbian Studies* 11: 1 (2007): 89–105.

Gosling, Ju. 'Virtual World of Girls Index: The History of Girls' School Stories', 1998. http://www.ju90.co.uk/his.htm. Last accessed 20 March 2013.

Goswami, Parimal. *Marke Lengey* (We Shall Fight and Win). Kolkatta: Bibhash Corner, 1950.

Govindan, Padma P. and Bisakha Dutta, '"From Villain to Traditional Housewife!": The Politics of Globalization and Women's Sexuality in the "New" Indian Media' In *Global Bollywood*, ed. Anandam P. Kavoori and Aswin Punathambekar. New Delhi: Oxford University Press, 2009, 180–202.

Gramsci, Antonio. *Selections from the Prison Notebooks of Antonio Gramsci*, ed. and trans. Quintin Hoare and Geoffrey Nowell Smith. New York: International Publishers, 1971.

Grosz, Elizabeth. *Volatile Bodies –Toward a Corporeal Feminism*. Bloomington and Indianapolis: Indiana University Press, 1994

Guha, Ramachandra. *A Corner of a Foreign Field: The Indian History of a British Sport*. London: Picador, 2002.

Guha, Ramachandra. *The States of Indian Cricket: Anecdotal Histories*. Delhi: Black Kite, 2005.

Gunter, Barrie. *Children as Consumers: A Psychological Analysis of the Young People's Market*. New York: Routledge, 1998.

Guttmann, Alan. *Games and Empires: Modern Sports and Cultural Imperialsim*. New York: Columbia University Press, 1994.

Gupta, Shubhra. 'How to be a Sport', in 'Eye', *Sunday Express*, 17 September, 2013.

Haigh, Gideon. 'International men of mystery', *ESPN cricinfo*, April 28, 2008, http://www.espncricinfo.com/magazine/content/story/347392.html. Last accessed 3 July 2012.

Hansen, Mark. *How We Became Posthuman: Virtual Bodies in Cybernetics, Literature, and Informatics*. London: University of Chicago Press, 2001.

———. *Embodying Technesis: Technology Beyond Writing*. Michigan: University of Michigan Press, 2000.

Haraway, Donna. 'A Cyborg Manifesto: Science, Technology, and Socialist-Feminism in the Late Twentieth Century', In *Simians, Cyborgs, and Women: The Reinvention of Nature*. New York: Routledge, 1991.

Hargreaves, John. *Sport, Power and Culture*. Cambridge: Polity, 1986.

Harvey, David. *The Condition of Postmodernity*. Oxford: Blackwell, 1990.

Harvie, Robin. *The Lure Of Long Distances: Why We Run*. New York: Public Affairs, 2011.

Hayles, Katherine. *How We Became Posthuman: Virtual Bodies in Cybernetics, Literature, and Informatics*. Chicago and London: University of Chicago Press, 1999.

———. 'Virtual Bodies and Flickering Signifiers', *October* 66: 1993, 69–91.

Huizinga, Johan. *Homo Ludens: A Study of the Play-Element in Culture*, London: Routledge, 1938.

———. 'Nature and significance of play as a cultural phenomenon'. In *The Ethics of Sports: A Reader*, ed. Mike McNamee. London: Routledge, 2010, 29–32.

Hunt, Peter. 'Narrative Theory and Children's Literature', *Children's Literature Association Quaterly*, 9, 4, Baltimore,: The John Hopkins University Press, 1984–85, 191–94. doi: 10.1353/chq.0.0415. http://muse.jhu.edu/journals/chq/summary/v009/9.4.hunt.html. Last accessed 25 March 2013.

Hurka, Thomas. 'Games and the good—I'. In *The Ethics of Sports: A Reader*, ed. Mike McNamee. London: Routledge, 2010, 52–61.

Iqbal. Dir. Nagesh Kukunoor, Mukta Films, 2005.

Jacobson, Lisa. *Raising Consumers: Children and the American Mass Market in the Early Twentieth Century*. New York: Columbia University Press, 2004.

James, C.L.R. 'Garfield Sobers'. In *Cricket: The Great All-Rounders*, ed. John Arlott. London: Pelham Books, 1969, 155–69.

———. *Beyond a Boundary*. Durham: Duke University Press, 1993.

Jameson, Fredric. 'Imaginary and the Symbolic in Lacan: Marxism, Psychoanalytic Criticism and the Problem of the Subject', *Yale French Studies*, 1977.

———. *The Political Unconscious: Narrative as a Socially Symbolic Act*. London: Routledge, 1989

———. *Postmodernism: Or, The Cultural Logic of Late Capitalism*. Durham: Duke University Press, 1991.

Kapadia, Novy. 'Witness to an era, a profile of Harnam Singh', The *Telegraph*, Calcutta: 11 February 1983.

Kellner, Douglas. *Media Culture: Cultural Studies, Identity and Politics between the Modern and the Postmodern*. New York: Routledge, 1995.

King, C. Richard and David J. Leonard, eds *Visual Economies of/ in Motion: Sport and Film*, New York: Peter Lang, 2006.

Kipling, Rudyard. 'If—', *The Collected Poems of Rudyard Kipling*. Kent: Wordsworth Editions, 1994.

Kirby, Vicki. *Telling Flesh–The Substance of the Corporeal*. New York and London: Routledge, 1997.

Knights L.C. *Explorations: Essays in Criticism Mainly on the Literature of the Seventeenth Century*. London: Chatto & Windus, 1958.

Lacan, Jacques. *The Seminar, Book XI. The Four Fundamental Concepts of Psychoanalysis*, trans. Alan Sheridan. London: Hogarth Press and the Institute of Psycho-Analysis, 1977.

———. *Ecrits*, ed. Alan Sheridan. London: Routledge, 1992

Lagaan. Dir. Asutosh Gowariker. Aamir Khan Productions, 2001.

Landy, John. *The Gigantic Book of Running Quotations*, ed. Amby Burfoot and Hal Higdon. New York: Skyhorse Publishing, 2008.

———. *The Quotable Runner*, ed. Mark Will-Weber. New York: Breakaway Books, 1995.

Lanier, Jaron. *You Are Not a Gadget: A Manifesto*. New York: Alfred A. Knopf, 2010.

Latimer, Joanna and Michael Schillmeier, eds *Un/Knowing Bodies*. Oxford: Blackwell Publishing Ltd., 2009.

Lewin, Kurt, Donald K. Adams and Karl E. Zener, eds *A Dynamic Theory of Personality: Selected Papers*. London: McGraw Hill, 1959.

Lomax, David. *BBC 1*, 'Panorama' 20 June 2001. Last accessed 30 Sept.2013.

Lyotard, Jean-Francois. *The Postmodern Condition: A Report on Knowledge*, trans. Geoffrey Bennington and Brian Massumi. Manchester: Manchester University Press, 1984.

Mahapatra, Dhananjay. 'Lack of a law saved Azhar, Jadeja', The *Times of India*, 26 May 2013.

Majumdar, Boria. 'Don't take Cricket Fans for a Ride', The *Times of India*, 9 June 2013.

———. 'The Vernacular in Sports History', *Economic and Political Weekly* XXXVII, 29 (20, July 2002): 3069–75.

Majumdar, Boria and Kausik Bandyopadhyay, 'Cricket as Everyday Life: World Cup 2003', *Economic and Political Weekly* XXXIX, 14/15 (3 April 2004): 1450–54.

———. *Goalless: The Story of a Unique Footballing Nation*. New Delhi: Penguin Viking, 2006.

Majumdar, Boria and Nalin Mehta. *India and the Olympics*. New Delhi: Harper Collins, 2008.

Mangan, J.A. *Athleticism in the Victorian and Edwardian Public School: The Emergence and Consolidation of an Educational Ideology*. London and Portland, Oregon: Frank Cass, 1981.

———. *The Games Ethic and Imperialism: Aspects of the Diffusion of an Ideal*. Harmondsworth: Viking, 1986.

Mangan, J.A. and Fang Hong, eds *Sports in Asian Society: Past and Present*. London: Frank Cass, 2003.

Marks, Laura. 'Video Haptics and Erotics', *Screen* 39(4): 1998, 331–349.

Marqusee, Mike. *Anyone but England: Cricket and the National Malaise*. London: Verso 1994.

Maslow, Abraham. 'A Theory of Human Motivation', *Psychological Review*, 50(4)1943: 370–96.

Mason, Tony. 'Football on the Maidan: Cultural Imperialism in Calcutta'. In *The Cultural Bond: Sport, Empire, Society*, ed. J.A. Mangan. London: Frank Cass 1992, 142–53.

Mauss, Marcel. 'Techniques of the Body', in *Techniques, Technology and Civilisation*, ed. Nathan Schlanger. New York: Berghahn/Durkheim Press, 2006, 77–95.

Meerabai Not Out. Dir. Chandrakant Kulkarni, 2008, India: Sony Pictures India, 2009, VCD.

Memon, Ayaz. 'Rip the Veil of Silence'. *Times of India*, 30 May 2013.

Menon, K.N.K. 'Vintage Soccer'. In the *Souvenir* of the 59th IOC-Senior National Football Championship, ed. Novy Kapadia. Delhi: 2004, 47–49.

Menon, Suresh. 'The Loneliness of the long-distance cricketer', *ESPN cricinfo,* 24 February 2008, http://www.espn.cricinfo.com/magazine/content/story/337858.html. Last accessed 3 July 2012.

Merleau-Ponty, Maurice. *The Primacy of Perception*. Illinois: Northwestern University Press, 1964.

Mickenberg, Julia L. 'American Studies and Childhood Studies: Lessons from Consumer Culture', *American Quarterly*, 58, 4, Baltimore: The John Hopkins University Press, 2006, 1217–27. doi: 0.1353/aq.2007.0014. http://muse.jhu.edu/journals/american_quarterly/v058/58.4mickenberg.html. Last accessed 25 March 2013.

Miller, Toby. *Sportsex*. Philadelphia: Temple University Press, 2001.

Mitra, Soumen. 'Babu at Play: Sporting Nationalism in Bengal: A Study of Football in Bengal, 1880–1911'. In *Bengal: Yesterday and Today* ed. Nisith Roy and Ranjit Roy. Calcutta: Papyrus, 1991.

Mitra, Soumen. 'Nationalism, Communalism and Sub-Regionalism: A Study of Football in Bengal 1880–1950'. Unpublished M.Phil Thesis, Jawaharlal Nehru University, New Delhi, 1988.

Mukherjee, Sumit. 'Football in Colonial Bengal in Nationalist Perspective'. *90 Minutes*, 1, 4, Oct.-Dec. 2009, 36–42.

Mukhopadhyay, Sarat Kumar. 'Chhoto Golpo o Moti Nandy' [Short Stories and Moti Nandy], in *Proma*: Special Moti Nandy Number, 29 (1415/2008).

Mukhopadhyay, Sarat Kumar. Speech at Moti Nandy's memorial meeting, January 2010 (unpublished).

Mulvey, Laura. 'Visual Pleasure and Narrative Cinema'. *Screen* 16, 3 (Autumn 1975): 6–18.

Murakami, Haruki. *What I Talk About When I Talk About Running: A Memoir*, tr. Philip Gabriel. London: Vintage, 2009.

Nair, Patchy. 'Meerabai Not Out entertains in parts'. *rediffMOVIES* (blog), rediff.com, December 5, 2008, http://www.rediff.com/movies/2008/dec/05meerabai-not-out-entertainment.htm. Accessed on 6 January 2012.

Nandy, Ashis. *An Ambiguous Journey to the City: The Village and Other Odd Ruins of the Self in Indian Imagination*. New Delhi: Oxford University Press, 2001.

_____. 'The Tao of Cricket' in *A Very Popular Exile*. Oxford India Paperbacks, New Delhi: Oxford University Press, 2011, iv–150.

_____. Interview by Ajoy Ashirwad Mahaprashasta, 'It has become a real business,' *Frontline*, 28 June 2013.

_____. Preface to the OUP Edition, *A Very Popular Exile*. Oxford India Paperbacks, Oxford University Press: New Delhi 2011, ix–xx.

Nandy, Moti. 'Calcutta Soccer'. In *Calcutta: The Living City*. ed. Sukanta Chaudhuri, vol II. New Delhi: Oxford University Press, 1990, 316–20.

_____. 'Football and Nationalism'. In *The Calcutta Psyche*, ed. Geeti Sen. New Delhi: India International Centre, 1991, 249–50.

_____. *Dashti Kishor Upanyas* [Ten Novels for Young Adults]. Calcutta: Ananda Publishers, 2010.

_____. *Striker, Stopper*. Trans. Arunava Sinha. Gurgaon: Hachette India, 2010.

_____. *Striker/Stopper*. Trans. Mihir K. Das. Calcutta: Orient Longman, 1994.

Nature 432(2004): 345–52.

Nel, Philip. 'Is There a Text in This Advertising Campaign?: Literature, Marketing, and Harry Potter', *The Lion and the Unicorn*, 29, 2, Baltimore: The John Hopkins University Press, 2005). 236–67. doi: 10.1353/uni.2005.0031. http://muse.jhu.edu/journals/lion_and_the_unicorn/v029/29.2nel.html. Last accessed 25 March 2013.

Novak, Michael. *The Joy of Sport: End Zones, Bases, Baskets, Balls, and the Consecration of the American Spirit*. New York: Basic Books, 1975.

Orwell, George. 'The Sporting Spirit'. In *The Penguin Essays of George Orwell*. Harmondsworth: Penguin, 1994.

Piaget, Jean. *The Child's Conception of the World*. Lanham, Maryland: Rowman & Littlefield, 2007 (First Published 1951).

———. *Play, Dreams and Imitation in Childhood*, New York: Routledge, 1999 (First Published 1951).

Pimental, Ken and Kevin Texeira. *Virtual Reality: Through the New Looking Glass*. London: Mcgraw-Hill School Education Group, 1992.

Poulton, Emma and Martin Roderick. 'Introducing Sport in Cinema', *Sport in Society* 11, 2/3 (March/May 2008): 107–16.

Quigly, Isabel. *The Heirs of Tom Brown: The English School Story*. Oxford: Oxford University Press, 1984.

Rajan, Amol. *Twirlymen: The Unlikely History of Cricket's Greatest Spin Bowlers*. London: Yellow Jersey Press, 2011.

Raley, Rita. 'e-Empires'. *Cultural Critique*, 57.1. (Spring 2004): 115–37.

———. *Tactical Media*. Minneapolis: University of Minnesota Press, 2009.

Ray, Manas. 'Growing Up Refugee.' *History Workshop Journal*, issue 5, 2002.

Raychaudhuri, Tapan. *Bangalnama*. Kolkata: Ananda Publishers, 2009.

Redhead, Steve. *Paul Virilio: Theorist for an Accelerated Culture*. Edinburgh: Edinburgh University Press, 2004.

———. 'Those Absent from the Stadium are Always Right: Accelerated Culture, Sport Media, and Theory at the Speed of Light.' *Journal of Sport & Social Issues* August 2007, 31.3: 226–41.

Reng, Ronald. *A Life Too Short: The Tragedy of Robert Enke*, tr. Shaun Whiteside. London: Yellow Jersey Press, 2011.

Robertson, E. Arnot. 'Potting Shed of the English Rose'. *The Old School*. ed. Graham Greene. Oxford: Oxford University Press, 1984, 153–64.

Roche, Maurice. *Mega Events and Modernity: Olympics, Expos and the Growth of Global Culture*. London: Routledge, 2000.

Rodrigues, Mario. *Batting for the Empire: A Political Biography of Ranjitsinghji*. New Delhi: Penguin, 2003.

Rowe, David. *Popular Cultures: Rock Music, Sport and the Politics of Pleasure*. London: Sage, 1995.

_____. *Sport, Culture and The Media: The Unruly Trinity*. 2nd edn, Buckingham: Open University Press, 2004.

Rowling, J.K. *Harry Potter and the Philosopher's Stone*. London: Bloomsbury, 1997.

_____. *Harry Potter and The Prisoner of Azkaban*. London: Bloomsbury, 1999.

_____. *Harry Potter and The Goblet of Fire*. London: Bloomsbury, 2000.

_____. *Quidditch Through The Ages by Kennilworthy Wis*, London: Arthur A. Levine, 2001.

Roy, Maitreyi B. *Calcutta Slums: Public Policy in Retrospect*. Kolkata: Minerva, n.d.

Russell, J.S., 'The value of dangerous sport'. In *The Ethics of Sports: A Reader*, ed. Mike McNamee. London: Routledge, 2010, pp. 441–55.

Salen, Katie and Eric Zimmerman, eds *The Game Design Reader: A Rules of Play Anthology*. Cambridge, Mass.: MIT Press, 2005.

Sammond, Nicholas. *Babes in Tomorrowland: Walt Disney and the Making of the American Child 1930–1960*. Durham: Duke University Press, 2005.

Schwartzman, Helen B. 'The Anthropological Study of Children's Play', *Annual Review of Anthropology*, 5, Sao Paolo, California: Annual Reviews, 1976, 289–328. http://www.jstor.org/stable/2949315 (Last accessed 25 March 2013)

Sen, Dwaipayan. 'Wiping the Stain off the Field of Plassey: Mohun Bagan in 1911', *Soccer and Society* 7.2.-3, London: 2006, 208–32.

Shilling, Chris. *The Body in Culture, Technology and Society*. London: Sage, 2005.

Shoonya. Dir. Arindam Mitra, 2007.

Sillitoe, Alan. *The Loneliness of the Long Distance Runner*. London: Harper Collins, 2007.

_____. *Life without Armour: An Autobiography*. New York: Robson Books Ltd., 1995; reprt. 2004.

Singh, Balbir. *The Golden Hat Trick: My Hockey Days*. New Delhi: Vikas Publishing House, 1977.

Singh, G. Nandy, Cdr. 'Future Goal of Indian Hockey'. In the *45th Nehru Hockey Tournament Annual Souvenir*, ed. M.N. Shome. New Delhi: 2008, 54–57.

Sinha, Mrinalini. *Colonial Masculinity: the 'Manly Englishman' and the 'Effeminate Bengali' in the late nineteenth century*. Manchester: Manchester University Press, 1995.

Small, Helen. 'The Loneliness of the Long-Distance Runner in Browning, Sillitoe, and Murakami', *Essays in Criticism*, 60:2 (2010).

Sobchack, Vivian. 'New Age Mutant Ninja Hackers: Reading Mondo 2000'. In *Flame Wars: The Discourse of Cyberculture* , ed. M. Dery. Durham, NC: Duke University Press, 1993.

Sophia, Zoe. 'Virtual Corporeality: A Feminist View', *Australian Feminist Studies* 15: 1992, 11–24.

Sorley, Charles. 'The Song of the Ungirt Runners'. In *Marlborough and other Poems*. Cambridge: Cambridge University Press, 1916.

Stone, Allucquere Roseanne. 'Will the Real Body Please Stand Up?'. In *Cyberspace: First Steps*, ed. M. Benedikt. Cambridge, Mass.: MIT Press, 1992.

Stutley, Margaret and James. *A Dictionary of Hinduism*. London: Routledge and Kegan Paul, 1977.

Sugden, John and Alan Tomlinson, eds *Power Games: A Critical Sociology of Sport*. London: Routledge, 2002.

Suits, Bernard, 'Construction of a definition'. In *The Ethics of Sports: A Reader*, ed. Mike McNamee. London: Routledge, 2010, 17–28.

Summerfield, Penny. 'Cultural Reproduction in the Education of Girls: A Study of Girls' Secondary Schooling in two Lancashire Towns, 1900–50'. In *Lessons for Life: The Schooling of Girls and Women*, ed. Felicity Hunt. Oxford: Basil Blackwell, 1987, 149–70.

Sutton-Smith, Brian. *The Ambiguity of Play*. Cambridge, Mass.: Harvard University Press, 1997.

Sutton-Smith, Brian et al. 'Developmental structures in fantasy narratives', *Human Development* 19 (1976): 10.

Tadié, Alexis, 'Running for Freedom: The Politics of Long-Distance Running in Modern Fiction'. Unpublished paper presented at the International Conference on 'Sport and the Nation', Jadavpur University, January 2012.

Thapar, Romila. *From Lineage to State: Social Formations in the Mid-First Millennium B.C. in the Ganga Valley*. New Delhi: Oxford University Press, 1990.

Tomlinson, Alan. 'Pierre Bourdieu and the Sociological Study of Sport: Habitus, Capital and Field'. In *Sport and Modern Social Theorists*, ed. Richard Giulianotti. London: Palgrave Macmillan, 2004, 161–72.

Turkle, Sherry. *The Second Self: Computers and the Human Spirit*. New York: Simon and Schuster, 1984.

Turner, Victor. 'Body, Brain and Culture', *Zygon* 18, 3 (1983): 221–45.

Vasudevan, Ravi. *The Melodramatic Public: Film Form and Spectatorship in Indian Cinema*. Ranikhet: Permanent Black, 2010.

Virdi, Jyotika. *The Cinematic ImagiNation: Indian Popular Films as Social History*. Ranikhet: Permanent Black, 2003.

Virilio, Paul. *Speed and Politics: An Essay on Dromology*, trans. Mark Polizzotti. New York: Semiotext(e), 1986.

_____. *War and Cinema: The Logistics of Perception*, tr. Patrick Camiller. London: Verso, 1989.

_____. *Open Sky*, tr. Julie Rose. London: Verso, 1997.

_____. *The Information Bomb*, tr. Chris Turner. London: Verso, 2000.

Walsh, Adrian and Richard Giulianotti. *Ethics, Money and Sport: This Sporting Mammon*. New York: Routledge 2007.

Whitehead, Lana. *The Ivory Tower and Harry Potter: Perspectives on a Literary Phenomenon*. Columbia, Missouri: The University of Missouri Press, 2002.

Wilkinson, Sheena. *Friends in the Fourth*. London: Bettany Press, 2007.

Williamson, Martin. 'Those two little pals of mine', *ESPN cricinfo*, June 24, 2006, http://www.espncricinfo.com/magazine/content/story/251196.html. Last accessed 3 July 2012.

Winder, Robert. 'A Dying game. Why would a cricketer commit suicide?' The *New Statesman*, 19 June, 2000, http://www.newstatesman.com/node/137938. Last accessed 3 July 2012.

Zatopek, Emil. 'The Warm Up'. *Runner's World*, 43:9 (2008).

Zipes, Jack. 'The Age of Commodified Fantasticism: Reflections on Children's Literature and The Fantastic', *Children's Literature Association Quaterly*, 9, 4, 1984–85, 187–90. doi: 10.1353/chq.0.0316, http://muse.jhu.edu/journals/childrens_literature_association_quarterly/v009/9.4.zipes.html. Last accessed 25 March 2013.

_____. Sticks *and Stones: The Troublesome Success of Children's Literature from Slovenly Peter to Harry Potter*. London: Routledge, 2002.

About the Contributors

SOHINI BANERJEE did her Masters in English Literature from Jadavpur University and has joined the University of Massachusetts, Amherst in Fall 2013 as a Ph.D. student in the Department of English. Her primary areas of interest are Modernism/Modernity, Postcolonialism, Cultural Studies and the Novel.

MAITRI BARUAH is an Assistant Professor in the Department of English at Hans Raj College, University of Delhi. Her current research project is a critical investigation of the relationship between the print/public sphere and theatrical practices in late nineteenth century colonial Assam.

SUPRIYA CHAUDHURI is Professor (Emeritus) in the Department of English at Jadavpur University, Kolkata. Her areas of scholarly interest are early modern English and European literature, nineteenth and twentieth century cultural history, critical theory, translation, and the philosophy and culture of sport. Recent publications include *Petrarch: the Self and the World* (2012), co-edited with Sukanta Chaudhuri; *Sport, Literature, Society: Cultural Historical Studies* (2013), co-edited with Alexis Tadié and J.A. Mangan; and *Reconsidering English Studies in Indian Higher Education* (Routledge, 2015), with Suman Gupta, Richard Allen and Subarno Chattarji.

ARATRIKA DAS is currently pursuing a Ph.D. at Department of English, University of Delhi on the figure of a nineteenth century vampire.

Mithuraaj Dhusiya teaches at the Department of English, Hans Raj College, University of Delhi. He is currently pursuing his Ph.D. on Indian horror films from the Department of English, University of Delhi. His research interests include the study of popular cultural forms, especially cinema. In addition to papers presented at international and national conferences, his publications include articles on several aspects of the Indian horror film.

Boria Majumdar is regarded as one of India's leading sports analysts and broadcasters. He was a Rhodes Scholar at the University of Oxford, where he obtained his D.Phil. in history. He has written extensively on Indian sport and politics and has covered the Indian Premier League for six seasons.

Niha Masih is a journalist and documentary photographer, currently with NDTV. Her work has been published in several newspapers and magazines, both national and international. Niha shot two photographic series for the Delhi Commons project—one on the destruction and reconstruction of Connaught Place and another on tourists at India Gate.

Iram Ghufran is a national award-winning film-maker and an artist. Her work has been shown in several international art and cinematic contexts: Berlin Film Festival, London Indian Film Festival, Experimenta, World Social Forum and ISEA among others. Iram is the initiator of Delhi Commons, a critical art project in response to the Commonwealth Games in Delhi. She was the recipient of the Pro Helvetia Swiss Arts Council residency for 2012.

Novy Kapadia is an Associate Professor, Department of English, SGTB Khalsa College, University of Delhi and also a versatile sports commentator and analyst for both radio and television. Football is his forte but he maintains the same level of excellence in other sports and in both Hindi and English. At present, Novy is a football columnist with several newspapers and sports journals. He won the Wills Award for Excellence in Sports Journalism in 1986 for his article 'The Other Side of the Medal'. He has covered several international sports events, the latest being the 2010 World Cup football tournament in South Africa and 2012 London Olympics.

Sanam Khanna teaches English Literature at Kamala Nehru College, University of Delhi. Her areas of interest are Young Adult Fiction, Children's Literature, Culture Studies, Media Studies, Science Fiction, and Literary Theory. Her publications include, among others, critical essays on news coverage, Victorian Literature and European drama. She has also co-edited a reader of seminal works in Indian Literature from ancient times to the present, titled, *Indian Literature: An Introduction*.

Arindam Mitra studied English at Jadavpur University and was a Media professional in Kolkata till he ventured into film making. He produced the controversial film 'Black Friday' on the Bombay blasts (dir. Anurag Kashyap) and has written and directed the sports film 'Shoonya' which has been shown at a number of film festivals abroad. He lives and works in Bombay. Arindam was a keen sportsman and was a University Blue in rowing.

Paromita Patranobish is a Ph.D. student at the Department of English, University of Delhi. Her research interests include Virginia Woolf, philosophies of the body, Modernism, and children's literature.

Debjani Sengupta completed her doctoral thesis on the Partition of Bengal and its literatures. She has edited *Mapmaking: Partition Stories from Two Bengals* (2011) and has co-edited with Selina Hossain (Bangladesh) a collection of South Asian feminist stories titled *Dakkhin Asiar Naribadi Golpo* (2008). She teaches at Indraprastha College for Women, University of Delhi and has contributed translations from Bangla to the *Oxford Anthology of Bengali Literature*, Vol. 2 (2010) and *The Essential Tagore* (2011).

Aishwarya Subramanian holds a B.A. in English Literature from the University of Delhi, and an M. Phil in Popular Literature from Trinity College, University of Dublin. She has previously worked in the field of children's publishing as an editor and has also worked as a freelance editor, critic and columnist. Her research has focused upon children's literature and its historical contexts, and she will be beginning a Ph.D. in British children's literature at the end of Empire in 2013.

ANAS TABRAIZ is deeply interested in psychoanalysis and linguistics and is working on a doctoral dissertation on 'The Pursuit of Ethical Silence in the works of J.M. Coetzee' at Jawaharlal Nehru University, Delhi.

POONAM TRIVEDI was Associate Professor in English at Indraprastha College, University of Delhi. Her main areas of interest are in Shakespeare Studies, Shakespeare in India, performance and film versions, women in Shakespeare, Indian theatre and the culture of sport. Her main publications (co-edited) are *Re-playing Shakespeare in Asia* (2010) and *India's Shakespeare: Translation, Interpretation and Performance* (2005 and 2006). She has authored a CD-ROM 'King Lear *in India*' (2006) and has published articles in *The Shakespearean International Yearbook, Shakespeare Survey, Cambridge Companion to Shakespeare on Stage, Borrowers and Lenders, Literature and Film Quarterly, Hamlet Studies* and other national and international journals. She was the secretary of the Shakespeare Society of India from 1993-99 and is currently the vice-chair of the Asian Shakespeare Association.

Index